ceac

101 RECIPES FOR

Preparing Food in Bulk

Everything You Need to Know About Preparing, Storing, and Consuming

D0897504

BY RICHARD HELWEG

101 Recipes for Preparing Food in Bulk: Everything
You Need to Know About Preparing, Storing, and Consuming

Copyright © 2011 Atlantic Publishing Group, Inc.
1405 SW 6th Avenue • Ocala, Florida 34471 • Phone 800-814-1132 • Fax 352-622-1875
Website: www.atlantic-pub.com • E-mail: sales@atlantic-pub.com
SAN Number: 268-1250

No part of this publication may be reproduced, stored in a retrieval system, or transmitted in any form or by any means, electronic, mechanical, photocopying, recording, scanning, or otherwise, except as permitted under Section 107 or 108 of the 1976 United States Copyright Act, without the prior written permission of the Publisher. Requests to the Publisher for permission should be sent to Atlantic Publishing Group, Inc., 1405 SW 6th Avenue, Ocala, Florida 34471.

Helweg, Richard, 1956-
  101 recipes for preparing food in bulk : everything you need to
know about preparing, storing, and consuming / by Richard Helweg.
     p. cm.
  ISBN-13: 978-1-60138-360-0 (alk. paper)
  ISBN-10: 1-60138-360-6 (alk. paper)
  1. Quantity cooking. 2. Cookbooks. I. Title. II. Title: One
hundred and one recipes for preparing food in bulk. III. Title: One
hundred one recipes for preparing food in bulk.
  TX820.H44 2011
  641.7'9--dc22
                            2011011087

LIMIT OF LIABILITY/DISCLAIMER OF WARRANTY: The publisher and the author make no representations or warranties with respect to the accuracy or completeness of the contents of this work and specifically disclaim all warranties, including without limitation warranties of fitness for a particular purpose. No warranty may be created or extended by sales or promotional materials. The advice and strategies contained herein may not be suitable for every situation. This work is sold with the understanding that the publisher is not engaged in rendering legal, accounting, or other professional services. If professional assistance is required, the services of a competent professional should be sought. Neither the publisher nor the author shall be liable for damages arising herefrom. The fact that an organization or website is referred to in this work as a citation and/or a potential source of further information does not mean that the author or the publisher endorses the information the organization or website may provide or recommendations it may make. Further, readers should be aware that Internet websites listed in this work may have changed or disappeared between when this work was written and when it is read.

TRADEMARK DISCLAIMER: All trademarks, trade names, or logos mentioned or used are the property of their respective owners and are used only to directly describe the products being provided. Every effort has been made to properly capitalize, punctuate, identify, and attribute trademarks and trade names to their respective owners, including the use of ® and ™ wherever possible and practical. Atlantic Publishing Group, Inc. is not a partner, affiliate, or licensee with the holders of said trademarks.

PROJECT MANAGER: Amy Moczynski • EDITORIAL ASSISTANT: Sarah Ann Beckman
BOOK PRODUCTION DESIGN: T.L. Price • design@tlpricefreelance.com
PROOFREADER: C&P Marse • bluemoon6749@bellsouth.net
COVER DESIGN: Meg Buchner • meg@megbuchner.com
BACK COVER DESIGN: Jackie Miller • millerjackiej@gmail.com

Printed on Recycled Paper

Printed in the United States

A few years back we lost our beloved pet dog Bear, who was not only our best and dearest friend but also the "Vice President of Sunshine" here at Atlantic Publishing. He did not receive a salary but worked tirelessly 24 hours a day to please his parents.

Bear was a rescue dog who turned around and showered myself, my wife, Sherri, his grandparents Jean, Bob, and Nancy, and every person and animal he met (well, maybe not rabbits) with friendship and love. He made a lot of people smile every day.

We wanted you to know a portion of the profits of this book will be donated in Bear's memory to local animal shelters, parks, conservation organizations, and other individuals and nonprofit organizations in need of assistance.

– Douglas & Sherri Brown

PS: We have since adopted two more rescue dogs: first Scout, and the following year, Ginger. They were both mixed golden retrievers who needed a home.

Want to help animals and the world? Here are a dozen easy suggestions you and your family can implement today:

- *Adopt and rescue a pet from a local shelter.*
- *Support local and no-kill animal shelters.*
- *Plant a tree to honor someone you love.*
- *Be a developer — put up some birdhouses.*
- *Buy live, potted Christmas trees and replant them.*
- *Make sure you spend time with your animals each day.*
- *Save natural resources by recycling and buying recycled products.*
- *Drink tap water, or filter your own water at home.*
- *Whenever possible, limit your use of or do not use pesticides.*
- *If you eat seafood, make sustainable choices.*
- *Support your local farmers market.*
- *Get outside. Visit a park, volunteer, walk your dog, or ride your bike.*

Five years ago, Atlantic Publishing signed the Green Press Initiative. These guidelines promote environmentally friendly practices, such as using recycled stock and vegetable-based inks, avoiding waste, choosing energy-efficient resources, and promoting a no-pulping policy. We now use 100-percent recycled stock on all our books. The results: in one year, switching to post-consumer recycled stock saved 24 mature trees, 5,000 gallons of water, the equivalent of the total energy used for one home in a year, and the equivalent of the greenhouse gases from one car driven for a year.

Table of Contents

Chapter 4: Breakfast 69

Chapter 10: Side Dishes............. 159

Table of Contents

Chapter 11: Dinner Main Dishes.. 181

Table of Contents

Introduction

There are many reasons why you would consider cooking in bulk and making any of the recipes in this book. There are many good reasons why you will find this book on cooking food in bulk to be a valuable addition to your cookbook library. You may have a garden that produces prodigious amounts of vegetables and/or fruits in the summer months. You might be a member of a local CSA (Community Supported Agriculture) farm and regularly receive large amounts of produce. Perhaps you regularly take part in potluck dinners where you must prepare a dish to feed a large number of people. You might find that cooking and freezing meals at a time that is convenient for you is a good way to manage those times when you would like to have dinner for your family but you do not have the time to prepare a meal. You might be someone who enjoys taking advantage of sales at supermarkets and purchases meat and produce in large quantities.

This book will take you through the process of preparing to shop, cook, preserve, and serve large amounts of food. This book will guide you through every aspect of cooking in bulk to make it as manageable as cooking regular-sized meals. The book details all the essential appliances and utensils you need in your kitchen, as well as how to take inventory of the supplies and foods you already have. This book provides tips so you know where and how to do your grocery shopping. In addition to these basic details, you will learn everything you need to know to prepare yourself for cooking day, from deciding whether you should cook solo or with a partner, to how to prepare, cook, cool, and properly store your meals. Once you are ready to eat your frozen meal, this book tells you how to thaw and reheat each recipe and how to detect foods gone bad — which probably will not happen if you follow the simple instructions in this book.

Included in this book are more than 100 recipes that detail the ingredients and methods for preparing food for 100 servings. Whether you are making breakfast, lunch, dinner, dessert, or snacks for a wedding or a soccer team, everything you need to know is here. The companion CD-ROM included in the back of the book has all the recipes in the book plus an additional 1,700 bulk food recipes. Another great feature about the CD-ROM is that it has the ability to scale a recipe. For example, if you are planning a party for 150 guests, simply key in 150 and the recipe will change all the quantities for you.

CHAPTER

Getting Started

ONE

Planning

Whether you are cooking meals for your family over the course of a week, cooking in bulk for 100 people, or cooking a quantity of food to be frozen for a later date, the better you plan, the easier and more cost-effective your task will be. Planning to make food in bulk will take in numerous factors, all of which will determine how you will proceed with your task, where you will procure your ingredients, how much the venture will cost you, how you will preserve the fruits of your labor, and how and when you may prepare and consume the food you prepare.

HINT: There are many facilities that have commercial kitchens that are underutilized. Consider churches, schools, county extension services, even restaurants that might only be open for dinner. Be creative; all they can do is say no.

A good plan will ensure that you do not find yourself without the proper equipment, ingredients, and space to preserve and/or cook your recipes. If you plan to cook in bulk, you will need to do the following:

- ❏ Decide what you will be making
- ❏ Inventory your kitchen for ingredients and equipment you have on hand

- ❏ Prepare a shopping list of ingredients and equipment you will need to carry out your plan
- ❏ Prepare your workspace
- ❏ Set aside the time needed to carry out your plan
- ❏ Prepare the space you will need to freeze or store any food you make that will not be served immediately
- ❏ Prepare a way to serve food that will be served immediately
- ❏ Clean up

If you consider your needs in each of these areas before you proceed with your task, you will save time and money.

Deciding what to make

The factors that will determine what you make will stem from any one of a number of situations. You may have a garden full of tomatoes that are about to ripen, or you may have been asked to bake for a large birthday party. You might have a household full of kids who absolutely love lasagna, but you rarely have the time to make it with your busy schedule. Whatever the reason for your need or desire to cook in bulk, the situation will guide your decisions on how to plan for the task.

Once you decide what it is you would like to prepare, find a recipe that you and your family and friends will love. This book contains more than 100 tested recipes for preparing food in bulk, and the Resources section of the book has detailed instructions on the basics for freezing and canning things from your garden or your kitchen. Know what you are getting into before you begin. Check out the recipes and, if you plan on freezing or canning, go over the resources. This information will help as you proceed to the next steps of your planning.

HINT: Look into wholesale food companies in your area, such as Sysco, Cheney Brothers, and **www.bulkfoods.com**. Many will deliver to you, and some are open to the general public.

Inventorying your kitchen for ingredients and equipment you have on hand

Before you go out to buy that large stockpot needed to make 100 portions of chicken broth, look around your kitchen. If you are new to cooking large quantities of food, there may be necessary equipment or ingredients you do not have, but before you run out and purchase anything, it is always good to know what you have and what you need. The necessary equipment, like the necessary ingredients, will be dictated by what you plan to make, so be sure you have a solid idea as to your needs based on what you aim to accomplish. It is here that you will start your shopping list. Decide what you are making, and then compare that to what you have so you know what you need to buy. Knowing this information will make putting together your shopping list a little easier, and it may also save you some money.

As you think about your needs prior to embarking on this large-scale cooking adventure, you should consider the important issue of storage space. Although cabinet or shelf space to store jars of canned tomato sauce may not be difficult for you to come up with, you may be hard-pressed to find freezer space to stock 100 portions of chicken pot pie. As you inventory the equipment you have on hand, you should consider the space available in your freezer.

If you are seriously considering upgrading your freezer to handle larger quantities of food, or if you are just due to purchase a new freezer, consider these recommendations provided by the U.S. Environmental Protection Agency and the U.S. Department of Energy:

What else should I look for when buying a freezer?

Ask for an ENERGY STAR model.

When buying a freezer from a retailer, request an ENERGY STAR qualified model to be sure it is energy efficient.

Check the yellow EnergyGuide label.

Use this label to determine the model's energy use, compare the energy use of similar models, and estimate annual operating costs.

Purchase an appropriately sized freezer.

Generally, the larger the freezer, the greater the energy it consumes. Also, consider whether an upright or chest freezer better meets your needs. An upright freezer has a front-mounted door like a refrigerator and shelves that allow for easy organization. Although a chest freezer typically requires more floor space, it is usually more energy efficient because the door opens from the top and allows less cold air to escape.

Consider a manual defrost model.

Manual defrost freezers use half the energy of automatic defrost models, but they must be defrosted periodically to achieve the energy savings. Do not allow frost to build up more than ¼ inch.

Best Practices

Follow these guidelines to reduce the amount of energy your freezer uses:

❏ Set the appropriate temperature. Keep the temperature at 0 degrees Fahrenheit.

❏ Avoid extreme temperatures. Unless you live in a mild climate, keep your freezer indoors, such as in the basement. Extreme temperatures are hard on the compressor and can reduce the life of your freezer.

❏ Allow air circulation behind the freezer. Leave a few inches between the wall or cabinets and the freezer.

❏ Check the door seals. Make sure the seals around the door are airtight. If not, replace them.

❏ Keep the door closed. Minimize the amount of time the freezer door is open.

❏ If you buy a new freezer, be sure to recycle your old one. Many appliance retailers will pick up and recycle your old freezer when you purchase a new one.

HINT: Buy produce that is seasonally available and, when possible, buy in bulk. Farmers markets, farm stands, and big box stores often offer substantial savings on seasonal and bulk items.

HINT: When preparing your bulk food shopping list and menu, think about making a little extra for people in need. Consider the elderly, disabled, and anyone in need in these tough economic times. You will feel great about helping others while helping yourselves.

Preparing a shopping list of ingredients and equipment you will need

As you prepare to cook, it is wise to keep the old adage "measure twice and cut once" in mind. As you make your shopping lists, check them twice. Again, the place to start is with your recipe. Whether you use a recipe from this book or from some other source, be sure to read it over carefully and note your needs. You have already done your in-home inventory, so you know what you have. The recipe will tell you what you need.

Note: There is a full explanation of equipment you may require later in this chapter.

If you are new to cooking in bulk, you may not have a lot of the equipment that some of the recipes call for. Rather than running out to purchase a steam-jacketed kettle that many recipes call for, consider using the alternative large stockpot. If you do not own a large stockpot, ask a friend or neighbor to borrow one. If you enjoy the process of cooking food in bulk, then you can go out and purchase a nice stockpot. Also, offer to share some of your soup with the neighbor who allowed you to borrow that pot.

HINT: Big box stores such as Sam's Club, Costco, and others are ideal for home cooking. Bulk foods cost 30 percent to 95 percent less than similar smaller packaged products.

As you list your equipment needs, think about the equipment you will need that is not indicated in the recipe. Example: If you are making soup, you will need several large slotted spoons and ladles. If you are making baked goods, you may need a spatula or two. Check your knives. Do you have knives that will cut the beef you need to make the stew?

Chapter 1: Getting Started

Examine every step of the recipe, and consider the requirements for each step of your activity. The more careful you are about reading your recipe, the less chance there is that you will find you do not have the wire whisk needed to beat the egg whites.

As you start to put together your shopping list of ingredients, there are several things to keep in mind:

- ❏ Storage
- ❏ Quantity
- ❏ Fresh vs. Prepared
- ❏ Service

Storage — Consider what you will do with the ingredient when you get it home or to the location where you plan on cooking. If you buy large amounts of food that need to remain refrigerated, you need a place to keep them until you are ready to use them. Likewise, if you need freezer space to store those frozen strawberries until you put them on top of cheesecakes, make sure that adequate freezer space is available before you bring anything home from the store.

Quantity — Be very careful to shop for the amount of ingredients you will need. This advice is given not only to be sure you have enough of something, but also so you do not buy too much. One of the primary reasons people cook food in bulk is to save money. You will not be saving money if you throw spoiled food away because you bought too much. On the other hand, if you have space to store that extra 50 pounds of beef that you got a great deal on, by all means, buy and store.

Fresh vs. Prepared — Many of the recipes you will make can be made with either fresh or frozen (or otherwise preserved) ingredients. Keep in mind, however, that if you plan on freezing your food after preparation, you will want to start with ingredients that are as fresh as possible. Some foods, such as fish, should not be refrozen after they are thawed. Other foods, such as vegetables and fruits, change in consistency with refreezing, and you may not get the outcome you expect. If you plan to refreeze meat or vegetables, be sure to handle them properly. *Be sure to read Chapter 2 in this book on freezing before you proceed.*

Service — Think about how and when you are going to serve the food you are making. If you are making cheesecake that you plan on freezing and will, eventually, serve with fresh fruit on top, you may not need to buy the fruit when you shop for the ingredients to make the cheesecake. Many recipes that you will make to preserve (whether you freeze or can them) may be enhanced with the addition of a fresh ingredient at the time of serving. Take this into account when you shop.

HINT: Involve family, friends, neighbors, and your children in preparing food. This will be a fun social and learning event for all involved.

When you make a shopping list, make sure to write down the item you need, as well as the total amount you need for bulk cooking. To calculate this, simply multiply the needed ingredients by the number of batches you want. If you find larger-sized cans of the ingredients you need, you will not have to spend 15 to 30 minutes in front of a can opener opening multiple standard-size cans. Dividing your list between what you need to get in bulk from the warehouse stores and what you can get at your grocery store is the best way to maximize your time on the day you shop.

Breaking down the shopping lists further is also a big help. Divide what you need into categories such as dairy, meat, and vegetables, and make sure you get enough for every recipe. For example, if you have more than one dish that calls for chicken, add up how much you need for all your recipes, and be sure to purchase that amount. When you get home, divide up the chicken to match the recipes that call for it. Have a miscellaneous column on your shopping list for all the items you will need while cooking, including freezer bags, foil, labels for freezer containers, rubber gloves, trash bags, permanent markers, dish detergent, an apron with pockets, and various snacks to stop yourself from eating the ingredients.

Be sure to check advertisements before making your decision on where to do the majority of your shopping. Most grocery store chains have some form of protein on sale from week to week, which can help stretch your budget. If you are taking on the bulk cooking with a partner and you are splitting the shopping, make sure your lists do not have duplicate ingredients. If you are going to shop in the supermarket for meat, try calling the meat department, and ask if there are discounts for buying in bulk. Ask if they have limits on how much you are able to buy at one time. If you need meats mixed, ground, sliced, or cubed, the meat department will do that for you if you call ahead and give them enough time. You may want to call two to three days before you plan on shopping so the butcher has enough time to fill your order. You also may want to consider buying jars of chopped, minced, or pureed garlic, and frozen, diced onions to save you time and the tears.

Preparing your workspace

You now know what you are going to make and what you will need to make it. Sometime between the planning, the shopping, and the actual cooking, you need to prepare your workspace. In most cases, this means you will need to prepare your kitchen, but this prep work may also include other areas of your house or

the place in which you will be preparing your food. The most important thing you need to do is to clean your workspace. Cleaning to prepare your workspace also means cleaning the equipment you will use to prepare, store, and/or serve your food. If you have a small space and are limited in equipment, you may also need to work out a plan to clean as you work.

Every inch of your kitchen should be cleaned. Clean your appliances such as your refrigerator, stove, and oven, and wash your pots, pans, spoons, and ladles.

Cleaning up the area, courtesy of the USDA

Contact with botulinum toxin can be fatal, whether it is ingested or enters through the skin. This toxin can occur in improperly processed home canned foods. Take care to avoid contact with suspect foods or liquids. Wear rubber or heavy plastic gloves when handling suspect foods or cleaning up contaminated work surfaces and equipment. Use a fresh solution of one part unscented liquid household chlorine bleach (5 percent to 6 percent sodium hypochlorite) to five parts clean water to treat work surfaces, equipment, or other items, including can openers and clothing, that may have come in contact with suspect foods or liquids. Spray or wet contaminated surfaces with the bleach solution, and let stand for 30 minutes. Wearing gloves, wipe up treated spills with paper towels, being careful to minimize the spread of contamination. Dispose of these paper towels by placing them in a plastic bag before putting them in the trash. Next, apply the bleach solution to all surfaces and equipment again, let stand for 30 minutes, and rinse. As a last step, thoroughly wash all detoxified counters, containers, equipment, clothing, etc. Discard gloves when the cleaning is complete. (Note: Bleach is an irritant itself and should not be inhaled or allowed to come in contact with the skin.)

If you are cooking in your home, you need to ensure that as you clean and prepare to cook, there is limited activity in the kitchen. Most people's kitchens are the central activity hubs of the household, especially if they have children. Help to prepare your workspace by preparing those who live in your house for the day of cooking you have planned. If your cooking is going to take an entire day, be sure the day's meals are easy ones that do not require cooking.

HINT: As an added bonus, you will save money on energy costs by batch cooking and doubling recipes. A little extra time and money spent one day cooking in bulk will result in long-term savings and less stress when deciding what to have for dinner.

Setting aside the time needed to carry out your plan

As you read through this book, you will see that cooking in bulk is not something you can enter into without planning and devoting a considerable amount of time. Planning for the actual cooking is a process that may take you a couple of days. If you need to shop for your ingredients, you should plan to spend at least a couple of hours doing so. The prep work of cleaning and washing any fruit, vegetables, or other food that needs cleaning will take some time.

You cannot do it all in one day. Plan first, and shop after you plan. Clean your space the night before you cook. Plan for your cooking and subsequent cleanup to take an entire day. The more you are able to prepare before cooking day, the better off you will be. If you are going to be cooking with a friend or a group, dividing the prep work should be easy; if you are cooking alone, see if you can find someone willing to help out. Examples of prep work you may need to do include the following:

- Removing skin from chicken
- Cooking and draining the pasta. If you are putting it in sauces, stocks, or broths, only cook it half way
- Making the rubs, barbeque sauces, and marinades for your meat products
- Making your slow-cooking meal
- Chopping and steaming fresh vegetables
- Browning any of your ground meats
- Dicing or grinding your ham
- Making all your sauces

▶ Cooking and dicing your poultry

▶ Soaking and cooking all your dry beans

As you are doing prep work, separate what you need for every recipe into its own bag so you do not run the risk of using too much of one item in one recipe and not having enough for the other recipes. Measure out your dry and wet ingredients, and put them into bowls. Wrap the tops of the bowls with plastic wrap. You can leave the dry ingredients on the counter, provided you do not have a cat or dog that will get on the counter in the middle of the night. Place the wet ingredients in bowls as well, wrap the bowls in plastic wrap, and place them inside the refrigerator.

No matter what you are making or when you are making it, you will need to carefully schedule and plan your activities. Your plan will include your recipe(s) and your timeline of what needs to be done and when.

Preparing the space you will need to freeze or store your food

If you do not plan to serve the food you prepare immediately, be sure to take some time prior to cooking to make storage space. Clean out your freezer and make room in your refrigerator. Be sure the containers you will be using to store your prepared dishes are clean and ready to be used. Viable options for storing food for a short period of time are coolers or deep freezers for frozen foods.

If you plan on immediately serving some or all of the food you prepare, be sure your service plates, trays, tables, spoons, ladles, and other utensils are clean and ready to go. Be sure that if your dishes need to be kept warm or cold, you are prepared to hold your food at the proper temperature to keep the food safe and tasty. Most recipes in this book suggest proper temperatures and methods of keeping your prepared dishes safe as you serve.

Cleaning up

Make a cleanup plan a part of your scheduled cooking activity. It is often possible to clean as you go. If you find that you have time while you are waiting for things to bake, cool, boil, or roast, plan to do some preliminary cleanup so you are not left with a mountain of work after you cook. Washing dishes as you go and keeping the floor swept are two easy ways to make cleanup a little more manageable. You may also consider scheduling your cooking day for a day when the trash is collected in your neighborhood. Planning this will mean you will not have a large amount of food refuse sitting for several days in your trash bin.

Shopping

Choosing your shopping site

Knowing the value of a warehouse store, such as Sam's, Costco, or BJ's Wholesale, is one of the most important parts of shopping. Shopping at a warehouse store is especially convenient for purchasing items such as cooking oil, flour, sugar, nuts, cheeses, freezer bags, disposable gloves, wider width  aluminum foil, and plastic wrap. You save more money at a warehouse store than at a grocery store, even if you use grocer or manufacturer coupons. The cost of an annual membership to these stores, which is around $45 per person, is a concern for some people, but if you know someone who already has a membership, ask them to take you shopping one day. If you are going to bulk cook with a friend, split the cost of the membership; often when you purchase a membership, you receive a second card for free. For instance, Sam's Club charges $42 for a year membership with the added advantage of receiving a second card for free. You can pick who you want to give the second card to. If you split that cost in half with a friend, it is $21 each, and the savings you receive on your shopping trips will far outweigh the cost of the membership. If you are going to cook in a group or a co-op, see if the warehouse gives discounts for joining as a group.

If you have never been to a warehouse store, make sure you have plenty of time to do your shopping. Allow two to three hours for the shopping trip. Completing your shopping in one day will save you time and prevent you from having to make more than one trip; this way, you have more time to spend in the kitchen to prep and cook your meals. You can choose to stock up on nonperishable items for the month when there are sales. As far as fruits, vegetables, dairy products, and meats are concerned, it is best to purchase them within two or three days of when you are going to use them. Always remember to check dates on the items you purchase to ensure their freshness.

Always shop at least two days before you are going to cook. This gives you enough time to get your prep work done before the big cooking day. If you shop during peak business hours, between 5 p.m. and 7 p.m., you will probably upset a few people in line behind you at the register. Instead, opt to shop in the early morning, early afternoon, or late in the evening to avoid the glares and grumbles of people behind you in line. If you are cooking with a friend or a group of friends and you are doing all the shopping, separate the ingredients each person needs on the belt to save time when you are trying to figure out who gets what. If you separate your items on the belt at the register as they are being rung up, then those items can be bagged together, which will make it easier when it comes time to give each person what they need. If you order large quantities of a sale item from your grocer, they will sometimes waive quantity limits if you call them three to four days in advance.

Do all your shopping for nonperishable items first. Then visit the meat, dairy, and frozen food sections to help keep your items cold for a longer period of time. The warehouse store, Sam's Club, offers something called Click 'n' Pull®, which allows you to get on their website before 5 p.m. and click on the items you wish to purchase. The store then pulls it for you to pick up the next day. This service is included in your membership fee. This is a time-saving feature because they essentially do the shopping for you.

There are also websites where you can purchase items you need by the case and they will ship it to you, even if they are not in your area. Two examples are Bulk Food (**www.bulkfood.com**) and Dutch Valley (**www.dutchvalleyfoods.com**). The difference between online-only stores and the warehouse stores in your area is that perishable items are not available through the online stores.

Equipment

Every kitchen should have certain items to meet basic cooking needs. It is important to invest in the best quality of pots and pans that you can afford. If taken care of, you can enjoy them for years, instead of having to buy new ones every two years. Buying kitchen equipment that you know will serve several functions, such as blenders, food processors, and sheet pans, is a smart investment. Remember to buy only what is needed; there is no point in going crazy at a kitchen store and buying equipment that most likely will never be used. The following are the essential pots, pans, utensils, bowls, storage materials, and miscellaneous other useful gadgets for the kitchen.

HINT: Auction sites such as **www.Ebay.com** are great resources for buying used and new commercial food service equipment.

To prepare the recipes included in this book, you will need to have a range with a working oven and cooktop, a refrigerator/freezer, and a microwave oven. Before you start, you would do well to check the reliability of your oven by setting it for 350 or 400 degrees and placing an oven thermometer inside. You may need to adjust times or temperatures of the recipes if your oven has an uneven or unreliable thermostat.

Appliances

▸ A *blender* is used to blend, emulsify, or purée food. It can pull double duty as both a food processor and a blender.

▸ A *hand mixer* is a frequently used, motorized appliance that combines ingredients. Mixers usually come with specialty attachments, including a wire whip, a dough hook, and flat beaters. The wire whips help to beat air into whipped mixtures, such as angel food cakes and whipped creams. The dough hook mixes and kneads yeast dough for bread, and the flat beater mixes everything.

▸ A *slow cooker* retains low heat over a long period of time so a meal can be prepared in the morning and ready to eat at dinnertime. Although some models can be pricey, slow cookers are an investment worth the expense, especially for families who rarely have time to sit down and enjoy a meal together. The slow cooker comes in various sizes, from 16 ounces to 7 quarts, and it allows you to have a full meal in one pot. A removable interior makes cleaning easy. Although ten to 30 minutes are required before placing the meal in the slow cooker, you can avoid spending hours in the kitchen.

▸ A *food processor* helps chop, shred, slice, and blend food, making meal preparation easier. To use a food processor, an item simply needs to be sliced in half, placed in the food processor, and pulsed, which consists of pushing the processor's button a few times. This helps to easily chop food items without having to take the time to do it manually.

▶ A *grater* is a hand-held tool that has slits on one side and holes on the other. A grater is used to shred cheeses or vegetables.

▶ An ***immersion blender***, also known as the stick blender, is a handheld blender that is tall, narrow, and has a rotating blade at one end that spins at various speeds. Stick blenders help purée large batches easily. Especially helpful when cooking soup, the immersion blender can be placed directly in the pot, turned on, and moved in a circular motion, avoiding pouring batches of soup into a blender.

▶ A ***waffle iron*** is not necessary unless your family particularly enjoys homemade waffles. There are several types of waffle irons on the market. Belgian waffle irons give you oversized, round waffles, and the standard waffle iron makes square waffles that fit perfectly into a toaster. A waffle iron has two cast iron plates that are hinged together and close to perfectly cook the batter placed inside.

▶ A ***toaster oven*** is a small electrical appliance used to toast or reheat. Toaster ovens make reheating small foods such as French toast or personal pizza simple. The toaster oven should be used when a microwave will not do, or when it is not worth heating the large oven for something that will take less than five minutes to reheat. Toaster ovens even help with meal preparation.

▶ A ***deep-fat fryer*** is a heated vessel used to submerge meat — most likely chicken — into heated fat. You can also make french fries and potato chips with this appliance. It comes with a basket, which makes submerging and retrieving the food easy. Fryers are available in different sizes and can be placed right on the countertop.

▸ *Pressure fryers* are used to heat meat and oil at a low temperature while a high amount of pressure is added so air, or steam, is not allowed to escape. This enables the meat to cook at a rate faster than standard frying. This appliance also comes with a basket to make it easier to drop and retrieve meat, and it comes in a counter top model.

Pots, pans, and skillets

▸ A set of three *sauté pans* is necessary, preferably without plastic handles so they can be placed under the broiler, which is close to the flame or heating element. A 6-inch pan is useful when making an omelet, frying an egg, or sautéing a small quantity of vegetables. An 8- or 12-inch pan helps sauté larger quantities of vegetables or chicken, or it can be used to sear a pork tenderloin before finishing it off in the oven. The final size is the 5-quart pan with a lid, which will hold large amounts of vegetables to make stews, braises, or pasta sauces.

▸ A *stockpot or Dutch oven* in an 8- or 12-quart size pot can be used to make soups or pastas. The Dutch oven is generally shorter and squatter and can be used for chili, braising a whole chicken, cooking stuffed cabbage, or cooking a pot roast — both on the stove and in the oven. If purchasing a Dutch oven, be sure it is made of cast iron.

▸ It is important to have a set of three *saucepans* that hold 1½ quarts, 2½ quarts, and 5 quarts. Having all three allows you to make three different sauces at once, melt butter, or make gravy. Depending on the amount of sauce you need, you will be able to use all three of these pots while bulk cooking for

a month and even during the reheating process. All three pots should be sturdy enough to use in the oven, as well as on the stove. They come in cast iron, stainless steel, or copper at any leading retail store.

▶ A *canning kettle* is a pot made especially for canning items. It has a wire rack to place jars that are being sterilized and sealed. Before canning items such as jellies, jams, soups, pickles, marinades, or sauces, it is wise to purchase one of these pots. This item is available at specialty cooking stores or online.

▶ One or two *rimmed baking sheets* in either the 15-inch by 12-inch or the 17-inch by 14-inch size help bake cinnamon rolls or jellyrolls, garlic bread, salmon, sheet cakes, or french fries. When purchasing baking sheets, make sure the size allows a 2-inch clearance on every side of your oven rack to provide an even distribution of heat.

▶ *Muffin tins* come in handy when baking muffins or cupcakes. Tin size varies from mini to regular — to even jumbo sized. The mini pans hold up to 24 bite-size muffins. Regular muffin tins hold a dozen muffins and are the size of the muffins mom used to make. Jumbo muffin tins hold eight muffins that are the same size as coffeehouse or bakery muffins. It might take six to ten bites to eat a whole one.

▶ *Electric skillets and griddles* help to sauté, brown meats, or cook bacon or sausage. The main difference between electric skillets and griddles is electric skillets have sides and a top, whereas an electric griddle is a flat surface. They range from 11 to 16 inches, which is recommended for home use. They are usually square or rectangular, but some are circular. They all plug into the wall. Skillets are used to simmer, warm, or cook food up to 400 degrees. Electric griddles come in sizes ranging from 9 ½ inches to 36 inches, the larger size being found in restaurants. A standard household griddle is 22 inches.

▶ *Large electric roasting pans* are important to have so you can roast a chicken or pot roast while using the oven to cook a meatloaf. The electric roasting pan plugs into the wall, and the temperature can be set anywhere from 200 to 450 degrees. Food is enclosed and cooks evenly because of an internal heating element that allows you to roast, bake, or steam your food. It differs from the electric skillet or griddle because it encloses the food, you can cook the food several different ways, and there is a timer; with the griddle or skillet you may not have a top, and you definitely will not have an automatic timer.

▸ **Steam-jacketed kettles** are used to prepare large quantities of food. You can use them for a wide range of items, such as sauces, soups, vegetables, and meat dishes. Water is heated in an outer layer of a kettle or pot. The water heats to become steam, which surrounds the food that is in an interior pot. The steam, or excess moisture, never comes into contact with the food, and the heat from the steam cooks the food. The flavor of the food remains undiluted by excessive moisture. A small steam-jacketed kettle costs about $2,000, while a large one can cost more than $20,000.

▸ **Steam tables** are large serving tables in which foods are kept warm by steam that circulates beneath the surface of the table.

All pots and pans should be a heavy grade, such as a heavy-duty stainless steal or cast iron. These materials last longer and withstand going from stovetop to oven.

Utensils

▸ A good set of **knives** is essential in food preparation. High-grade butcher blocks are convenient because they include a paring knife, an 8-inch chef's knife, a 6-inch utility knife, a fillet knife, a carving knife, and a sharpening knife, which is important should a blade become dull. A **paring knife** has many uses, such as peeling vegetables or fruits, de-veining

shrimps, removing seeds from hot peppers, and cutting small garnishes. This is the smallest of the knives in the butcher block. A **chef's knife** can be used to cut bone instead of using a cleaver. This knife is known as the all-purpose knife. **Utility** knives are used to cut cheeses and meats for sandwiches. They look like standard steak knives but lack serrated edges. A **fillet knife** is generally used to debone and fillet fish, and a **carving knife** is used to slice thin pieces of meat, such as hams, poultry, and roasts.

▶ *Kitchen shears* are handy tools that will most likely come with the butcher block knife set. These shears can be used for anything, such as **butterflying** — cutting along both sides of a chicken's backbone, pulling the backbone out, and pressing down on the chicken until it lays completely flat. Another use of shears is cutting the rope away from a pork roast. As they are extra sharp, keep them away from children.

▶ A *ladle* comes in handy when transferring soups, sauces, jellies, jams, pickled items, and salad dressings from their preparation devices to their storage containers. They come in both metal and plastic, so choose based on personal preference.

▶ A *spatula* is also needed; they can be either metal or plastic. It is best to have a couple so you can use them for more than one dish. These also come in handy when scraping down the sides of bowls and pots. Spatulas usually come in sets of two or three.

▶ *Mixing spoons* come in packages that contain anywhere from three to eight spoons. The more available in the kitchen, the better. It is best to have at least two sets — one set for dry ingredients and one for wet ingredients.

▶ A pair of *tongs* come in handy when flipping or transferring meat from one pan to another.

▶ The *wire whisk* is useful when making gravy, meringues, and other foods. Plastic whisks are available, but wire is best.

▶ A *vegetable peeler* is used to peel potatoes, carrots, zucchini, squash, cucumbers, and other vegetables.

▶ *Slotted spoons* help remove items that are soaking or cooking in liquid. These spoons ensure there is little to no liquid left when transferring an item from one dish to another. They are available in plastic or metal.

HINT: Check online for purchasing your equipment and small wares from sites that service restaurants and other food service establishments. Take a look at companies such as **www.bigtray.com**, **www.foodservicewharehouse.com**, and **www.webrestaurantstore.com**.

▶ You will also need two sets of *measuring cups*, one for wet ingredients and the other for dry. They come in two varieties: stand-up glass, which is one glass container with several measurements on it, or a set of plastic or metal cups that vary in size. They sometimes come hooked together on a ring.

▶ Two sets of *measuring spoons* are needed, either plastic or stainless steel, for wet and dry ingredients.

▶ A wood or plastic *rolling pin* is used to roll out dough.

Bowls and storage materials

▶ A set of *mixing bowls* is necessary. They are made of glass, plastic, or stainless steel, and they come in sets of three up to sets of six. The more on hand, the better. It is beneficial to have a set for dry ingredients and a set for wet ingredients.

▶ Glass *prep bowls* come in handy. These bowls are available in food retail stores and generally come in sets of eight. They vary in ounce sizes, from small enough to fit a teaspoon to large enough for a cup of ingredients. It is convenient and efficient to pre-measure ingredients, both wet and dry, and put them in these bowls.

▶ *Plastic storage containers* are available for individual purchase, or come in sets with as many as 50 pieces. These can be used to store anything from shredded, chopped, or grated ingredients, to soups, sauces, and stocks.

Although convenient, these containers may be ruined after several uses because they may warp and develop stains.

▸ *Resealable plastic storage bags* keep a variety of items fresh. Do not get the old-fashioned kind with a twist tie because they have a tendency to leak. Instead, purchase the locking bags. Every kitchen should have 1-quart, 1-gallon, and 2-gallon sized bags to store meat, salads, vegetables, soups, or sauces. These handy bags fit wherever needed. To freeze your items, make sure you use containers and bags that are specially made to go into the freezer. They last longer, and you will not run the risk of a bag or container breaking.

▸ *Plastic wrap* helps store cooking creations. There are many varieties of plastic wrap to choose from, but stay away from the colored variety. Not only does it make seeing what is wrapped inside difficult, but it also turns food another color, making it hard  to tell if the food is bad or still good to eat. Elastic edge plastic wrap, meant to fit over bowls, is not good for long periods of storage because it does not create the tight seal needed to keep air out. When it comes to plastic wrap, it is important to consider whether you want cling wrap, whether the wrap is microwavable, and if heavy-duty or thin wrap is preferred. Each plastic wrap has different results for each user, and some cooks may prefer one brand more than another. Try a couple options before settling on the one you like best. For longer periods of storage, the heavy-duty version is best.

▸ You will need *aluminum foil* for storing items up to two weeks, as well as for cooking. Decide whether you like nonstick, plain, heavy-duty, or standard weight. Olive oil and cooking sprays keep your food from sticking to the foil when you use it for cooking. The heavy-duty version tears less frequently, so you get more use out of this kind than with regular weight. Never use aluminum foil with foods that have a high acid content, such as foods cooked with tomatoes, wines, or vinegars. The acid will react with the metal, and the food will end up having a metallic taste.

▶ *Parchment paper* is great for baking cookies, brownies, cakes, and baked items that have a tendency to stick to pans. You can also use parchment paper when baking fish, chicken, and vegetables.

Miscellaneous gadgets

▶ *Cutting boards* should be in every kitchen. The plastic ones are inexpensive and more sanitary than wooden ones. There are glass versions available as well. You may choose which boards work best for you, but always buy a couple of them. You can buy them individually, or in sets of up to five. It is a common practice to have several colors and types of cutting boards that are used on the same type of food every time you use them. You can use one for chicken, one for fish, one for beef, one for pork, and one for vegetables so there is no cross contamination of the meats and vegetables. When washing your cutting boards, be sure to follow the cleaning instructions outlined earlier in this chapter.

▶ *Can openers* are a staple in every kitchen, even though a majority of standard-sized canned products come with a pop-top. There are both hand-held can openers and electrical ones. The electrical can opener opens cans faster than the hand-held option, but it may not be able to hold the weight of a large can.

▶ *Colanders* are used to strain pastas, vegetables, as well as a variety of other foods. You can purchase them individually, or in sets of three. They are available in plastic, copper, stainless steel, enamel, and mesh varieties. It is best to own one set of the plastic, copper, stainless steel, or enamel variety, in addition to a set of the mesh version. The mesh version can be used to sift dry ingredients when you are baking.

▶ *Oven mitts and potholders* are important to avoid burning yourself, or your countertops. Every kitchen should have a couple sets of potholders and oven mitts.

▶ *Rubber, plastic, or latex gloves* are necessary when you mix things with your hands or debone a chicken. You can choose the version you like best, but make sure to try each so you know which ones work for your cooking needs. You can clean and reuse rubber gloves, but you must be sure to clean thoroughly, or you run the risk of contaminating other meals with bacteria. Plastic or latex gloves are disposable and safer for mixing.

▶ *Spring mechanism cookie scoops* help you make desserts or breakfast dishes, such as muffin mixes, or fruits. The scoops spoon out the exact measurements you need — from 2 teaspoons to 3 tablespoons. The lever-activated spring mechanism attached to the scoop makes releasing its contents easy.

▶ *Pastry brushes* are good for brushing on sauces and marinades. You can also egg wash the crusts on casseroles and quiches with these brushes.

▶ A *bulb baster* helps baste meat while it is cooking to prevent it from drying out. The baster is a long, cylindrical tube that has a bulb on the end that you squeeze. It allows you to gather the meat's juices so you can squeeze them on top of the meat.

▶ A *kitchen timer* will help you cook your meals to perfection. If you have more than one, you can set them for different projects going on at once — just be sure to place a piece of paper or an index card underneath each one so you know what it is set for.

▶ *Instant read thermometers* that range from 0 to 220 degrees and can be inserted at least a couple of inches into the food are desirable. "Instant read" means it indicates the temperature very quickly, which is important when you are increasing the heat of your food and you need to know exactly what the temperature is in an instant. You will probably find

that two thermometers will come in handy, as it is often good to know the temperatures of several items being cooked simultaneously. Often, you will find that one of your thermometers is not clean when you need it, so having a second thermometer will be useful. Also, you will find it useful if you have the kind of thermometers that can clip onto the edge of a pot. To test to see if your thermometers are accurate, boil some water and check the reading of the thermometer. If you get a reading of 212 degrees, your tool is working properly.

*Note that all recipes and directions in this book refer to temperatures using the Fahrenheit scale.

CHAPTER

Food Preservation

TWO

Freezing Foods

Preserving foods through freezing only became available in much of the world since the invention of refrigerators and freezers about 75 years ago. However, many cultures have been freezing foods for millennia. People who lived in extremely cold climates, such as the Arctic Circle, dug storage places for the meat from hunting, or built a cache out of rocks. The meat was protected from predators, and when the people needed some food, they would chop a hunk off the frozen meat and cook it.

Other early cultures invented clever ways to keep food frozen during the summer months. The Chinese used ice cellars more than 3,000 years ago. The ancient Incas, living in the Andes, learned how to freeze-dry food by removing the water content during the freezing process. In warmer climates, the Egyptians and Indians discovered they could produce ice crystals by causing clay jars to evaporate water quickly. In addition, many cultures, including the Greeks and Romans, collected snow and ice from mountains during the winter months to line cellars that would keep food frozen during the summer.

Today, freezing is the safest, quickest, and easiest method to store food until you are ready to eat it. Freezing is also an economical method because you can buy meat and produce when it is on sale or in season and pack it away for later. Whether you have a large chest freezer or a refrigerator/freezer combination, this chapter will explain how to pack and freeze foods properly. This chapter discusses how to keep frozen foods tasting as delicious as possible and how long you should keep items in your freezer. It will also show you what to do when something goes wrong — such as handling a power outage or an unexpected thaw.

Freezer options

There are two types of freezers that you can use to store all of your bulk items: an upright freezer and a chest freezer. An upright freezer can range in size from 12 to 30 cubic feet. Some come with a sliding basket, or drawer, that comes in handy when making items in bulk by giving you a little more room to pack the bigger items on the shelves. Others have an optional icemaker, but these can take up room in the freezer. There are certain benefits to having an upright freezer. For instance, they take up less floor space than a chest freezer of the same capacity. You can store your food on shelves, which makes it easier to find. The only problem is that the temperature in the door space will be warmer than the temperature at the back of the freezer, unlike a chest freezer.

A chest freezer comes in a size of 2 to 28 cubic feet. These models are generally cheaper than the upright models, and they give you more usable space to pack the food into. You can use boxes or baskets for more optimal usage of space. This type of freezer can be more cost-efficient to operate. With the food being more tightly packed together, the packages will hold in the chill better. Less cold air escapes with a chest freezer than an upright freezer.

Freezing occurs when food is kept at 0 degree Fahrenheit (-18 degrees Celsius) for 24 hours or longer. Of course, the amount and texture of the food determines how quickly it will reach the optimal freezing state. Once the food is completely frozen, bacteria, yeasts, and molds that could cause food to spoil are rendered completely inactive. This means that while the bacteria is still present, it does not reproduce and cannot spoil the food. Some bacteria are destroyed by freezing, but many can begin to multiply once the food is thawed and begin to cause illness again. It is possible that sub-zero freezing can destroy trichina and other parasites, but it is still a good idea to rely on proper cooking to kill any parasites. Freezing also changes the enzymes present in food. This can be especially important in fruits and vegetables that may continue to ripen slightly while they are frozen. In these cases, a few extra steps, described in this chapter, are needed to stop the enzymatic process.

All methods of preservation will change the flavor and texture of the food. Freezing can toughen some produce and soften other foods. In addition, food can take on a stale "freezer taste" or absorb odors from newly frozen foods. To prevent this, defrost the refrigerator occasionally and wipe it down with cleaner and a wet rag. Frost-free freezers, which are standard appliances today, should not require that you remove ice but will still benefit from a periodic cleaning. Between cleanings, keep an open box of baking soda in the freezer to absorb odors and ensure foods have the best taste possible. Change the box every three to four months — you can also pour it down your kitchen sink to get rid of odors there.

Problems with freezing

You may notice two problems in your freezer — foods that take on a tough, dried-out texture and foods entirely covered with ice crystals. Neither of these conditions is dangerous to your health, but they will not add to your enjoyment of the food. Freezer burn happens when food is inadequately wrapped against the cold, and frozen air dries out the surface and damages the fibers of the food.

Ice crystals generally form when food is not packed properly or freezes too slowly. *Later in this chapter, you will find tips on how to package food to protect it against freezer burn.* Large ice crystals will form on food as it slowly releases moisture directly from the produce or meat. When you defrost these products, you end up with a great deal of water and a tough, dry portion of food. Ice crystals also form when a freezer has fluctuations in temperature that may cause slight thawing — again, releasing moisture from your food. An older or malfunctioning freezer will most likely cause temperature fluctuations, so it is smart to check your freezer now and then for a stable, cold environment. Food that has been frozen long past its lifetime will also be susceptible to ice crystals, but it is not harmful.

You will be most successful at freezing foods, and will produce food with the best possible quality, if you use containers, bags, and wraps designed for the freezer. These are designed to be thick enough to keep moisture in and freezer odors out. Plastic wrap and sandwich bags are not thick enough and often leave gaps that will cause freezer burn on your food. Foil is a good freezer wrap, but the disadvantage is that it is hard to tell what food is under the layer of foil. Plastic containers and casserole dishes designed to go from freezer to oven (or vice versa) are good choices as well, but some plastic containers can give your food a plastic taste — especially when new. Some people also use vacuum-seal machines that remove the air from a thick plastic bag and then seal the open edge with heat.

Regardless of the storage container you use, always write the date and the contents of the package on the outside. Nothing is more frustrating than riffling through anonymous packages looking for that bag of eggplant from last month.

Freeze smarter

There are ways to freeze smarter so your food will taste better and your freezer will be more energy-efficient. Cold foods need much less energy to freeze than hot ones, so wait for hot foods to cool before freezing. If you live in a cold climate, you can save energy by placing the warm container outside and letting the weather cool it for you. Then place it in the freezer at a spot where there is plenty of space around the container so cold air can circulate around it. Once it is frozen solid, you can place it with the rest of the foods.

Remember to freeze food in small portions. The food will freeze faster and will taste fresher when it is thawed, and your freezer will have to produce less cold air to keep the food frozen. Freezing food in serving portions is also a smart idea; it can be hard to chip one chicken breast out of a package of six, or remove a few slices of bread from a frozen loaf. However, if you individually wrap meats or other foods, you can take out just what you need and save the rest.

When sealing the bags, make sure you remove as much air from the bag as you can. Any air remaining in the bag can cause freezer burn or allow condensing moisture to create ice crystals. If you use a container rather than a bag, make sure that the food fills the entire container. On the other hand, if freezing soups, sauces, or stews, leave some headspace at the top of the container to prevent the liquid, which expands as it freezes, from freezing to the lid — or popping the lid right off the container.

Foods that do not freeze well

▶ Buttermilk

▶ Eggs in the shell, whether cooked or raw

▶ Raw egg yolks

▶ Any products made of eggs, such as pudding, custard sauces, or pastries and cakes containing custard

▶ Sour cream or dips made with sour cream

▶ Whipped topping, including those in a frozen carton, an aerosol can, or prepared from a mix

▶ Whipped cream and half-and-half

▶ Yogurt

▶ Prepared salads: egg, chicken, ham, tuna, and macaroni salads

▶ Opened bottles of salad dressing

▶ Lettuce and other salad greens

▶ Radishes

▶ Green onions

▶ Cucumbers

▶ Opened cans of meat, poultry, fish, or seafood

These foods do not freeze well for a variety of reasons. Some foods, such as buttermilk, yogurt, and sour cream, will separate when frozen. Lettuce and salad greens will wilt when frozen. Opened cans of meat, poultry, fish, or seafood will become dry and change in consistency when frozen.

Tips for Freezing Foods

Always make sure the recipe you are bulk cooking can be frozen. You do not want to make multiples of your family's favorite recipes, only to find out it will not freeze well. If you buy big a package of meat and freeze the entire package instead of breaking it into smaller packages, you will have to defrost and cook the entire package in a few different recipes before you attempt to refreeze the meat again. Here are some other tips on how to freeze different kinds of foods:

▶ A hard-boiled egg will get rubbery when it has been frozen and then thawed, but if you cut it up into fine pieces before you freeze it, this will not happen.

▶ Sauces, gravies, or any other liquid thickened with cornstarch and flavored with mild seasonings have a tendency to separate when you reheat them. If the sauce is frozen as a part of a dish with other ingredients, the quality will be better after thawing. Consider canning sauces that you do not plan on mixing with other ingredients.

▶ If you plan to use raw vegetables in a recipe that is intended to be frozen, blanch the vegetables beforehand to lock in the flavor and nutrients. **Blanching** simply means placing vegetables in boiling water for a very short amount of time. Blanching keeps vegetables from breaking down during the thawing process. *You will learn how to blanch later in this chapter.*

▶ Instead of using raw vegetables, you can use the frozen variety, which will save you some time. Green peppers, onions, and celery are the exception. Even fresh, these vegetables are easy to use and freeze better than any other vegetables due to their water content.

▶ Eat ham, bacon, and other cured meats within a month's time of freezing because they lose all their color and flavor if left in the freezer any longer. Cured meats are meats that were preserved by being salted, smoked, or aged.

▶ Some seasonings become stronger in flavor, while others lose their flavor when frozen. Salt, celery, and green peppers all lose a little flavor. Salt may leave your recipe with a metallic taste. Flavors that become stronger during the freezing period are black pepper, cloves, bay leaves, onions, sage, and artificial vanilla. When you freeze foods, remember to adjust the spices by adding a little more or less, according to the spice you are working with. Another option is to leave seasoning out completely and add it during the reheating process.

▶ If you plan on deep frying meals, be aware they will not remain crispy after you thaw and reheat them. Also, their flavor can alter after time in the freezer.

▶ If you use egg and milk substitutes in recipes, such as soy milk, powdered milk, or lactose-free milk, these items will freeze quite well.

▶ For pasta, rice, or bean recipes that involve any stock, broth, or sauce, under cook the pasta, rice, or beans by at least half the recommend time; failing to do this results in the dish having a mushy consistency when you thaw and reheat.

▶ Lettuce, cucumbers, tomatoes, and radishes freeze well, but they do not maintain their original consistency when thawed. Tomatoes, for example, freeze, thaw, and reheat fine as part of a sauce, but not as a fresh vegetable. For these foods, it is best to not freeze them. Instead, keep them on hand, and add them to the recipe before serving.

Fresh vegetables require special attention before freezing. It is important to choose good, fresh vegetables for your recipes. Clean and trim off any inedible parts, and then cut the vegetables into the sizes needed for your recipes. Once cut, you can blanch the vegetables using one of three ways: microwave blanching, stovetop steaming, or boiling water blanching.

Blanching vegetables before using them in recipes helps maintain freshness and crispness when you are ready to use them or store them. Microwave blanching consists of pouring ¼ cup of water in a round, microwave-safe bowl. Place the vegetables in the container, using no more than 4 cups of a leafy vegetable such as spinach, or 2 cups of non-leafy vegetables. Cover the container with microwavable plastic wrap. If you have a turntable in your microwave, make sure the bowl has enough room to move freely. Microwave the vegetables on high, keeping in mind that time will vary, depending on the vegetable. Once the vegetables are blanched, spread them out in a single layer on a baking sheet or tray to cool for five minutes. You can then use the vegetables in recipes, or you can freeze them by themselves to be used at a later time.

To stovetop steam the vegetables, you need a pan with a wire basket, or a steamer basket that can fit into an 8-quart size pot. Pour 1 inch of water in the pot, and bring it to a rolling boil. Place your vegetables into the basket — no more than 1 pound at a time — and set the basket into the water. Steaming time will vary depending on the vegetable you are blanching. Once the vegetables are steamed, remove the basket, plunge the vegetables into cold water or an ice bath, or run cold water over them. This will stop the cooking process. Drain the vegetables well, and use them in your recipes or freeze them by themselves.

To use the boiling water method of blanching, you need a large pot that you can place at least 1 gallon of water in for every pound of vegetables you are blanching. The water must come to a rolling boil before you can plunge the vegetables into the water. Once the water returns to a boil, begin timing your vegetables. When the allotted time is up, remove the vegetables with a slotted spoon, steamer basket, or a strainer with a handle. Cool the vegetables in cold water, or an ice bath, or by running cold water over the top of them. The chart below will give you the time for each of the methods listed.

Blanching Chart

Vegetable	Microwave Blanching	Stovetop Steaming	Boiling Water Blanching
Beets	n/a	n/a	30 to 45 minutes
Broccoli	5 minutes	3 to 5 minutes	2 to 4 minutes
Brussels sprouts	4 minutes	6 minutes	4 minutes
Cabbages wedges	2 minutes	4 minutes	3 minutes
Carrots	2 to 5 minutes	4 to 5 minutes	2 to 5 minutes
Cauliflower	5 minutes	5 minutes	3 minutes
Celery	3 minutes	4 minutes	3 minutes
Corn on the cob	n/a	n/a	6 to 8 minutes
Corn cut from the cob	4 minutes	6 minutes	4 minutes
Green beans	3 minutes	4 minutes	3 minutes
Peas, all types	4 minutes	6 minutes	4 minutes
Potatoes, cut	10 minutes	12 minutes	10 minutes
Spinach, or other greens	n/a	3 minutes	2 minutes
Sweet potatoes	Cook until soft	Cook until soft	Cook until soft
Zucchini, cubed	2 to 3 minutes	2 to 3 minutes	2 to 3 minutes

* N/A = blanching these items on the stovetop or microwave is not possible.

No blanching is needed for: mushrooms, onions, peppers, tomatoes, or shredded zucchini.

Choosing Storage Options

Freezer bags

Most people choose to use freezer bags as their container of choice because they allow you to store anything, and they are easy to label. If you have a small chest freezer, or just the freezer that comes with your refrigerator, using freezer bags to store your food is your best bet. You can make them almost completely flat, or you can bend and shape them to fit into the space available. When you are on the hunt for storage bags, make sure you get freezer bags and not standard food storage bags.

Here are some additional tips for storing food in freezer bags:

▶ Never reuse a bag unless it only contained dry ingredients such as breadcrumbs. You do not want to have a cross contamination of foods or recipes.

▶ Do not store any food that contains a bone in freezer bags. The bone could create a hole in the bag, and the contents will leak all over your freezer.

▶ You can fit baking dishes and pie dishes into 1- or 2-gallon freezer bags.

▶ Make sure when you store items in containers that you add just enough so that when you thaw and reheat the item, there will not be any leftovers.

Always make sure you remove air completely from the bags before you place them in the freezer. If there is air, oxidation will occur inside the bags and spoil your food. There are a few methods for removing air from freezer bags.

One method of removing air is called the **squeegee method**. To use this method, seal your bag from one corner to the other, leaving a small gap in one corner. Then, use the palm of your hand to squeeze the air out from the bottom to the top, flattening the bag as you go along. Once all the air is pushed out of the bag, finish sealing it. This method works best for stews, chicken, noodles, and meatloaf mixtures, known as **formless foods.**

You can also use the **straw method** for removing air. Place cooled food, or a pan containing food, into a freezer bag. Take an ordinary drinking straw and place it in the opening of the bag. Hold onto the straw tightly and seal the bag to the straw so that no air can return into the bag. Then simply suck the air out of the bag through the straw until the bag is completely flat. Once flat, remove the straw quickly and finish sealing the bag. Make sure the straw does not touch the food, especially if the food is raw. As long as the straw does not touch raw meat, you run no risk of getting sick. This method works best when the food is lumpy, such as chicken, fish fillets, steaks, and various chops. It also works well for food being stored in its container, such as a pie.

You could also use a vacuum sealer, which is a machine that seals plastic bags or containers by sucking all the air out to preserve what is inside. These are best used on lumpy foods, or the foods stored in a dish. The only time you can use one of these on a soup, sauce, or stock is when the machine has a stopping mechanism that allows you to control when the suction ends so you can seal the bag.

Plastic containers

You can purchase plastic containers that can be used for freezer storage just about everywhere. You can reuse them until a crack forms or the seal around the rim no longer holds. They are easier to stack if you have a big freezer. Ones specially designed for freezer use are a bit more expensive, but they are well worth it because they last longer. Do not overfill freezer containers; always leave a ½-inch gap at the top so the liquid can expand properly. This prevents the item from pushing the top off the container.

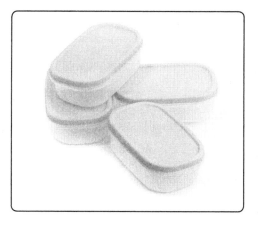

You have the option of storing casseroles and quiches in the container you cooked them in, but be aware that these dishes take up more room, and you may run out of dishes. You can stock up on disposable freezer bags and containers relatively easily by going to your local grocery store.

Glass dishes

The beauty of storing food in a glass dish is that you can prepare, freeze, thaw, and reheat all in the same dish. However, remember to always thaw your dish out completely before placing it in the oven because the rapid temperature change can cause your dish to break. Also remember to never place it in the freezer while it is still hot. You must let the entire container cool down first, wrap it in aluminum foil or freezer paper, which is a heavy white paper with plastic coating on one side, and then place it inside a freezer bag before placing it into the freezer.

Metal/foil pans

Metal or foils pans are another storage option. Aluminum pans may not stack properly in your freezer until they are completely frozen, so you run the risk of losing valuable storage space while they are freezing.

There is always the **frozen block trick** if you do not have enough containers to freeze your items in. To do this, line one of your dishes with the freezer wrap of your choice, either plastic wrap or aluminum foil, leaving an inch or two extra over the sides of the dish. Place the cooled food into the dish, and put it into the freezer until the meal is firm. After the meal is frozen, remove the dish by grabbing the excess wrap and pulling it out of the dish. Then finish wrapping the food either in aluminum foil or plastic wrap, place it back in the freezer, and store it until you are ready to use it. Do not forget to label the bag. Experimenting with your container options allows you to find the best one for you. When you choose your containers, do so wisely so you can cut back on waste and leftovers.

Freezer Storage Times

The following chart shows various foods that freeze well, and the foods' recommended storage times. These times are for quality purposes.

If you take a food out of the freezer and are unsure about its quality after you defrost it, smell it to determine if it still good. If it smells odd, off, or rancid, discard it. If a food smells fine, but looks odd, it is still probably good enough to serve cooked in a stew or soup. You can cook suspect foods first, and if they taste good after cooking, use them as ingredients.

Item	Months
Bacon and sausage	1 to 2
Egg whites or egg substitutes	12
Frozen dinners and entrees	3 to 4
Gravy, meat, or poultry	2 to 3
Ham, hot dogs, and lunch meats	1 to 2
Meat, uncooked roasts	4 to 12
Meat, uncooked steaks or chops	4 to 12
Meat, uncooked ground	3 to 4
Meat, cooked	2 to 3
Poultry, uncooked whole	12
Poultry, uncooked parts	9
Poultry, uncooked giblets	3 to 4
Poultry, cooked	4
Soups and stews	2 to 3
Wild game, uncooked	8 to 12

Information courtesy of the USDA Food Safety and Inspection Service, public domain fact sheet
at **www.fsis.usda.gov/Fact_Sheets/Focus_On_Freezing**.

Defrosting Food

When you are ready to eat something that you froze, how you defrost it will have an effect on the food's flavor, texture, and it could even have an effect on your health. The best way to thaw meat or a dairy product, for example, is to remove it from the freezer several days before it is to be cooked, place it in the refrigerator, and let it thaw slowly. Applying heat 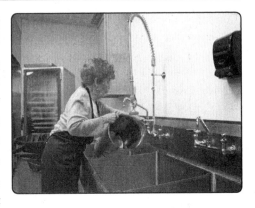 quickly will start the multiplication process of any dangerous organisms. *Never* leave meat out at room temperature to thaw.

A quicker method is to keep the meat in a plastic bag and submerge it in cool water until it is thawed. This could take several hours depending on the size of the meat portion, but again, it will slow the growth of bacteria and parasites. Using the microwave to defrost your meat is also a good option, but watch the process so the meat is not browned or overheated in some areas and still frozen in others. Any quick acceleration of heat will affect the inactive microorganisms in the food.

Vegetables can be cooked from their frozen state — there is no need to thaw them. Any fruits or vegetables that will be used raw can be thawed in the refrigerator, where they will keep some firmness while defrosting. Fruits and vegetables do not pose as much health threat as defrosting as meats. Many fruits and vegetables may lose liquid during the defrosting process, so you may want to drain them before using.

What to do when your freezer stops working

It could happen at any time — your freezer could fail, and then all of your investment in food and time could be lost. Your freezer may have mechanical problems, or someone could accidentally change the temperature, or a power failure could occur. A terrible thunderstorm could knock your power out for a week.

It is wise to know ahead of time what you should do to minimize your losses and prevent illness due to spoiled food. At the moment of an emergency, you may have other things to worry about. So ahead of time, find local commercial or institutional freezers that may accept your food should you experience appliance failure. You should also attempt to locate a dry ice supplier. If your area is subject to frequent power failures or you know there is a scheduled outage, set your freezer temperature between -10 degrees and -20 degrees so that the food will be colder during the outage and less likely to thaw.

Once your freezer stops working, keep the door closed at all times. A freezer packed with foods that are frozen solid will continue to keep those foods frozen for about two days if the doors are kept shut. Putting blankets or other types of insulating objects around the freezer will also help keep foods cold, but be sure not to close off air vents in case the freezer starts up again. Separate the meat from other foods so that if the meat thaws, it will not drip juices onto other food.

Next, determine the cause of the equipment failure. It could be as simple as an accidental disconnection, a tripped circuit breaker, a blown fuse, or an electrical shortage. In these cases, fix the problem as quickly as possible, and then check for any food that might be thawing. If the problem is the result of a power failure, contact the utility company to find out how long it will be before power is restored.

If the problem is not a simple one, or the result of a power failure, check the operating instructions for your freezer to see if there are any additional solutions before you call a technician. You might save yourself a service call.

Protect your food from thawing

Though a sealed freezer that is not operational may keep food frozen for a day or two, it is wise to plan ahead to protect your food from thawing. If you are in the middle of winter and temperatures will be well below 0 degrees for several days, you could pack your food in coolers and store them in a garage or shed, but do not store the cooler in sunlight. You might want to ask a friend or neighbor if you can store your food in their freezers — or perhaps distribute the food among several freezers. You could also check with a school, church, or social organization to see if they have freezer space for you to use temporarily. If there is a local freezing plant in your area, you may ask to store your food there.

When you move your food, be sure to protect it from thawing, as well. Place the packages into insulated coolers or boxes that are lined with Styrofoam, thick layers of newspaper, or blankets. Once you take the food out of your freezer, get it to an operating freezer as soon as possible.

If you cannot find another freezer to store your food, you might be able to purchase dry ice and place it in your freezer to keep things cold. Check your phone book or the Internet for a local place that sells dry ice or carbonic gas. A full 20-cubic foot freezer will use a 50-pound cake of dry ice to keep the packages frozen for three to four days; a 10-cubic foot freezer will use a 25-pound cake. Note that if your freezer is half full, it will need more dry ice to keep it cold because the more frozen items in the freezer, the more stable the temperature in the freezer will remain. When you buy dry ice, ask the company to cut it to the right size for you, and have them wrap each piece in plastic or other protective material. Dry ice is dangerous; you can lose layers of skin or give yourself frostbite by touching it with bare skin. Handle it quickly, and always wear protective gloves to prevent the ice from burning your hands.

Place heavy cardboard or newspapers on top of your frozen food packages, put the dry ice on top of the cardboard, and close the freezer. Make sure the freezer is not opened again unless you must replace the dry ice or the freezer is working again. The dry ice will gradually form a vapor that you can dispel by opening the door. The vapor is harmless and will dissipate quickly.

If you had to move your food to another freezer, this is the perfect time to unplug it, defrost, and clean it out. Use mild cleaners and wipe it down one last time with plain water so the freezer will not impart any chemical taste to the foods that will be put back. While your freezer is not in use, leave the door open slightly to air it out. As a safety precaution for young children, be sure the door is propped so it cannot be closed.

What to do with thawed foods

Some thawed foods can be refrozen; others should be kept refrigerated and eaten quickly. Some foods must be discarded after a thaw. Note that refreezing a food will break down its texture and taste. If you find you have too much edible thawed food to eat in the next few days, contact a church, shelter, or charitable organization to share your food before it spoils. Or feel free to share your extra helpings with neighbors.

Here are some guidelines for food that is thawed:

Food	How to Handle
Baked goods	If the product is still solidly frozen, it can be returned to the freezer. Baked goods that are partially or completely thawed will have a poor texture and flavor if re-frozen. Instead, refrigerate the product, and eat within the next few days.
Cheese	If the product is still solidly frozen, it can be returned to the freezer. If the cheese started to thaw, do not refreeze because the flavor and texture will degrade. Refrigerate the cheese, and use as soon as possible.
Fish	If the package is solidly frozen, it can be returned to the freezer. If the meat thawed but is still cold, check for bad smell or discoloration. If it looks and smells normal, cook and eat immediately. If the fish reached room temperature, it should be thrown away.

Food	How to Handle
Frozen fruit juices	Juices that are still frozen can be returned to the freezer. Thawed juices should be refrigerated and used in the same time frame as fresh juice.
Frozen prepared foods	If the package still has a layer of ice crystals, it can be refrozen. Completely thawed foods should be cooked and eaten immediately. If the product reached room temperature, it should be thrown away.
Fruits	Check the package. If the food is mostly thawed but does not smell "off" or look spoiled or discolored, it can be refrozen; however, it may lose some taste and texture. Thawed fruits may be used in cooking or making jams, jellies, and preserves.
Ice cream	Discard thawed or partially thawed ice cream or frozen desserts.
Meat	Check the package. If the food is mostly thawed but does not smell "off" or look spoiled or discolored, it can be used within the next day or two. If the package is still very cold or mostly frozen or has a layer of ice crystals, it can be refrozen after packaging in a new wrap. If the meat reached room temperature, it should be thrown away.
Poultry	If the package is still very cold or mostly frozen or has a layer of ice crystals, it can be refrozen after packaging in new wrap. If the meat thawed but is still cold, check for bad smell or discoloration. If it looks and smells normal, cook, and eat immediately. Make sure poultry juices from thawed meat do not touch any other food.
Smoked or cured meat	If the package is still frozen or very cold, it can be placed back in the freezer. Check for bad smell or discoloration of thawed meat; if it looks and smells normal, refrigerate, and use within a day or two.
Vegetables	If the package is still very cold or mostly frozen or has a layer of ice crystals, it can be refrozen after packaging in new wrap. Thawed vegetables will lose most of the flavor and texture if you attempt to refreeze them; instead, refrigerate, and cook within the next few days.

CHAPTER

Beverage Recipes

THREE

There are a wide variety of recipes in the next few chapters, everything from soup to nuts, as the saying goes. You may find a bread recipe in the breakfast section, and you may discover a great lunch recipe in the dinner main dish section. Every recipe is apportioned for 100 servings. The serving size is noted with each recipe.

Most of the recipes here can be preserved in some way or another. Each recipe includes a note with the suggested manner of preservation, whether it be freezing or canning. Some recipes, though they are preservable, may not be worth the effort to do so. The first recipe, coffee, is a good example of such a recipe. These recipes are commonly prepared for large numbers of people and are meant to be served immediately. You will note that there is a suggested way to freeze coffee, but it may not really worth the effort. On the other hand, you may find a creative way to use frozen coffee, such as in a coffee smoothie.

Also note that there are recipes that should be preserved as component parts or those that should only be partially preserved. A good example of such a recipe is spaghetti and meatballs. With this dish, you would can the sauce, freeze the meatballs, and cook the pasta fresh or pre-dried.

Though there are notes in each of the recipes on freezing or canning, you should carefully read the sections on freezing and canning if you plan on engaging in this activity with the food you prepare.

Coffee

Serving size: 8 oz.

■ Ingredients

1 pound (2 quarts 2½ cups) coffee, roasted, ground

■ Directions

1. Place filter paper in brewing funnel.
2. Spread coffee evenly in filter.
3. Slide funnel into brewer; place empty pot on heating element.
4. Press switch to start automatic brewing cycle.
5. Let water drip through completely; discard grounds.

■ Notes

Serve coffee within 30 minutes.

Check water temperature. The water filtered through the grounds must be 200 degrees to ensure that the coffee from the brewing chamber will be at least 190 degrees.

For one pot: Use 2½ ounces or ¾ cup roasted, ground coffee. One pot makes 11 5-ounce portions or seven 8-ounce portions.

Coffeemaker production rates: It takes two to three minutes to reach optimal water temperature and an average of four minutes for a pot to brew. With an average time of seven minutes per pot of coffee, expect to create eight pots in an hour.

For 5-ounce portions: In Step 1, use 1 ½ pounds or 1 ⅞ quarts roasted, ground coffee to make 10 pots.

For stronger brew, use 2 ¹³⁄₁₆ pounds or 3 ½ quarts roasted, ground coffee for 8-ounce portion; for 5-ounce portion, use 2 pounds or 2 ½ quarts roasted, ground coffee.

■ Freezing instructions

This recipe can be frozen in individual portions or larger quantities. Freeze in plastic microwavable containers. You may also consider freezing in ice cube trays.

Reheat in microwave.

Hot Tea

Serving size: 8 oz.

■ Ingredients

8 ounces (1 ¼ cups) loose black tea

54 ⅓ pounds (6 gallons 2 quarts) boiling water

■ Directions

1. Place tea in a cloth bag large enough to hold three times the amount.
2. Tie top of bag with cord long enough to facilitate removing the tea bag. Tie the cord to handle of urn or kettle.
3. Place tea bag in urn or kettle.
4. Boil water, and pour the water over tea bag. Cover and allow the tea to steep three to five minutes. Do not agitate or stir.
5. Remove tea bag.
6. Cover. Keep hot, but do not boil.

Notes

If loose tea, not enclosed in a cloth bag, is placed in the urn or kettle, strain tea after it has steeped for five minutes.

Never boil tea as this produces a bitter flavor.

Schedule preparation so no more than 15 minutes will elapse between preparation and service. Hold tea at temperatures of 175 to 185 degrees.

For 5-ounce portions, use 1 ¾ cups loose tea and 4 gallons of water.

100 8-ounce individual tea bags may be used. Place on serving line for self-service.

Freezing instructions

You can freeze in individual portions or larger quantities. Freeze in plastic microwavable containers, or consider freezing in ice cube trays.

Reheat in microwave.

Grapefruit and Pineapple Juice Cocktail

Serving size: 8 oz.

Ingredients

4 ⅛ pounds (1 quart 2 ⅝ cups) frozen grapefruit juice from concentrate

14 ⅓ pounds (1 gallon 2 ½ quarts) canned, unsweetened pineapple juice

12 ½ pounds (1 gallon 2 quarts) water

4 pounds (1 gallon 1 quart) ice cubes

Directions

1. Combine grapefruit and pineapple juices with water; stir.
2. Cover, and refrigerate.

3. Add ice just before serving.

■ Freezing instructions

This juice mixture can be frozen in individual portions or larger quantities. Freeze in plastic containers, or consider freezing in ice cube trays.

Orange and Pineapple Juice Cocktail

Serving size: 8 oz.

■ Ingredients

15 ⅜ pounds (1 gallon 3 quarts) orange juice

14 ⅓ pounds (1 gallon 2 ½ quarts) canned, pineapple juice, unsweetened

4 pounds (1 gallon 1 quart) ice cubes

■ Directions

1. Combine orange and pineapple juices; stir.

2. Add ice just before serving.

■ Freezing instructions

You can freeze this cocktail in individual portions or larger quantities. Freeze in plastic containers, or consider freezing in ice cube trays.

Lemonade

Serving size: 8 oz.

■ Ingredients

7 pounds (1 gallon) granulated sugar

12 ½ pounds (1 gallon 2 quarts) water

2 ⅛ pounds (1 quart) lemon juice

37 ⅝ pounds (4 gallons 2 quarts) cold water

9 ⅝ pounds (3 gallons) ice cubes

■ Directions

1. Dissolve sugar in water, and allow it to cool.
2. Add juice and water to sugar solution. Mix thoroughly. Cover, and refrigerate.
3. Add ice just before serving.

■ Freezing instructions

Lemonade may be frozen in individual portions or larger quantities. Freeze in plastic containers. You may also consider freezing in ice cube trays.

Fruit Punch

Serving size: 8 oz.

■ Ingredients

4 ¼ pounds (2 quarts 1 ⅝ cups) granulated sugar

12 ½ pounds (1 gallon 2 quarts) water

3 ⅔ pounds (1 quart 2 cups) frozen grapefruit juice, from concentrate

1 ⅛ pounds (2 cups) lemon juice

6 ⅝ pounds (3 quarts) canned pineapple juice, unsweetened

33 ½ pounds (4 gallons) cold water

9 ⅝ pounds (3 gallons) ice cubes

■ Directions

1. Dissolve sugar in water. Cool.
2. Add juices and water to sugar solution. Mix thoroughly. Cover, and refrigerate.
3. Add ice just before serving.

■ Notes

In Step 2, 1 ½ gallons of canned grapefruit juice may be used. Reduce water to 2 ¾ gallons per 100 servings.

In Step 2, 2 quarts of fresh lemon juice may be used. Reduce water to 3 ½ gallons per 100 servings.

■ Freezing instructions

Can be frozen in individual portions or larger quantities. Freeze in plastic containers. You may also consider freezing in ice cube trays.

Lime Lemon Punch

Serving size: 8 oz.

■ Ingredients

7 pounds (1 gallon) granulated sugar

12 ½ pounds (1 gallon 2 quarts) water

1 ⅛ pounds (2 cups) lemon juice

5 ⅞ pounds (2 quarts 3 ¾ cups) lime juice

39 ¾ pounds (4 gallons 3 quarts) water

½ ounce (1 tablespoon) green food coloring

9 ⅝ pounds (3 gallons) ice cubes

■ Directions

1. Dissolve sugar in water. Cool.
2. Add juices, food coloring, and water to sugar solution. Mix thoroughly. Cover, and refrigerate.
3. Add ice just before serving.

■ Notes

In Step 2, 2 quarts of fresh lemon juice may be used. Reduce water to 3 ½ gallons per 100 servings.

■ Freezing instructions

Can be frozen in individual portions or larger quantities. Freeze in plastic containers. You may also consider freezing in ice cube trays.

CHAPTER

Breakfast

FOUR

NOTE: Oven directions and usage may vary from recipe to recipe and depend on the type of oven you use. If a recipe calls for a convection oven, you may use a conventional oven, though you should set your temperature 25 degrees higher than the recipe directs. Alternatively, you may use a convection oven when a conventional oven is called for if you reduce the temperature by 25 degrees. The cooking times of convection and conventional ovens will be the same when the temperatures are adjusted accordingly. Food cooked in a convection oven should not be covered as this will negate the airflow of the fan used in convection ovens. Meats cooked in convection ovens tend to be dry.

Streusel Coffeecake

Serving size: 1 piece
Pan size: 16 x 24 x 1 (two pans)

■ Ingredients

6¾ ounces (1 cup) dry, active yeast

1 pound (2 cups) warm water

1⅝ pounds (3 cups) water

1¼ pounds (2¼ cup) whole eggs

1⅛ pounds (2⅝ cups) granulated sugar

1¾ ounces (¾ cups) dry, nonfat milk

1⅞ ounces (3 tablespoons) salt

7⅞ pounds (1 gallon 2½ quarts) wheat bread flour

14½ ounces (2 cups) softened shortening

¾ cup egg wash (*see recipe below*)

3 quarts streusel topping (*see recipe below*)

2 cups vanilla glaze (*see recipe below*)

■ Directions

1. Sprinkle yeast over water. Do not use water over 110 degrees as this will kill the yeast. Mix well. Let stand five minutes; stir. Set aside for use in Step 3.

2. Place water, eggs, sugar, milk, and salt in mixer bowl. Using dough hook, mix at low speed just until blended.

3. Add flour and yeast solution to the water and egg solution. Mix at low speed for one minute or until all flour mixture is incorporated into liquid.

4. Add shortening; mix at low speed for one minute. Continue mixing at medium speed for ten minutes or until dough is smooth and elastic. Dough temperature should be between 78 degrees and 82 degrees.

5. Cover the mixture, and set it in a warm place (80 degrees) about 1½ hours or until double in bulk.

6. Divide dough into two pieces of 6-pound, 8-ounce sections. Shape into a rectangular piece. Let rest ten to 20 minutes.

7. Roll each piece of dough into a rectangular sheet, about 18 inches wide, 25 inches long and ½-inch thick. Fit into greased sheet pans, pressing against sides. The edges should be thicker than the center.

8. Poke holes in the dough with a fork.

9. Prepare one-fourth recipe egg wash recipe (below) per 100 portions. Brush about ⅓ cup on dough in each pan.

10. Prepare one serving streusel topping recipe (below); sprinkle 1 ½ quart topping over dough in each pan.

11. Proof dough (allow it to rise) for 20 to 35 minutes.

12. Bake at 375 degrees for 30 to 35 minutes or until golden brown, or in 325 degree convection oven 15 minutes on high fan, open vent.

13. Prepare two-thirds the recipe for vanilla glaze (below) per 100 portions. Drizzle about 1 cup over each cake while hot.

14. Cut each pan into six pieces by nine pieces.

Egg wash

■ Ingredients

8 ounces (¾ cup 3 tablespoons) whole eggs

⅞ ounce (¼ cup 2 ⅓ tablespoons) nonfat dry milk

1 pound (2 cups) water

■ Directions

1. Combine eggs, milk, and water; mix well. Refrigerate at 41 degrees or lower until ready to use.

2. Brush over shaped dough before or after proofing.

Streusel topping

■ Ingredients

1⅔ pounds (1 quart 2 cups) general-purpose wheat flour

1 pound (3¼ cups) packed brown sugar

7 ounces (1 cup) granulated sugar

½ ounce (2 tablespoons) ground cinnamon

1¼ pounds (2½ cups) butter

■ Directions

1. Place flour, sugars, and cinnamon in mixer bowl; blend thoroughly at low speed for two minutes.
2. Add butter or margarine to dry ingredients; blend at low speed 1½ to two minutes or until mixture resembles coarse cornmeal. Do not overmix.
3. Sprinkle over sweet rolls and coffeecakes before baking.

■ Notes

If butter or margarine is too soft, a mass will form and mixture will not be crumbly.

Vanilla glaze

■ Ingredients

1⅝ pounds (1 quart 2 cups) sifted powdered sugar

1½ ounces (3 tablespoons) softened butter

6¼ ounces (¾ cup) boiling water

¼ ounce (¼ teaspoon) vanilla extract

■ Directions

1. Combine powdered sugar, butter, boiling water, and vanilla, and mix until smooth.

2. Spread glaze over baked sweet rolls or coffeecakes. Coat or dip fried doughnuts in glaze.

■ Freezing instructions
You may freeze streusel coffee cake with vanilla glaze by placing it in an airtight plastic container before freezing. For best results, freeze the baked good without the glaze, and apply glaze just prior to serving.

To serve, allow item to thaw in refrigerator or at room temperature. Reheat in microwave in individual serving portions. You may also reheat larger quantities in an oven preheated to 300 degrees. Heat covered item for approximately 20 minutes.

Cinnamon Rolls

Serving size: 1 roll
Pan size: 16 x 24 x 1 (two pans)

■ Ingredients
6¾ ounces (1 cup) dry active yeast

1 pound (2 cups) warm water

1⅝ pounds (3 cups) water

1¼ pounds (2¼ cups) whole eggs

1⅛ pounds (2⅝ cups) granulated sugar

1¾ ounces (¾ cup) dry nonfat milk

1⅞ ounces (3 tablespoons) salt

7⅞ pounds (1 gallon 2½ quarts) wheat bread flour

14½ ounces (2 cups) softened shortening

1 pound (2 cups) butter

3 cups cinnamon sugar filling (*see below*)

■ Directions

1. Sprinkle yeast over water, but make sure the water's temperature does not reach over 110 degrees. Mix well. Let stand five minutes, stir, and set aside for use in Step 3.

2. Place water, eggs, sugar, milk, and salt in mixer bowl. Using dough hook, mix at low speed just until blended.

3. Add flour and yeast solution to mixture created in Step 2. Mix at low speed for one minute or until all flour mixture is incorporated into liquid.

4. Add shortening, and mix at low speed for one minute. Continue mixing at medium speed for ten minutes or until dough is smooth and elastic. The dough's temperature should be between 78 degrees and 82 degrees.

5. Cover the mixture, and allow it to sit in a warm place (around 80 degrees) about 1 ½ hours or until double in bulk.

6. Divide the dough into three pieces, 4 pounds 5 ounces each, and shape into a rectangular piece. Let rest ten to 20 minutes.

7. Roll each piece of dough into a rectangular sheet, about 18 inches wide, 36 inches long, and ¼ inch thick.

8. Melt butter or margarine. Brush ½ cup on each sheet of dough. Set aside remainder for use in Step 10.

9. Prepare one portion cinnamon sugar filling for 100 servings. Sprinkle 1 ½ cups cinnamon sugar mixture over each sheet of dough.

10. Roll each piece tightly to make a long slender roll. Seal edges by pressing firmly. Elongate roll to 35 inches by rolling back and forth on countertop. Brush 2 tablespoons of butter or margarine on each roll.

11. Using a dough cutter, slice each roll into 34 pieces about 1 inch wide.

12. Place cut side down on lightly greased sheet pans in rows five by eight.

13. Allow the dough to rise until double in bulk.

14. Bake at 375 degrees for 20 to 25 minutes or until golden brown, or in 325 degree convection oven 15 minutes on high fan, open vent. Allow the mixture to cool.

15. Glaze, if desired, with one portion vanilla glaze recipe per 100 portions. Brush about 1 cup on rolls in each pan.

Cinnamon sugar filling

■ Ingredients

1 ounce (¼ cup ⅓ tablespoon) ground cinnamon

1 pound (3 ¼ cup) packed brown sugar

■ Directions

1. Combine cinnamon and brown sugar.

■ Notes

Granulated sugar may be substituted for brown sugar.

■ Freezing instructions

You may freeze cinnamon rolls with vanilla glaze by placing them in an airtight plastic container before freezing. For best results, freeze the baked good without the glaze, and apply glaze just prior to serving.

To serve, allow item to thaw in refrigerator or at room temperature. Reheat in microwave in individual serving portions. You may also reheat larger quantities in an oven preheated to 300 degrees. Heat covered item for approximately 20 minutes.

Doughnuts

Doughnuts may be cooked in a deep-fryer or in a large frying pan

■ Ingredients

5 ½ pounds (1 gallon 1 quart) general-purpose wheat flour

3 ⅞ ounces (½ cup) baking powder

1 ⅝ ounces (½ cup 2 ⅔ tablespoons) nonfat dry milk

⅝ ounce (1 tablespoon) salt

¼ ounce (1 tablespoon) ground nutmeg

7¼ ounces (1 cup) shortening

1½ pounds (3⅜ cups) granulated sugar

1¼ pounds (2¼ cups) whole eggs

2 pounds (3¾ cups) water

½ ounce (1 tablespoon) vanilla extract

■ Directions

1. Sift together flour, baking powder, milk, salt, and nutmeg. Set aside for use in Step 5.

2. Place shortening and sugar in mixer bowl; cream at medium speed until light and fluffy.

3. Add eggs to mixture; beat at medium speed until light and fluffy.

4. Combine water and vanilla. Add to creamed mixture.

5. Add dry ingredients to creamed mixture, adding about one-third flour mixture each time. Blend at low speed after each addition. Do not overmix. Let dough rest for ten minutes.

6. Roll dough ⅜-inch thick on well-floured board; cut with doughnut cutter.

7. Fry one minute on each side or until golden brown. Drain on absorbent paper.

■ Notes

In Step 5, dough may be chilled one hour to make handling easier.

Omit steps 6 and 7 if dough machine is used.

■ Freezing instructions

You may freeze doughnuts by placing them in an airtight plastic container before freezing.

To serve, allow item to thaw in refrigerator or at room temperature. Reheat in microwave in individual serving portions. You may also reheat larger quantities in a 300 degree oven. Heat covered item for approximately 20 minutes.

Hot Oatmeal

Serving size: ¾ cup

■ Ingredients

6 pounds (1 gallon, ⅜ quarts) rolled cereal oatmeal

1 ⅞ ounces (3 tablespoons) salt

41 ¾ pounds (5 gallons) boiling water

■ Directions

1. Add cereal and salt to boiling water; stir to prevent lumping.
2. Return to a boil, reduce heat, and simmer one to three minutes, stirring occasionally.
3. Turn off heat. Let stand ten minutes before serving.

■ Freezing instructions

Freeze individual servings of prepared oatmeal in small freezer bags. To reheat, remove oatmeal from freezer bags, and place in a bowl. Cover the bowl, and microwave for approximately three to four minutes, stirring every minute.

Breakfast Burrito

Serving size: 1 burrito

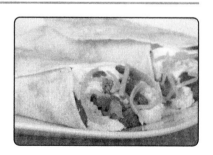

■ Ingredients

7 ½ pounds (3 quarts 2 cups) egg whites

7 ½ pounds (3 quarts 2 cups) whole eggs

2 ⅔ pounds (2 quarts ⅝ cups) shredded cheddar cheese

2 pounds cooked pork sausage, diced

2 pounds (1 quart 1 cup) fresh tomatoes, chopped

1 pound (2 ⅝ cups) fresh onions, chopped

⅓ ounce (1 tablespoon) ground black pepper

½ ounce (3 tablespoons) crushed oregano

2 ounces (¼ cup ⅓ tablespoon) nonstick cooking spray

9 ½ pounds (100 count) 8-inch flour tortillas

■ Directions

1. Combine egg whites and eggs. Blend thoroughly.

2. Combine cheese, sausage, tomatoes, onions, pepper, and oregano, and mix thoroughly.

3. Lightly spray griddle with nonstick cooking spray. Pour about 1 quart egg mixture on 325 degree lightly sprayed griddle. Cook until partially set. Add 6 ounces cheese-sausage mixture. Cook until cheese is melted and eggs are firm. Internal temperature must reach 145 degrees or higher for 15 seconds.

4. Place tortillas on lightly sprayed griddle, and heat for 30 seconds on each side.

5. Place about ½ cup cooked egg mixture in center of each tortilla; fold tortilla to cover eggs and form burrito.

6. Hold for service at 140 degrees or higher. This step is not necessary if you plan on freezing the burritos.

■ Notes

In Step 2, 3 ¼ pounds of canned diced tomatoes may be used per 100 portions. Drain before using.

■ Freezing instructions

Freeze individual servings of prepared breakfast burritos in small freezer bags. To reheat, remove breakfast burritos from freezer bags, and place on a dish. Cover the dish with a paper towel, and microwave for approximately three to four minutes.

Breakfast Pizza

Serving size: 1 piece
Pan size: 18 x 18 (4 pans)

■ Ingredients

2 ounces (¼ cup ⅓ tablespoon) nonstick cooking spray

16 pounds pizza dough (*see recipe below*)

4 ⅓ pounds (2 quarts) canned tomato sauce

3 pounds raw turkey bacon

15 ½ pounds (1 gallon 3 quarts) pasteurized egg substitute

¼ ounce (⅛ teaspoon) salt

⅛ ounce (⅛ teaspoon) ground black pepper

6 pounds (1 gallon 2 quarts) low-fat cheddar cheese, shredded

5 ½ pounds (2 quarts 3 ⅞ cup) frozen shredded hash browns

■ Directions

1. Lightly spray sheet pans with nonstick cooking spray.

2. Shape dough into four 4-pound pieces. Let dough rest 15 minutes. Place dough pieces on lightly floured working surface. Roll out each piece to ¼-inch thickness. Transfer dough to pans, pushing dough slightly up edges of pans. Gently prick dough with a fork to prevent bubbling.

3. Using a convection oven, bake eight minutes at 450 degrees on high fan, open vent until crusts are lightly browned. If using a conventional oven, bake at 475 degrees.

4. Spread 2 cups tomato sauce evenly over crust in each pan. Set aside for use in Step 7.

5. Cook bacon until lightly browned. Drain on absorbent paper, and chop finely.

6. Add salt and pepper to eggs. Blend well, and scramble eggs until just set. Do not overcook. Pasteurized eggs will be safe at an internal temperature of 145 degrees but will not set until they reach 160 degrees.

7. Distribute 1 ½ quarts cheese over sauce on each crust.

8. Distribute 1 ½ quarts scrambled eggs over cheese on each pan.

9. Distribute 1 ¼ cups bacon over eggs on each pan.

10. Distribute 1 quart shredded potatoes over bacon in each pan.

11. Bake another eight minutes or until crust is browned and hash browns begin to turn golden brown. Make sure you are baking on high fan, open vent. Internal temperature must reach 145 degrees or higher for 15 seconds.

12. Cut into five rows and five columns (25 pieces each pan).

13. Hold for service at 140 degrees or higher. This step is not necessary if you plan on freezing the pizzas.

■ Freezing instructions

Breakfast pizza should be frozen prior to Step 11 of above directions. Freeze individual servings of prepared breakfast pizzas in small freezer bags. You can freeze larger portions by wrapping in plastic wrap. To reheat, remove breakfast pizza from freezer bags, and place on a dish. Preheat oven to 400 degrees, and bake for 14 to 18 minutes.

Pizza dough

■ Ingredients

2 ⅜ ounces (¼ cup 2 tablespoons) dry active yeast

9 ⅜ ounces (1 ⅛ cup) warm water

3 ⅛ pounds (1 quart 2 cups) cold water

6 ⅝ pounds (1 gallon 1 ½ quarts) wheat bread flour

1 ounce (1 tablespoon) salt

2 ⅓ ounces (¼ cup 1 ⅔ tablespoon) granulated sugar

7 ⅔ ounces (1 cup) salad oil (any kind of vegetable oil used in salads)

▪ Directions

1. Sprinkle yeast over water. Make sure the water's temperature is not above 110 degrees. Mix well. Let stand for five minutes, and stir.

2. Place water, flour, salt, sugar, and salad oil in mixer bowl in order listed. Add yeast solution.

3. Using a dough hook, mix at low speed about eight minutes until dough is smooth and elastic. Dough temperature should be between 86 degrees and 88 degrees.

4. Divide dough, and shape into four balls. Cover the dough, and let it rise in warm place for one and a half to two hours or until double in bulk.

5. Proceed with intended recipe.

▪ Freezing instructions

You may freeze the dough after Step 4. Wrap balls of dough in plastic wrap, and place the wrapped dough in freezer bags and into the freezer. Allow to thaw overnight in refrigerator prior to use.

Cheese Omelet

Serving size: 1 omelet

▪ Ingredients

20 pounds (2 gallons 1⅓ quarts) whole eggs

2 ounces (¼ cup ⅓ tablespoon) nonstick cooking spray

3¼ pounds (3 quarts 1 cup) shredded cheddar cheese

▪ Directions

1. Place thawed eggs in mixer bowl. Using wire whip, beat just enough to thoroughly blend.

2. Lightly spray griddle with nonstick cooking spray. Pour ⅓ cup egg mixture for individual omelets on 325 degree griddle.

3. Cook until bottom is golden brown. Do not stir. If necessary, gently lift cooked portion with a spatula to permit uncooked mixture to flow underneath. Sprinkle about 2 tablespoons cheese over each omelet when partially set. Continue cooking until eggs are set and well done.

4. Internal temperature must reach 145 degrees or higher for 15 seconds, 155 degrees for fresh shell eggs.

5. Fold omelet in half or into thirds, making a long oval-shaped omelet.

■ Freezing instructions

Although it is not recommended to freeze egg dishes such as cheese omelets, you may freeze the eggs. Whisk the eggs just until blended and pour them into freezer containers. Seal the containers tightly, and label with the number of eggs and the date. Freeze. You may thaw the frozen eggs overnight in the refrigerator or by placing the frozen containers in cool water.

Scrambled Eggs

Serving size: ⅓ cup

■ Ingredients

20 pounds (2 gallons 1⅓ quarts) whole eggs

3⅞ ounces (½ cup) salad oil

■ Directions

1. Beat eggs thoroughly.

2. Pour about 1 quart eggs on 325 degree lightly greased griddle. Cook slowly until there is no visible liquid egg, stirring occasionally.

3. Internal temperature must reach 145 degrees or higher for 15 seconds, 155 degrees for fresh shell eggs.

4. Hold for service at 140 degrees or higher.

■ Notes

You can also prepare this meal using the oven. Using a convection oven, bake at 350 degrees for 18 to 25 minutes on high fan, closed vent. Standard ovens should be set to 375 degrees. After 12 minutes, stir every five minutes. You may bake the eggs in a large, well-oiled baking dish.

■ Freezing instructions

Although it is not recommended to freeze egg dishes, you may get a head start in your egg dish preparation by freezing the eggs. You may whisk the eggs just until blended and pour them into freezer containers. Seal the containers tightly, and label with the number of eggs and the date. Freeze. You may thaw the frozen eggs overnight in the refrigerator or place the frozen containers in cool water.

Grilled Bacon

Serving size: 2 slices

■ Ingredients

12 pounds raw, sliced bacon

■ Directions

1. Place bacon slices on 350 degree griddle. Grill approximately five minutes, turning once after three minutes, until slightly crisp. Remove excess fat as it accumulates on griddle.
2. Drain thoroughly. Place on absorbent paper or in perforated steam table pan.
3. Hold for service at 140 degrees or higher.

■ Freezing instructions

Wrap individual portions in paper towels. Place the wrapped portions into a freezer bag. Freeze and store for up to six weeks. Reheat in frying pan directly from the freezer. Heat on medium high for about a minute or until desired doneness is achieved. You may also reheat bacon in the microwave. The time will vary depending on the wattage of your particular microwave, but usually about 30 seconds will achieve desired doneness.

Corned Beef Hash

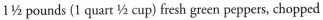

Serving size: 3 ½ ounces
Use a large roasting pan for this recipe.

■ Ingredients

15 pounds raw corned beef

2 ½ pounds (1 quart, 3 ⅛ cups) fresh onions, chopped

1 ½ pounds (1 quart ½ cup) fresh green peppers, chopped

½ cup shortening

10 pounds (1 gallon 3 ¼ quarts) fresh white potatoes

14 ⅝ pounds (1 gallon, 3 quarts) boiling water

½ ounce (⅜ teaspoon) salt

1 ⅝ pounds (3 cups) reserved stock (*see step 1 below*)

⅛ ounce (¼ teaspoon) ground black pepper

2 ounces (¼ cup ⅓ tablespoon) nonstick cooking spray

■ Directions

1. Place whole pieces of corned beef in steam-jacketed kettle or stockpot; cover with water. Bring to a boil. Cover, reduce heat, and let it simmer for 2 ½ hours. Remove scum as it rises to surface. Remove from heat; reserve stock for use in Step 5.

2. Hold stock at 140 degrees or higher.

3. Let corned beef stand 12 to 20 minutes; chop finely.

4. Sauté onions and peppers in shortening or salad oil about ten minutes or until tender. Stir frequently.

5. Place potatoes in boiling salted water. Return to a boil. Reduce heat, and cook ten minutes or until tender. Drain.

6.   Combine beef, vegetables, potatoes, stock, and pepper, mixing thoroughly.

7.   Lightly spray each pan with nonstick cooking spray. Place about 1 ½ gallons corned beef mixture into each lightly sprayed steam table pan.

8.   Using a convection oven, bake 25 minutes in 325 degree oven (350 degrees in a conventional oven) or until lightly browned high fan, open vent.

9.   Internal temperature must reach 145 degrees or higher for 15 minutes.

■ Notes

In steps 1 and 2, 9 pounds 15 ounces precooked corned beef may be used per 100 portions. Follow steps 3 and 4. In Step 5, use 3 cups water for reserved stock. Follow steps 6 and 7.

■ Freezing instructions

Allow the mixture to cool, and place individual portions in freezer bags. Freeze. Allow it to thaw overnight in refrigerator. Remove from freezer bags, and place on a small dish. Cover, and reheat in microwave for 3 to 4 minutes.

Hash Browned Potatoes

Serving size: ⅔ cup

■ Ingredients

31 pounds (5 gallons 2 ½ quarts) fresh potatoes, peeled and cubed

20 ⅞ pounds (2 gallons 2 quarts) boiling water

¼ ounces (⅛ teaspoon) salt

1 ⅓ pounds (3 cups) vegetable shortening, melting

1 ⅞ ounces (3 tablespoons) salt

⅛ ounces (⅓ teaspoon) ground black pepper

■ Directions

1.   Cover potatoes with boiling salted water, bring to a boil, reduce heat, and simmer 15 minutes or until tender. Do not overcook. Drain well.

2. Spread a layer of potatoes over well-greased griddle at 400 degrees. Cook ten minutes or until golden brown on one side.

3. Turn potatoes; cook ten minutes or until golden brown.

4. Sprinkle with salt and pepper.

■ Freezing instructions

Allow potatoes to cool, and place individual portions in freezer bags. Freeze. Allow them to thaw overnight in refrigerator. Remove from freezer bags, and place on a small dish. Cover, and reheat in microwave for three to four minutes. May also be reheated in frying pan over medium-high heat.

Home Fried Potatoes

Serving size: ⅔ cup

■ Ingredients

1 ⅞ pounds (1 quart) salad oil

35 pounds (6 gallons 1 ½ quarts) fresh potatoes, peeled and sliced

1 ⅞ ounces (3 tablespoons) salt

⅛ ounce (⅓ teaspoon) ground black pepper

■ Directions

1. Spread a layer of potatoes on well-greased griddle.

2. Cook on 400 degree griddle for about 25 minutes, turning occasionally to ensure even browning.

3. Sprinkle with salt and pepper.

4. Hold at 140 degrees or higher for service.

■ Freezing instructions

Freeze cut potatoes before you cook them by placing the cut potatoes in boiling water for two minutes. Remove from water, drain, and allow them to cool. Place potatoes in freezer bags and freeze. You may cook potatoes directly out of freezer by starting at Step 2 of above recipe and cooking for about five minutes longer.

Buttermilk Pancakes

Serving size: 2 pancakes

■ Ingredients

9 ⅞ pounds (2 gallons 1 quart)
general-purpose wheat flour

3 ⅞ ounces (½ cup) baking powder

2 ⅜ pounds (1 quart ½ cup) dry buttermilk
powder

1 ounce (2 tablespoons) baking soda

1 ⅞ ounce (3 tablespoons) salt

12 ⅓ ounces (1 ¾ cup) granulated sugar

2 ⅔ pounds (1 quart 1 cup) whole eggs

13 pounds (1 gallon 2 ¼ quarts) water

1 pound (2 cups) salad oil

2 ounces (¼ cup ⅓ tablespoon) nonstick cooking spray

■ Directions

1. Sift together flour, baking powder, dry buttermilk, salt, sugar, and baking soda.

2. Add eggs and water; mix at low speed about one minute or until blended.

3. Blend in salad oil or melted shortening for about one minute.

4. Lightly spray griddle with nonstick cooking spray. Pour ¼ cup batter onto hot griddle. Cook on one side one and a half to two minutes or until top is covered with bubbles and underside is browned. Turn; cook on other side one and a half to two minutes.

■ Freezing instructions

Place cooled pancakes in freezer bag. Freeze. Reheat in microwave in a covered dish. Each portion will take about two minutes to reheat.

French Toast

Serving size: 2 slices

■ Ingredients

5 ¾ pounds (2 quarts 3 cups) water

10 ⅝ ounces (1 ½ cups) granulated sugar

5 ⅝ ounces (2 ⅜ cups) nonfat dry milk

7 /12 pounds (3 quarts 2 cups) whole eggs

11 pounds (200 slices) white bread, sliced

2 ounces (¼ cup and ⅓ tablespoon) nonstick cooking spray

■ Directions

1. Place water in a mixer bowl.
2. Combine water, milk, and sugar, blending well. Whip on low speed until dissolved, about one minute.
3. Add eggs to ingredients in mixer bowl; whip on medium speed until well blended, about two minutes.
4. Dip bread in egg mixture to coat both sides. Do not soak.
5. Lightly spray griddle with nonstick spray. Place bread on griddle, and cook on each side about one and a half minutes or until golden brown.
6. Internal temperature must reach 145 degrees or higher for 15 seconds.

■ Freezing instructions

Place cooled French toast in freezer bag. Freeze. Reheat in toaster.

Stovetop Granola

Serving size: ¾ cup

■ Ingredients

¾ pound (1 ½ cups and 1 tablespoon) olive oil

13 pounds (50 cups) rolled oats

4 ½ pounds (8 ⅓) cups butter

34 ounces (3 cups and 2 tablespoons) honey

64 ounces (8 ⅓ cups) packed brown sugar

50 ounces (12 ½ cups) almonds, chopped

50 ounces (8 ⅓ cups) cranberries, dried

■ Directions

1. Heat the oil in a large skillet over medium-high heat. Add oats, then cook and stir until they begin to brown and crisp, which should take about five minutes. Remove from heat, and spread out on a cookie sheet to cool.

2. Melt the butter in the same pan over medium heat. Stir in the honey and brown sugar; cook, stirring constantly, until bubbly. Return the oats to the pan. Cook and stir for another five minutes or so. Pour out onto the cookie sheet, and spread to cool.

3. Once cool, transfer to an airtight container, and stir in the almonds and dried cranberries. Any additional nuts and fruit can be stirred in at this time, also.

4. Granola will keep for three months in a sealed airtight container.

CHAPTER

Breads

F I V E

Baking Powder Biscuits

Serving size: 1 biscuit
Bake on large cookie/baking sheet

■ Ingredients

6 ⅝ pounds (1 gallon 2 quarts) general-purpose wheat flour

3 ⅝ ounces (1 ½ cups) nonfat dry milk

5 ⅞ ounces (¾ cups) baking powder

1 ½ ounces (2 ⅓ tablespoons) salt

12 ounces (1 ⅝ cups) shortening

3 ⅞ pounds (1 quart 3 ½ cups) water

2 ounces (¼ cup ⅓ tablespoon) nonstick cooking spray

■ Directions

1. Sift together flour, milk, baking powder, and salt into mixer bowl.

2. Blend shortening at low speed into dry ingredients until mixture resembles coarse cornmeal.

3. Add water; mix at low speed only enough to form soft dough.

4. Place dough on lightly floured board. Knead lightly for one minute or until dough is smooth.

5. Roll or pat out to a uniform thickness of ½-inch.

6. Lightly spray each pan with nonstick cooking spray. Cut with 2 ½ inch floured biscuit cutter. Place 50 biscuits on each pan.

7. Using a convection oven, bake at 350 degrees (375 degrees in a conventional oven) for 15 minutes or until lightly browned on low fan, open vent.

8. After the biscuits cools, they can be frozen in quart-sized freezer bags for up to two months. Freeze four to six biscuits per freezer bag. To use, remove from freezer four to six hours before using, and allow to thaw at room temperature in the freezer bags.

■ Freezing instructions

Place cooled biscuits in freezer bag. Freeze. Allow to thaw overnight (six to eight hours) at room temperature.

Cheese Biscuits

Serving size: 1 biscuit
Bake on large cookie/baking sheet

■ Ingredients

6 ⅝ pounds (1 gallon 2 quarts) general-purpose wheat flour

3 ⅝ ounces (1 ½ cups) dry nonfat milk

5 ⅞ ounces (¾ cup) baking powder

1 ½ ounces (2 ⅓ tablespoons) salt

1 pound (1 quart) grated cheddar cheese

12 ounces (1 ⅝ cup) shortening

3 ⅞ pounds (1 quart 3 ½ cups) water

2 ounces (¼ cup ⅓ tablespoon) nonstick cooking spray

■ Directions

1. Sift together flour, milk, baking powder, and salt into mixer bowl. Add grated cheddar cheese to sifted dry ingredients.
2. Blend shortening at low speed into dry ingredients until mixture resembles coarse cornmeal.
3. Add water; mix at low speed only enough to form soft dough.
4. Place dough on lightly floured board. Knead lightly for one minute or until dough is smooth.
5. Roll or pat out to a uniform thickness of ½ inch.
6. Lightly spray each pan with nonstick cooking spray. Cut with 2½-inch floured biscuit cutter. Place 50 biscuits on each pan.
7. Using a convection oven, bake at 350 degrees (375 degrees in a conventional oven) for 15 minutes or until lightly browned on low fan, open vent.

■ Notes

For browner tops: In Step 1, add ½ cup of granulated sugar per 100 portions to dry ingredients.

■ Freezing instructions

Place cooled biscuits in freezer bag, and place into freezer. Allow biscuits to thaw overnight at room temperature.

Blueberry Muffins

Serving size: 1 muffin

■ Ingredients

5 pounds (1 gallon ½ quart) general-purpose wheat flour

2½ pounds (1 quart ⅝ cup) granulated sugar

3⅝ ounces (1½ cups) dry nonfat milk

3⅞ ounces (½ cup) baking powder

⅝ ounces (1 tablespoon) salt

3 ⅔ pounds (1 quart 3 cups) warm water

1 ¾ pounds (3 ¼ cup) whole eggs

1 ⅝ pounds (3 cups) canned unsweetened applesauce

11 ½ ounces (1 ½ cup) salad oil

2 ¼ pounds (1 quart) canned blueberries, drained

1 ½ ounces (3 tablespoons) nonstick cooking spray

▉ Directions

1. In mixer bowl, sift together flour, sugar, milk, baking powder, and salt.

2. Add warm water, eggs, applesauce, and salad oil; mix at low speed until dry ingredients are moistened, which should take about 15 seconds. Scrape down sides and bottom of mixer bowl, and continue to mix at low speed another 15 seconds. Do not overmix. Batter will be lumpy.

3. Rinse blueberries, and drain them well. Fold into batter.

4. Lightly spray muffin cups with nonstick cooking spray. Fill each muffin cup two-thirds full.

5. Using a convection oven, bake at 350 degrees (375 degrees in a conventional oven) 23 to 26 minutes with open vent, fan turned off the first ten minutes, and then low fan. Remove muffins from oven, and let cool.

▉ Notes

In Step 3, 2 pounds (1 ½ quarts) frozen blueberries (thawed) may be substituted.

▉ Freezing instructions

Place cooled muffins in freezer bag. Freeze. Allow them to thaw overnight at room temperature. May reheat for 30 seconds in microwave.

Banana Bread

Serving size: 1 slice
Pan size: 1 ½ quart bread pans (10 pans)

■ Ingredients

1 pound (1 ⅛ cup) shortening

2 ⅔ pounds (1 quart 2 cups) granulated sugar

1 ⅞ pounds (3 ½ cups) whole eggs, frozen

8 ounces (1 cup) canned applesauce, unsweetened

5 ¼ pounds (2 quarts 2 ⅝ cups) fresh bananas, mashed

2 ⅝ pounds (2 quarts) unsalted nuts, coarsely chopped

3 ⅞ pounds (3 quarts 2 cups) general-purpose wheat flour

2 ⅔ ounces (¼ cup 2 tablespoon) baking powder

⅜ ounces (⅓ teaspoon) salt

2 ounces (¼ cup ⅓ tablespoon) nonstick cooking spray

■ Directions

1. Cream shortening and sugar in mixer bowl at medium speed for two minutes until light and fluffy.

2. Add eggs and applesauce to mixture. Mix at medium speed for one minute.

3. Add bananas and nuts to egg mixture, and mix at medium speed until blended.

4. Sift together flour, baking powder, and salt.

5. Add dry ingredients to banana mixture; beat at low speed about 30 seconds. Continue beating 30 seconds longer or until blended. Do not overmix.

6. Lightly spray each pan with nonstick cooking spray. Pour about 2 quarts of batter into each sprayed and floured loaf pan. Spread batter evenly.

7. Using a convection oven, bake at 325 degrees (350 degrees in a conventional oven) for 70 to 75 minutes or until done on low fan, open vent.
8. Let bread cool in pans for five minutes, then remove from pan and place on wire rack to cool completely.
9. Refrigerate at 41 degrees or lower overnight.

■ **Freezing instructions**

Place cooled loaves in freezer bags and into the freezer. Allow to thaw overnight at room temperature.

Pumpkin Bread

Serving size: 1 slice
Pan size: 1 ½ quart bread pans (10 pans)

■ **Ingredients**

1 ½ pounds (2 ⅞ cups) whole eggs

3 ½ pounds (3 quarts) general-purpose wheat flour

1 ¼ ounces (2 tablespoons) salt

⅓ ounces (⅓ teaspoon) baking powder

1 ⅓ ounces (2 ⅔ tablespoons) baking soda

⅓ ounces (1 tablespoon) ground cinnamon

¼ ounce (1 tablespoon) ground allspice

⅓ ounce (1 tablespoon) ground nutmeg

¼ ounce (1 tablespoon) ground cloves

5 ¼ pounds (3 quarts) granulated sugar

1 ⅞ pounds (1 quart) salad oil

3 ¾ pounds (1 quart 3 cups) solid packed canned pumpkin

1 pound (2 cups) water

10 ⅓ ounces (2 cups) unsalted nuts, coarsely chopped

10 ¼ ounces (2 cups) raisins

2 ounces (¼ cup ⅓ tablespoon) nonstick cooking spray

■ Directions

1. Beat eggs in mixer bowl at medium speed for three minutes or until lemon colored.

2. Blend flour, salt, baking powder, baking soda, cinnamon, allspice, nutmeg, and cloves together in separate bowl.

3. Add flour mixture, sugar, salad oil, pumpkin, water, nuts, and raisins to beaten eggs.

4. Beat on low speed for one minute or until well blended. Do not over beat.

5. Lightly spray each pan with nonstick cooking spray. Pour about 7 ½ cups of batter into each sprayed pan.

6. Using a convection oven, bake at 325 degrees (350 degrees in a conventional oven) for about 70 minutes or until done on low fan, open vent. Let pans cool five to ten minutes before removing bread from pans.

7. Allow the loaves to cool thoroughly, wrap in waxed paper, and store at room temperature overnight before slicing.

8. Cut 25 slices per loaf.

■ Freezing instructions

Place cooled loaves in freezer bags. Freeze. Allow them to thaw overnight at room temperature.

Corn Bread

Serving size: 1 piece
Pan size: 16 x 24 x 2 (two pans)

■ Ingredients

3 ⅞ pounds (3 quarts 2 cups)
  general-purpose wheat flour

3 ⅔ pounds (3 quarts) cornmeal

6 ounces (2 ½ cups) nonfat dry milk

7 ounces (1 cup) granulated sugar

5 ⅞ ounces (¾ cup) baking powder

1 ½ ounces (2 ⅓ tablespoons) salt

1 ½ pounds (2 ⅞ cups) whole eggs

7 ⅞ pounds (3 quarts 3 cups) water

1 ½ pounds (3 cups) salad oil

2 ounces (¼ cup ⅓ tablespoon) nonstick cooking spray

■ Directions

1. Blend flour, cornmeal, milk, sugar, baking powder, and salt in mixer bowl.

2. Combine eggs and water; add to ingredients in mixer bowl. Blend at low speed about one minute, scraping down the sides of the bowl.

3. Add oil; mix at medium speed until blended.

4. Lightly spray each pan with nonstick cooking spray. Pour 1 gallon of batter into each pan.

5. Using a convection oven, bake at 375 degrees (400 degrees in a conventional oven) for 20 minutes or until done on low fan, open vent.

6. Cool; cut into rows of six slices by nine slices (54 pieces total per pan).

■ Notes

In Step 1, omit sugar if Southern-style cornbread is desired.

■ Freezing instructions

Place cooled bread in freezer bags. Freeze. Allow them to thaw overnight at room temperature.

French Bread

Serving size: 2 slices
Bake on large baking sheets

■ Ingredients

2 ounces (¼ cup 1 tablespoon) dry active yeast

12 ½ ounces (1 ½ cup) warm water

4 ⅝ pounds (2 quarts ¾ cups) cold water

2 ⅔ ounces (¼ cup 2 ⅓ tablespoons) granulated sugar

3 ounces (¼ cup 1 tablespoon) salt

10 ⅞ pounds (2 gallons 1 quart) wheat bread flour

2 ¾ ounces (¼ cup 2 ⅓ tablespoons) shortening

1 egg white wash (*see recipe below*)

■ Directions

1. Sprinkle yeast over water. Do not use temperatures over 110 degrees. Mix well. Let stand five minutes, then stir. Set aside for use in Step 3.

2. Place water, sugar, salt, and flour in mixer bowl.

3. Using dough hook, mix at low speed for one minute or until all flour mixture is incorporated into liquid. Add yeast solution, and mix at medium speed for five minutes.

4. Add shortening and continue mixing at medium speed for three minutes. Dough temperature should be between 78 degrees and 82 degrees.

5. Cover, and set the mixture in a warm place, around 80 degrees, for two and a fourth hours or until double in bulk.

6. Fold sides of the dough into center, and turn completely over. Let the mixture rest for 15 minutes.

7. Shape into 12 pieces that are 19 ounces each. Roll each piece into a smooth ball, and let it rest for ten minutes. Form each piece into a rope, 1¼ inches in diameter and 18 inches long by rolling it out with your hands. Place three loaves on each cornmeal-dusted pan. Use ⅛ cup cornmeal per pan.

8. Proof the dough at 90 to 100 degrees for 50 to 60 minutes or until doubled in bulk.

9. Brush top of each loaf with egg white wash (*see recipe below*). Cut six diagonal slashes, ¼ inch deep, on top of each loaf.

10. Bake for 30 minutes at 425 degrees (400 degrees in a convection oven) or until done.

11. When cool, cut 17 1-inch thick slices per loaf.

◼ Freezing instructions

Place cooled loaves in freezer bags. Freeze. Allow loaves to thaw overnight at room temperature. You may reheat them in the oven by wrapping loaves in aluminum foil and placing in 350-degree oven. Reheat in oven for about 20 minutes. You may freeze the loaves before or after you slice them.

Egg white wash

◼ Ingredients

5⅔ ounces (½ cup 2⅔ tablespoons) egg whites

1⅛ pounds (2¼ cup) water

◼ Directions

1. Beat egg whites and water together. Refrigerate at 41 degrees or lower until ready for use.

2. Brush wash over shaped dough before or after proofing.

White Bread

Serving size: 2 slices

Pan size: 1 ½ quart bread pans (8 pans)

■ Ingredients

1 ⅔ ounces (¼ cup ⅓ tablespoon) dry active yeast

12 ½ ounces (1 ½ cups) warm water

4 ⅛ pounds (2 quarts) cold water

5 ¼ ounces (¾ cup) granulated sugar

3 ounces (¼ cup 1 tablespoon) salt

4 ¼ ounces (1 ¾ cup) nonfat dry milk

9 ⅓ pounds (1 gallon 3 ¾ quarts) wheat bread flour

6 ⅓ ounces (¾ cup 2 tablespoon) shortening

■ Directions

1. Sprinkle yeast over water. Do not use a temperature over 110 degrees. Mix well. Let stand for five minutes, and stir. Set aside for use in Step 4.

2. Place water, sugar, salt, and milk in mixer bowl. Mix at low speed just enough to blend.

3. Add flour. Using dough hook, mix at low speed for one minute or until all flour is incorporated into liquid.

4. Add yeast solution, and mix at low speed for one minute.

5. Add shortening, and mix at low speed for one minute. Continue mixing at medium speed ten to 15 minutes or until dough is smooth and elastic. Dough temperature should be between 78 degrees and 82 degrees.

6. Cover the dough, and set it in warm place, approximately 80 degrees, for two hours or until double in bulk.

7. Fold sides into center, and turn dough completely over. Let it rest for 30 minutes.

8. Shape into approximately eight 1 ¾ pound pieces, and roll each piece into a smooth ball. Let the dough rest 12 to 15 minutes. Mold each

piece into an oblong loaf, and place each loaf seam-side down into lightly greased pan.

9. Allow the dough to proof at 90 to 100 degrees for about an hour or until double in bulk.

10. Using a convection oven, bake at 350 degrees (375 degrees in a conventional oven) until done, on low fan with open vent.

11. When cool, slice 25 slices, about ½ inch thick, per loaf.

■ Notes

In Step 8, when using 9 x 4 ¼ x 2 ¾ bread pans, scale into 12 18-ounce pieces.

■ Freezing instructions

Place cooled loaves in freezer bags, and freeze. Allow the loaves to thaw overnight at room temperature. You may freeze the loaves before or after you slice them.

Whole Wheat Bread

Serving size: 2 slices
Pan size: 1 ½ quart bread pans (eight pans)

■ Ingredients

1 ⅔ ounce (¼ cup ⅓ tablespoon) active dry yeast

12 ½ ounces (1 ½ cup) warm water

4 ⅛ pounds (2 quarts) water

4 ½ ounces (1 ⅞ cups) dry nonfat milk

10 ⅝ ounces (1 ½ cup) granulated sugar

2 ½ ounces (¼ cup ⅓ tablespoon) salt

4 ¼ pounds (3 quarts 2 cups) wheat bread flour

3 ½ pounds (3 quarts 1 cup) whole wheat flour

7 ¼ ounces (1 cup) softened shortening

■ Directions

1. Sprinkle yeast over water. Do not use on temperatures over 110 degrees. Mix well, and let it stand five minutes. Stir. Set aside for use in Step 4.

2. Place water, milk, sugar, and salt in mixer bowl. Using dough hook, mix at low speed about one minute until blended.

3. Combine flours thoroughly, and add to liquid in mixer bowl. Using dough hook, mix at low speed one minute or until the dry ingredients are incorporated into liquid.

4. Add yeast solution, and mix at low speed for one minute.

5. Add shortening, and mix at low speed for one minute. Continue mixing at medium speed for ten to 15 minutes or until dough is smooth and elastic. Dough temperature should be between 78 degrees and 82 degrees.

6. Cover the dough, and place it in a warm place (80 degrees) for two hours or until double in bulk.

7. Fold sides into center, and turn dough completely over. Let it rest 15 minutes.

8. Shape into approximately eight 1 ¾ pound pieces, and roll each piece into a smooth ball. Let the dough rest 12 to 15 minutes. Mold each piece into an oblong loaf, and place each loaf seam-side down into lightly greased pan.

9. Allow the dough to proof at 90 to 100 degrees for about an hour or until double in bulk.

10. Using a convection oven, bake at 350 degrees (375 degrees in a conventional oven) until done, on low fan with open vent.

11. When cool, slice 25 slices, about ½ inch thick, per loaf.

■ Freezing instructions

Place cooled loaves in freezer bags. Freeze. Allow them to thaw overnight at room temperature. You may freeze the loaves before or after you slice them.

Bagels

Serving size: 1 bagel
Bake on large baking sheet

■ Ingredients

3⅜ ounces (½ cup) dry active yeast

5¾ pounds (2 quarts 3 cups) warm water

7 ounces (1 cup) granulated sugar

3⅜ ounces (¼ cup 1⅔ tablespoon) salt

13⅞ pounds (2 gallons 3½ quarts) white bread flour

2 ounces (¼ cup ⅓ tablespoon) nonstick cooking spray

■ Directions

1. Sprinkle yeast over water in mixer bowl. Do not use temperatures about 110 degrees. Mix well. Let stand for five minutes, and stir.

2. Using a wire whip, add sugar and salt to yeast solution; stir until ingredients are dissolved.

3. Using a dough hook, add flour, and mix at low speed for one minute or until all flour is incorporated into liquid. Continue mixing at medium speed for 13 to 15 minutes until dough is smooth and elastic. (Dough will be very stiff.) Dough temperature should be between 78 degrees and 82 degrees.

4. Cover the dough, and let it rest 15 minutes.

5. Place dough on unfloured work surface. Divide dough into 3 ounce pieces, and knead briefly. Shape into balls by rolling in circular motion on work surface.

6. Place balls, in rows of four by six, on four ungreased sheet pans.

7. Cover the dough, and set in warm place (about 80 degrees) for about 15 to 20 minutes or until dough increases slightly in bulk.

8. Shape bagels like a doughnut, and flatten to 2½-inch circles, ¾ inch thick. Pinch center of each bagel with thumb and forefinger, and pull

gently to make a 1-inch diameter hole and a total 3½-inch diameter, keeping uniform shape. Place on four ungreased sheet pans in rows of four by six bagels per pan.

9. Allow the dough to proof at 90 degrees until bagels begin to rise, about 20 to 30 minutes.

10. Lightly spray five sheet pans with nonstick cooking spray. Sprinkle each pan with ½ cup cornmeal.

11. Add water to steam-jacketed kettle or stockpot. Bring to a boil, and then reduce heat to a simmer. Add ½ cup granulated sugar to water, and stir until dissolved. Gently drop bagels, one at a time, into water. Cook 30 seconds; turn; cook 30 seconds. Remove bagels with slotted spoon and allow them to drain. Place on sheet pans in rows of four by five.

12. Bake dough for 30 to 35 minutes or until golden brown and crisp in 400 degree oven. Remove from pans and cool on wire racks.

◾ Notes

In Step 1, use a 60-quart mixer for 100 portions, as dough is very stiff. If using 20 to 30 quart mixers, prepare no more than 50 portions at a time.

In steps 7 and 9, bagels should not double in bulk because the bagels will rise more in Step 11.

In Step 12, if you use a convection oven, bake at 350 degrees for 15 to 20 minutes on high fan, open vent.

◾ Freezing instructions

Place cooled bagels in an airtight freezer bag. Thaw overnight at room temperature. If you pre-slice the bagels prior to freezing them, you can toast the bagels right out of the freezer.

Hot Rolls

Serving size: 2 rolls

Bake on large baking sheet

■ Ingredients

4 ½ ounces (½ cup 2 ⅔ tablespoons) active dry yeast

1 ⅞ pounds (3 ½ cups) warm water

5 ¾ pounds (2 quarts 3 cups) cold water

1 ½ pounds (3 ½ cups) granulated sugar

3 ⅛ ounce (¼ cup 1 ⅓ tablespoon) salt

14 ½ pounds (3 gallons) wheat bread flour

4 ¼ ounces (1 ¾ cup) nonfat dry milk

1 ¼ pounds (2 ¾ cups) softened shortening

1 ounce (2 tablespoons) nonstick cooking spray

■ Directions

1. Sprinkle yeast over water. Do not use temperatures over 110 degrees. Mix well. Let stand five minutes, and then stir.

2. Place cold water in mixer bowl. Add sugar and salt and stir until dissolved. Add yeast solution.

3. Combine flour and milk, and add to liquid solution. Using dough hook, mix at low speed for one minute or until flour mixture is incorporated into liquid.

4. Add shortening, and mix at medium speed ten minutes or until dough is smooth and elastic. Dough temperature should be between 78 degrees and 82 degrees.

5. Cover the dough, and set it in a warm place, about 80 degrees, oen and a half hours or until double in size.

6. Divide dough into eight 2 pound 14 ounce pieces. Shape each piece into a smooth ball, and let them rest ten to 20 minutes.

7. Roll each piece into a long rope, about 32 inches, of uniform diameter. Cut rope into 25 1 ¾-ounce pieces about 1 ¼ inch long. Place rolls on a lightly sprayed sheet pan.

8. Allow the dough to proof at 90 degrees for about one hour or until double in bulk.

9. Using a 350 degree convection oven (375 degrees in a conventional oven), bake for ten to 15 minutes, or until golden brown, on high fan, open vent.

■ Freezing instructions

Place cooled rolls in freezer bags. Freeze. Allow them to thaw overnight at room temperature. You can reheat in oven by wrapping rolls in aluminum foil and placing in 350 degree oven. Reheat in oven for about 20 minutes.

C H A P T E R

Lunch

S I X

Barbecued Beef Sandwich (Sloppy Joes)

Serving size: 1 sandwich

■ Ingredients

18 ¾ pounds raw ground beef, 90 percent lean

5 ¼ pounds (3 quarts 3 cups) fresh onions, chopped

9 ½ pounds (1 gallon ½ quart) ketchup

2 ¼ ounce (¼ cup 2 tablespoon) dry mustard

¾ ounce (1 tablespoon) salt

1 ¼ ounce (¼ cup ⅓ tablespoon) packed brown sugar

1 pound (2 cups) distilled vinegar

2 pounds (3 ¾ cups) water

9 ½ pounds (100 count) sandwich buns, split

■ Directions

1. Cook beef until beef loses its pink color, stirring to break apart. Drain or skim off excess fat.
2. Combine onions, ketchup, mustard, salt, brown sugar, vinegar, and water. Add to beef.
3. Cover meat, and simmer 35 minutes. Stir occasionally to prevent scorching.
4. Internal temperature must reach 155 degrees or higher for 15 seconds to ensure that the meat is thoroughly cooked.
5. Place ½ cup of hot meat mixture on bottom half of bun. Top with second half of bun.

■ Freezing instructions

Place barbecued beef sandwich filling in airtight freezer container. Do not freeze filling on roll. Reheat filling in covered microwavable bowl for three to four minutes before placing on a fresh or reheated frozen roll. *Instructions for reheating the rolls are found in Chapter 5.*

Barbecued Pork Sandwich

Serving size: 1 sandwich

■ Ingredients

13 ½ pounds cooked pork, diced

3 ⅜ pounds (2 quarts 1 ⅝ cups) fresh onions, chopped

6 ⅓ pounds (3 quarts) ketchup

2 ¼ ounces (¼ cup 2 tablespoons) dry mustard

1 ounce (3 tablespoons) packed brown sugar

2 ⅓ pounds (1 quart ½ cup) water

9 ⅜ ounce (1 ⅛ cup) distilled vinegar

9 ½ pounds (100 count) sandwich buns, split

■ Directions

1. Combine onions, ketchup, mustard, brown sugar, water, and vinegar. Add to pork.

2. Cover, and let simmer 35 minutes. Stir occasionally to prevent scorching.

3. Internal temperature must reach 145 degrees or higher for 15 seconds.

4. Place ½ cup of hot mixture on bottom half bun. Top with second bun half.

■ Freezing instructions

Place barbecued pork sandwich filling in airtight freezer container. Do not freeze filling on roll. Reheat filling for three to four minutes in covered microwavable bowl before placing on a fresh or reheated frozen roll. *Instructions for the rolls are found in Chapter 5.*

Pizza Burger

Serving size: 1 sandwich

■ Ingredients

5 ¼ pounds (1 gallon 1 ¼ quarts) mozzarella cheese, sliced

Pizza sauce (*see Chapter 9*)

14 pounds (100 count) 3 ounce beef patty, raw

9 ½ pounds (100 count) hamburger buns

■ Directions

1. Grill patties on 350 degree griddle four minutes or until browned. Turn, and grill on other side for four minutes.

2. Internal temperature must reach 155 degrees or higher for 15 seconds.

3. Place one slice cheese on each patty. Continue to grill until cheese melts.

4. Heat sauce to boiling.

5. Spread 2 ½ tablespoons of pizza sauce on each hamburger. Cover with top bun.

■ Freezing instructions

The component parts of this recipe, except for the cheese, can all be frozen and/or canned. The dish, as a whole, can be made up of the preserved component parts. See recipe for each component part for freezing instructions.

French Bread Pizza

Serving size: 4 oz.
Prepare on a large cookie sheet.

■ Ingredients

Pizza sauce (*see recipe in Chapter 9*)

17 pounds French bread (*see recipe in Chapter 5*)

6 ½ pounds (1 gallon 2 ½ quarts) mozzarella cheese, shredded

4 ounces (1 ⅛ cup) Parmesan cheese, grated

■ Directions

1. Prepare pizza sauce according to recipe in Chapter 9, or use prepared pizza sauce.

2. Cut each loaf of bread lengthwise, and divide each half into three pieces. Place 12 pieces on each pan.

3. Spread 2 ⅓ tablespoons sauce over each piece.

4. Evenly distribute 1 ounce or ¼ cup shredded cheese over each piece.

5. Sprinkle ½ teaspoon grated cheese over mixture on each piece.

6. Using a convection oven, bake at 400 degrees (425 degrees in a conventional oven) for six minutes or until cheese starts to turn golden on high fan, closed vent.

7. Hold for service at 140 degrees or higher.

■ Freezing instructions

The component parts of this recipe, except for the cheese, can all be frozen and/or canned. The dish, as a whole, can be made up of the preserved component parts. See recipe for each component part for freezing instructions.

Veggie Burger

Serving size: 1 sandwich

■ Ingredients

7 ½ pounds (3 quarts 2 cups) egg whites

4 ½ pounds (1 gallon ½ quart) part skim mozzarella cheese, shredded

2 ⅞ pounds (2 quarts ¼ cup) fresh onions, grated

1 pound (1 ½ cups) soy sauce

8 ⅝ pounds (1 gallon 2 ¼ quarts) rolled cereal oatmeal

1 ⅝ pounds (1 quart 2 cups) shelled walnuts, chopped

2 ⅜ ounce (½ cup) garlic powder

¼ ounce (¼ cup ⅓ tablespoon) ground sage

2 ounces (¼ cup ⅓ tablespoon) nonstick cooking spray

9 ½ pounds (100 count) sandwich rolls, split

■ Directions

1. Place egg whites, cheese, onions, and soy sauce in mixer bowl. Using a dough hook, mix on low speed for one minute or until well blended.

2. Add oats, walnuts, garlic powder, and sage, and mix on low speed for one minute. Scrape down sides of the bowl, and continue mixing 30 seconds, or until well blended. Refrigerate mixture at least one hour to allow mixture to absorb moisture. Refrigerate at 41 degrees or lower.

3. Shape 100 balls that are 3-½ ounces each. Place 20 balls on each sheet pan. Cover with parchment paper, and press down onto burgers with another sheet pan to a thickness until the burgers are ½ inch thick. Mixture will be very moist and fragile.

4. Grill burgers on lightly sprayed griddle at 400 degrees for six minutes total, or bake on lightly sprayed sheet pans in a convection oven at 350 degrees (375 degrees in a conventional oven) for 15 to 20 minutes on high fan, open vent or until golden brown.

5. Internal temperature must reach 145 degrees or higher for 15 seconds to ensure that burgers are thoroughly cooked.

6. Serve on buns.

■ Freezing instructions

You may freeze the burgers, minus the buns, individually by placing them in freezer bags. Reheat the frozen burger directly out of the freezer by placing a small amount of olive oil in a frying pan and heating the burger over a medium high heat in the oiled pan.

Falafel

Serving size: 2 patties

■ Ingredients

6¾ pounds (10 cups) fava beans, soaked overnight and drained

6¾ pounds (10 cups) chickpeas, soaked overnight and drained

30 medium onions, chopped

10 small bunches of parsley, chopped

80 cloves garlic, crushed

¾ ounce (3⅓ tablespoons) ground coriander

¾ ounce (3⅓ tablespoons) cumin

4¼ ounces (6⅔ tablespoons) salt

½ ounce (3⅓ tablespoons) pepper

¼ ounce (2½ teaspoons) chili powder

2 ounces (3 ⅓ tablespoons) baking soda

Oil for frying (about ¼ cup)

■ Directions

1. Place fava beans, chickpeas, and onions in a food processor, and process until beans and chickpeas are very finely ground. Add remaining ingredients, except oil, and process to a dough-like paste. Form into patties about 3 inches in diameter. If patties tend to crumble, process further, or add a little flour.

2. Heat oil in a saucepan, and fry patties over medium heat, turning until they are golden brown on both sides.

3. Serve patties warm as main dish with fresh vegetables and sesame tahini sauce on the side or in sandwiches of half-rounds of pita bread stuffed with salad vegetables and topped with tahini sauce. Tahini is a mixture made from roasted sesame seeds and olive oil that is readily available in most large grocery stores.

■ Freezing instructions

Place cooled falafel balls in a freezer bag. Freeze. Reheat the falafel by placing the desired amount on a microwavable dish and covering them loosely. Heat in microwave for one to two minutes, or until slightly soft.

Red Beans and Rice

Serving size: 1 cup

■ Ingredients

5 ¾ pounds (3 quarts 2 cups) long grain rice

15 ⅛ pounds (1 gallon 3 ¼ quarts) cold water

1 ounce (2 tablespoons) salad oil

1 ¼ ounce (2 tablespoons) salt

3 pounds sliced bacon, raw

2 ⅛ pounds (1 quart 2 cups) fresh onion, chopped

27 ⅛ pounds (3 gallons) dark red canned kidney beans, including liquid

¼ ounce (1 tablespoon) ground black pepper

Less than ¹⁄₁₆ ounce (⅛ teaspoon) ground red pepper

1 ⅛ ounce (¼ cup) garlic powder

■ Directions

1. Combine rice, water, salt, and salad oil, and bring to a boil. Stir occasionally.

2. Cover tightly, and simmer 20 to 25 minutes. Do not stir.

3. Remove from heat; transfer to shallow serving pan.

4. Set rice aside for use in Step 6.

5. Cook bacon until crisp; drain. Set aside 2 ounces bacon fat per 100 servings for use in Step 6. Set aside bacon for use in Step 7.

6. Sauté onions in bacon fat about one to two minutes or until lightly browned. Drain thoroughly.

7. Combine sautéed bacon and onions with undrained kidney beans, peppers, and garlic powder.

8. Using a convection oven, bake at 325 degrees for 30 minutes on high fan, closed vent. Bake at 350 degrees in a standard oven.

9. Internal temperature must reach 145 degrees or higher for 15 seconds.

10. Serve ½ cup of beans over ½ cup of rice.

■ Freezing instructions

Freeze individual portions in airtight freezer containers. Reheat in a covered microwavable dish for a minute or two, stirring once or twice.

Chili Con Carne

Serving size: 1 cup

■ Ingredients

14 pounds raw ground beef

8 ½ ounces (2 cups) ground dark chili powder

1 ⅔ ounce (½ cup) ground cumin

2 ounces (½ cup) ground paprika

1 ⅞ ounce (3 tablespoons) salt

⅞ ounce (3 tablespoons) garlic powder

⅜ ounce (2 tablespoons) ground red pepper

33 ⅞ pounds (3 gallons 3 quarts) dark red canned kidney beans, including liquid

8 ⅓ pounds (1 gallon) reserved bean liquid

8 ⅓ pounds (1 gallon) water

6 ⅝ pounds (3 quarts) canned diced tomatoes, drained

2 pounds (3 ½ cups) canned tomato paste

3 ⅛ pounds (2 quarts 1 cup) fresh onions, chopped

■ Directions

1. Place beef in steam-jacketed kettle. Cook in its own juice until it loses its pink color, stirring to break apart. Drain or skim off excess fat.

2. Combine chili powder, cumin, paprika, salt, garlic powder, and red pepper. Stir into cooked beef.

3. Drain beans; reserve beans for use in Step 4. Combine bean liquid with hot water to make 2 gallons; reserve for use in Step 4.

4. Add beans, tomatoes, tomato paste, and onions to cooked beef; stir well. Add reserved bean liquid and hot water to the beef mixture; stir. Bring to a boil, cover, reduce heat, and simmer for one hour. Do not bring to a boil. Stir occasionally.

5. Internal temperature must reach 155 degrees or higher for 15 seconds.

■ Notes

In Step 3, 10 pounds dry kidney, pinto, or white beans may be substituted. Inspect the beans, removing discolored beans and foreign matter. Wash beans thoroughly. Cover with 6 gallons water, boil for two minutes, and turn off heat. Cover the pot, and let the beans soak for one hour. Bring beans to a boil, and add 1⅔ ounces or 2⅔ tablespoons salt. Cover, and simmer 1½ hours or until tender. If necessary, add more water to keep beans covered. Drain beans, and reserve them for use in Step 4. Combine bean liquid with hot water to make 2 gallons; reserve for use in Step 4.

■ Freezing instructions

Freeze individual portions in airtight freezer containers. Reheat in a covered microwavable dish for a minute or two, stirring once or twice.

Veggie Wrap

Serving size: 1 wrap

■ Ingredients

12⅜ pounds (100 count) 10-inch wheat tortillas

5 pounds fresh lettuce

6 pounds (3 quarts 3⅛ cups) fresh chopped tomatoes

3⅛ pounds (3 quarts ⅞ cup) fresh carrots, grated

3⅛ pounds (2 quarts 1½ cups) fresh green peppers, chopped

3⅛ pounds (1 gallon 1⅛ quarts) fresh whole mushrooms, sliced

3⅛ pounds (3 quarts ½ cup) fresh summer squash, diced

3⅛ pounds (2 quarts 3⅞ cups) fresh cucumber, chopped

6 ounces (1¾ cups) fresh green onion, sliced

5⅝ pounds (2 quarts 1 cup) fat-free creamy garlic salad dressing

Directions

1. Wrap tortillas in foil, and place in warm oven, about 150 degrees or warmer, for 15 minutes or until warm and pliable.

2. Cut lettuce into ½-inch strips.

3. Toss lettuce, tomatoes, carrots, peppers, mushrooms, squash, cucumbers, green onions, and dressing.

4. Place 5 ounces (about 1 cup) vegetable mixture on warmed tortilla.

5. Roll up tortilla, and wrap with parchment, wax paper, or foil.

6. Hold for service at 41 degrees or lower. Prepare in batches to prevent the lettuce from wilting and the tortillas from getting soggy.

Notes

These do not freeze well. Wraps such as this are best served fresh.

Baked Chicken

Serving size: 8 oz.

Ingredients

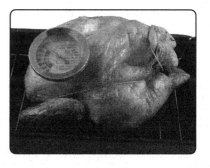

82 pounds eight piece cut chicken, skin removed

2 ⅛ ounces (¼ cup ⅔ tablespoons) nonstick cooking spray

2 ½ ounces (¼ cup ⅓ tablespoon) salt

⅞ ounce (¼ cup ⅓ tablespoon) ground black pepper

Directions

1. Wash chicken thoroughly under cold running water. Drain well. Remove excess fat.

2. Lightly spray sheet pans with nonstick cooking spray. Place chicken meat side up on each sheet pan.

3. Combine salt and pepper, mixing well.

4.   Sprinkle 1 tablespoon seasoning mixture evenly over chicken in each pan. Lightly spray chicken with cooking spray.

5.   Using a convection oven, bake 40 minutes at 325 degrees on high fan, closed vent. Bake at 350 degrees in a standard oven.

6.   Internal temperature must reach 165 degrees or higher for 15 seconds.

7.   Transfer chicken to steam table pans.

■ **Freezing instructions**

Place individual serving size portions of cooled baked chicken (without bones) in freezer bags. Make sure that you remove as much air as possible when sealing the bag. Freeze as quickly as possible. Allow to thaw overnight in refrigerator before using.

Baked Chicken and Noodles

Serving size: 1 cup

■ **Ingredients**

25 ⅛ pounds (3 gallons) boiling water

2 ¼ pounds (1 gallon 2 ¾ quarts) egg noodles

⅞ ounce (1 tablespoon) salt

25 pounds (2 gallons 2 quarts) chicken broth (*see recipe in Chapter 9*)

3 pounds (3 quarts) fresh onions, quartered

2 ¼ pounds (2 quarts) general-purpose wheat flour

4 ⅛ pounds (2 quarts) water cold

6 pounds (2 quarts 3 ½ cups) warm water

5 ⅜ ounce (2 ¼ cups) nonfat dry milk

1 ⅞ ounce (3 tablespoons) salt

¼ ounce (1 tablespoon) ground black pepper

¼ ounce (⅓ teaspoon) garlic powder

⅓ ounce (2 tablespoons) whole sweet basil, crushed

18 pounds cooked chicken, diced

1 pound (1 quart) breadcrumbs

6 ounces (¾ cup) melted butter

8 ounces (2 cups) cheddar cheese, shredded

■ Directions

1. Cook noodles in boiling salted water eight to ten minutes until tender. Drain. Use immediately in recipe preparation, or rinse with cold water, drain thoroughly, place in shallow containers, cover, and refrigerate.

2. Add onions to broth, and bring to a boil. Cover, reduce heat, and simmer eight to ten minutes until tender.

3. Blend flour and cold water together to make a smooth slurry. A slurry is a mixture of liquid (usually water) and "insoluble" matter. Add slurry to broth and onion mixture stirring constantly. Bring to a boil. Cover, reduce heat, and simmer ten minutes or until thickened, stirring frequently to prevent sticking.

4. Reconstitute milk in warm water (add the milk powder to the water). Add salt, pepper, garlic powder, and basil. Stir milk mixture into thickened broth, and bring to a boil. Cover, reduce heat, and simmer for two minutes.

5. Stir chicken and noodles gently into thickened sauce. Heat to a simmer.

6. Pour chicken and noodle mixture into ungreased steam table pans.

7. Combine crumbs, margarine or butter, and cheese. Sprinkle crumb mixture evenly over chicken and noodles in each pan.

8. Using a convection oven, bake 25 minutes at 325 degrees on high fan, open vent or until lightly browned. Bake at 350 degrees in a standard oven.

9. Internal temperature must reach 165 degrees or higher for 15 seconds.

■ Freezing instructions

This is a milk-based creamy dish that does not freeze well and is best enjoyed freshly made. However, you can freeze it in individual or larger portions. The soup base may separate as you thaw it. If this occurs, you can use a whisk to combine the soup. To reheat, place in a covered microwavable dish or a saucepan. Heat for several minutes or over a medium heat. If you plan to freeze this soup, do not freeze the noodles. Make the noodles as you reheat the soup, and add at this point.

Meatball Sandwich

Serving size: 1 sandwich

■ Ingredients

20 pounds lean, raw ground beef

2⅓ pounds (1 quart 2⅝ cups) fresh onions, chopped

2⅛ pounds (2 quarts 1 cup) finely ground dry breadcrumbs

12⅞ ounces (1½ cups) whole eggs

3 ounces (¼ cup 1 tablespoon) salt

¼ ounces (1 tablespoon) ground black pepper

8⅜ pounds (100 count) French rolls

38½ pounds (4 gallons) pizza sauce (*see recipe in Chapter 9*)

■ Directions

1. Combine beef, onions, breadcrumbs, eggs, salt, and pepper; mix lightly but thoroughly.

2. Shape into 300 1⅓ ounce meatballs. Place 100 meatballs on each pan.

3. Using a convection oven, bake 12 to 14 minutes at 350 degrees (375 degrees for a conventional oven) on high fan, closed vent or until browned.

4. Internal temperature must reach 155 degrees or higher for 15 seconds. Discard fat.

5. Slice rolls in half lengthwise with bottom half thicker than top. Place three meatballs on bottom half of each roll. Pour 4 ounces of pizza sauce over meatballs. Cover with top half of roll.

6. Serve hot.

7. Hold for service at 140 degrees or higher.

■ Freezing instructions

The component parts of this recipe (meatballs, sauce, and buns) can all be frozen and/or canned. The dish, as a whole, can be made up of the preserved component parts. See instructions for freezing and reheating the component parts of the dish in each of the individual recipes.

CHAPTER

Snacks

SEVEN

Granola Bars

Serving size: 1 bar
Pan size: 16 x 24 x 1 (two pans)

■ Ingredients

50 ounces (12 cups) quick-cooking rolled
  oats (not instant)

43 ounces (four 300 mL cans) condensed
  milk, sweetened

2 pounds (4 cups) semisweet chocolate chips

24 ounces (4 cups) wheat germ

15 ounces (3 cups) wheat bran

10 ounces (2 cups) oat bran

10 ounces (2 cups) margarine, melted

■ Directions

1. Combine oats, condensed milk, chocolate chips, wheat germ, wheat and
   oat brans, and margarine in large bowl.

2. Press into two greased, foil-lined 16 x 24 x 1 glass or metal cake pans.

3. Bake in 350 degree convection oven (375 degree conventional oven) for 15 to 20 minutes.

4. Allow to cool in pan before cutting into bars. Cut each pan into rows of six by nine for 54 bars each pan.

■ Freezing instructions

Cool completely prior to freezing. Wrap individual portions in wax paper to prevent from sticking. Place in an airtight plastic container or freezer bag, and freeze. Allow to thaw for six to eight hours at room temperature.

Oatmeal Cookies

Serving size: 2 cookies

■ Ingredients

2¼ pounds (2 quarts) general-purpose wheat flour

⅞ ounce (1 tablespoon) salt

⅜ ounce (⅜ teaspoon) baking soda

1⅓ ounces (2⅔ tablespoons) baking powder

12⅞ ounces (1½ cups) eggs, whole

4⅛ ounces (½ cup) water

⅞ ounce (2 tablespoons) vanilla extract

2 pounds (1 quart ½ cup) shortening

1½ pounds (3½ cups) granulated sugar

1⅓ pounds (1 quart ¼ cup) packed brown sugar

5⅛ pounds (3 quarts 3 cups) rolled oatmeal

1⅞ pounds (1 quart 2 cups) raisins

2 ounces (¼ cup ⅓ tablespoon) nonstick cooking spray

■ Directions

1. Sift together flour, salt, baking soda, and baking powder; set aside for use in Step 2.

2. Place eggs, water, vanilla, shortening, and sugars in mixer bowl. Beat at low speed for one to two minutes or until well blended. Add dry ingredients; mix at low speed for two to three minutes or until smooth.

3. Add rolled oats and raisins, and mix for about one minute.

4. Lightly spray each pan with nonstick cooking spray. Drop about 1 tablespoon of dough in rows of five by seven on lightly sprayed pans.

5. Using a convection oven, bake at 325 degrees for 13 to 15 minutes or until lightly browned on high fan, open vent. For standard ovens, increase temperature setting to 350 degrees.

6. Loosen cookies from pans while still warm.

■ Freezing instructions

Cool completely prior to freezing. Wrap individual portions in wax paper to prevent from sticking. Place in an airtight plastic container or freezer bag, and freeze. Allow to thaw for six to eight hours at room temperature.

Peanut Butter Cookies

Serving size: 2 cookies

■ Ingredients

1 ¾ pounds (1 quart) shortening

2 pounds (1 quart ½ cup) granulated sugar

1 pound (3 ¼ cups) packed brown sugar

1 ¼ pounds (2 ¼ cups) whole eggs

⅝ ounce (1 tablespoon) vanilla extract

2 ½ pounds (1 quart ½ cup) peanut butter

3 ⅓ pounds (3 quarts) general-purpose wheat flour

1 ⅓ ounces (2 ⅔ tablespoons) baking soda

⅜ ounce (⅓ teaspoon) salt

■ Directions

1. Place ingredients in mixer bowl in order listed. Mix at low speed one to two minutes or until smooth. Scrape down bowl once during mixing.

2. Divide dough into ten pieces about 1 pound 3 ounces each. Form into rolls about 20 inches long; slice each roll into 20 pieces, about 1 ounce each.

3. Place in rows, four by six, on ungreased sheet pans; using a fork, flatten to ¼-inch thickness, forming a crisscross pattern.

4. Using a convection oven, bake at 325 degrees for ten minutes or until lightly browned on high fan, open vent. Bake at 350 degrees in a standard oven.

5. Loosen cookies from pans while still warm.

■ Freezing instructions

Cool completely prior to freezing. Wrap individual portions in wax paper to prevent from sticking. Place in an airtight plastic container or freezer bag, and freeze. Allow to thaw for six to eight hours at room temperature.

Chocolate Chip Cookies

Serving size: 2 cookies

■ Ingredients

3 ⅝ pounds (3 quarts 1 cup) general-purpose wheat flour

¾ ounce (1 tablespoon) baking soda

1 ounce (1 tablespoon) salt

2 pounds (1 quart ½ cup) shortening

1 ⅛ pound (3 ½ cups) packed brown sugar

1 ½ pounds (3 ½ cups) granulated sugar

1 pound (1 ⅞ cups) frozen eggs, whole

1 ounce (2 tablespoons) warm water

½ ounce (1 tablespoon) vanilla extract

2 ¼ pounds (1 quart 2 cups) semisweet chocolate chips

▪ Directions

1. Sift together flour, baking soda, and salt. Set aside for use in Step 4.

2. Cream shortening in mixer bowl at medium speed about one minute. Gradually add sugars, and mix at medium speed for three minutes or until light and fluffy. Scrape down the sides of the bowl.

3. Combine slightly beaten eggs and water, and add gradually to creamed mixture. Blend thoroughly about one minute. Add vanilla, and mix thoroughly.

4. Add dry ingredients, and mix only until ingredients are combined, which should take about one minute.

5. Add chocolate chips, and mix on low speed about one minute or until evenly distributed.

6. Drop by tablespoons in rows, four by six, on ungreased pans.

7. Using a convection oven, bake at 325 degrees for ten to 12 minutes or until lightly browned on high fan, open vent. Set standard ovens to 350 degrees.

8. Loosen cookies from pans while still warm.

▪ Freezing instructions

Cool completely prior to freezing. Wrap individual portions in wax paper to prevent from sticking. Place in an airtight plastic container or freezer bag and freeze. Allow to thaw for six to eight hours at room temperature.

Fruit Freezer Pops

Serving size: 1 freezer pop

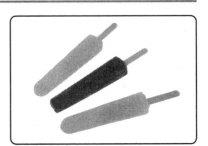

■ Ingredients

Half the recipe of fruit punch or lime lemon
  punch (*see Chapter 3*)

■ Directions

1. Pour punch into freezer pop forms
    or paper cups.
2. Cover the top of each cup with a strip of aluminum foil and poke a
    wooden stick through the center of the foil on each cup.
3. Freeze approximately four hours.

Yogurt Pops

Serving size: 1 pop

■ Ingredients

12 ½ pounds (25 cups) fresh fruit (blueberries, raspberries, strawberries, sliced
  bananas)

12 pounds (25 cups) plain or vanilla yogurt

1 ½ pounds (3 cups 2 tablespoons) granulated sugar

■ Directions

1. Place all ingredients into a blender.
2. Blend until fruit is chunky or smooth, as desired.
3. Pour punch into freezer pop forms or paper cups.
4. Cover the top of each cup with a strip of aluminum foil, and poke a
    wooden stick through the center of the foil on each cup.
5. Freeze approximately four hours.

CHAPTER

Appetizers

EIGHT

Pizza Treats

Serving size: 1 slice

■ Ingredients

4 pounds (1 gallon) pizza blend cheese, shredded (this can be a blend of mozzarella, Romano, and/or Parmesan cheese)

1 pound (1 ¾ cups) canned tomato paste

3 ⅞ ounces (½ cup) salad oil

7 ⅛ ounces (1 ½ cups) ripe, pitted olives, sliced and drained

1 pound (2 ⅝ cups) fresh onions, chopped

11 ⅞ ounces (2 ¼ cups) fresh green peppers, chopped

6 ¼ pounds (100 slices) French bread in ½-inch slices

■ Directions

1. Combine cheese, tomato paste, salad oil, olives, onions, and peppers. Blend well.

2. Spread 3 tablespoons of mixture on each slice of bread.

3. Place on ungreased pans. Using a convection oven, bake at 350 degrees for five minutes or until cheese is melted on low fan, open vent. Bake at 375 degrees in a standard oven.

■ Freezing Instructions

Freeze after Step 2 above. Individual portions may be wrapped in plastic wrap and frozen. May be baked directly from freezer in a preheated 400 degree oven for about ten minutes.

Swedish Meatballs

Serving size: 3 ½ oz.

■ Ingredients

2 pounds (1 gallon 2 ½ quarts) white bread, sliced

1 ¾ ounces (¾ cup) nonfat milk, dry

2 pounds (3 ¾ cups) warm water

10 ¾ ounces (1 ¼ cups) whole eggs

1 ¼ ounces (2 tablespoons) salt

⅛ ounce (⅓ teaspoon) ground nutmeg

⅛ ounce (¼ teaspoon) ground black pepper

⅛ ounce (¼ teaspoon) ground allspice

20 pounds raw ground beef, 90 percent lean

11 ¼ ounces (2 cups) fresh onions, chopped

25 pounds (2 gallons ½ quarts) beef broth

1 ⅜ pounds (1 quart 1 cup) general-purpose wheat flour

2 ⅝ pounds (1 quart 1 cup) water

¼ ounce (1 tablespoon) ground nutmeg

¼ ounce (1 tablespoon) ground black pepper

⅛ ounce (⅛ teaspoon) garlic powder

¼ ounce (1 tablespoon) ground paprika

■ Directions

1. Place bread in mixer bowl, and mix at medium speed for five minutes or until crumbs are formed.

2. Reconstitute milk by adding the water.

3. Blend in eggs, salt, nutmeg, pepper, and allspice. Pour over bread, and mix at low speed for 30 seconds. Let mixture stand ten minutes.

4. Add beef and onions to bread mixture. Mix at low speed for one minute. Do not overmix.

5. Shape into 300 balls weighing 1⅓ ounces; place 100 meatballs on each sheet pan.

6. Using a convection oven, bake at 350 degrees on high fan, closed vent eight to ten minutes or until browned and done. Bake at 375 degrees in a standard oven.

7. Internal temperature must reach 155 degrees or higher for 15 seconds.

8. Remove meatballs to steam table pans.

9. Hold at 140 degrees or higher for use in Step 10.

10. Prepare stock (*see Chapter 9, or make according to package directions.*)

11. Combine flour and water, stirring until smooth. Add to stock, and bring to a boil. Reduce heat, and allow to simmer for ten minutes or until thickened, stirring constantly.

12. Add nutmeg, pepper, and garlic powder, stirring well.

13. Pour 2¾ quarts gravy over meatballs in each pan.

14. Using a convection oven, bake at 350 degrees (375 degree conventional oven) for 15 minutes or until heated thoroughly on high fan, closed vent.

15. Internal temperature must reach 155 degrees or higher for 15 seconds.

16. Sprinkle each pan with 1 teaspoon paprika before serving.

■ Freezing Instructions

Freeze individual portions in airtight plastic containers. Cool completely prior to freezing. Freeze after Step 13 above. Allow portions to thaw overnight in refrigerator. Reheat in microwave approximately four to five minutes, stirring several times.

Baked Potato Skins

Serving size: 1 skin

■ Ingredients

16½ pounds (50) large baking potatoes

1 pound (2⅓ cups) vegetable oil

4 ounces (¾ cup 1 teaspoon) Parmesan cheese

2¼ ounces (2 tablespoons ¼ teaspoon) salt

1 ounce (1 tablespoon) garlic powder

1 ounce (1 tablespoon) paprika

½ ounce (1½ teaspoon) pepper

5 pounds (100 strips) cooked bacon, crumbled

5 pounds (18¾ cups) cheddar cheese, shredded

32 ounces (6¼ cups) sour cream

1 pound (50) green onions, chopped

■ Directions

1. Prick washed whole potatoes with a fork, and place on a large baking sheet.
2. Bake potatoes at 325 degrees in a convection oven (350 degrees in a conventional oven) for an hour.
3. Allow potatoes to cool.
4. Cut potatoes in half lengthwise; scoop out pulp, leaving a ¼-inch shell. (Save pulp for another use.)
5. Place potatoes skins on a greased baking sheet.
6. Combine oil, Parmesan cheese, salt, garlic powder, paprika, and pepper. Brush over both sides of skins.

7. Bake at 450 degrees in a convection oven (475 degrees in a conventional oven) for seven minutes, and then turn.

8. Bake until crisp, about seven minutes more.

9. Sprinkle bacon and cheddar cheese inside skins.

10. Bake until the cheese is melted.

11. Top with sour cream and onions, and serve immediately.

■ Freezing Instructions

Allow to cool prior to freezing. Wrap individual portions in wax paper, and place in freezer bags. Remove from wrapping, and reheat in preheated 375 degree oven for about 15 minutes.

Mini Quiche

Serving size: 1 mini quiche
Prepare this dish using muffin tins.

■ Ingredients

7 pounds (20 cups) fully cooked ham, diced

4 ½ pounds (16 cups) cheddar cheese

8 pounds (16 cups) chopped olives

12 ½ pounds (100) whole eggs

17 pounds (32 cups) half-and-half

4 pounds (8 cups) melted butter

2 ounces (100 drops) pepper sauce

4 pounds (16 cups 2 tablespoons) biscuit mix

1 ½ pounds (4 cups) Parmesan cheese

3 ounces (16 tablespoons) dry ground mustard

■ Directions

1. Combine ham, cheddar cheese, and olives in a large mixing bowl.
2. Divide mixture among 100 greased muffin cups.
3. In a mixing bowl, combine the remaining ingredients just until blended.
4. Pour over ham mixture.
5. Bake at 350 degrees in a convection oven (375 degrees in a conventional oven) for 20 to 25 minutes or until a knife inserted near the center comes out clean.
6. Let stand for five minutes before serving.

■ Freezing Instructions

Allow to cool prior to freezing. Wrap individual portions in wax paper, and place in freezer bags. To thaw, remove from wrapping, and reheat in preheated 375 degree oven for about 15 minutes. Do not reheat in microwave.

Crab Cakes

Serving size: 5 oz.

■ Ingredients

15 pounds cooked crabmeat

18⅛ pounds (4 gallons 3 quarts) breadcrumbs

2¼ ounces (¼ cup ⅓ tablespoon) mustard

3 ounces (¼ cup 2⅓ tablespoons) mayonnaise-type salad dressing

2 pounds (1 quart) melted butter

2 pounds (3¾ cups) whole eggs

2½ ounces (¼ cup ⅓ tablespoon) salt

⅓ ounce (1 tablespoon) ground black pepper

1¾ ounce (¾ cup) nonfat dry milk

2 pounds (3¾ cups) water

2 pounds (3 ¾ cups) whole eggs

2 ⅞ pounds (3 quarts) breadcrumbs

■ Directions

1. Remove any shell or cartilage from crabmeat.

2. Add breadcrumbs, mustard, salad dressing, butter or margarine, eggs, salt, and pepper, mixing lightly.

3. For each cake, measure ¼ cup of mixture. Form into cakes ½- to ¾-inch thick, about 2 ounces each.

4. Refrigerate at 41 degrees or lower.

5. Reconstitute milk by adding water, add eggs, and mix well.

6. Dip chilled crab cakes in milk and egg mixture, then in breadcrumbs. Shake off excess.

7. Fry at 350 degrees for two to three minutes or until golden brown.

8. Internal temperature must reach 145 degrees or higher for 15 seconds. Drain well in basket or on absorbent paper.

■ Freezing Instructions

Freeze after Step 6 above. Wrap individual portions in wax paper, and place in freezer bags. Freeze. Allow portions to thaw overnight in refrigerator prior to proceeding to Step 7.

Hummus

Serving size: 3 oz.

■ Ingredients

12 ½ (15.5 ounce) cans of canned
   chickpeas, drained

2 pounds (4 cups 2 tablespoons) Spanish
   manzanilla olives, pitted

¼ cup 1 teaspoon minced garlic

1 pound (2 ⅓ cups) olive oil

¾ pound (1 ½ cups 1 tablespoon) lemon juice

6 ounces (⅓ cup 1 tablespoon) fresh chopped basil

4 ounces (¼ cup 1 teaspoon) cilantro

Salt and pepper, to taste

■ Directions

1. Place garbanzo beans, olives, and garlic into the bowl of a blender or food processor.

2. Pour in olive oil and lemon juice; season with basil, cilantro, salt, and pepper.

3. Cover and puree until smooth.

4. Hummus can be served immediately, or covered and stored in the refrigerator until ready to use.

5. Serve with fresh vegetables, crackers, or flat bread.

■ Freezing Instructions

Place in airtight container(s) to freeze. Thaw overnight in refrigerator.

Buffalo Wings

Serving size: 3 wings

▆ Ingredients

Vegetable oil for deep frying (amount
   determined by your fryer)

90 pounds (300) chicken wings, tips
   removed, halved at joint

2 ½ pounds (3 cups 2 tablespoons) butter

½ pound (¾ cup 2 teaspoons) distilled white vinegar

2 pounds (3 ¾ cups 2 tablespoons) pepper sauce

Salt and pepper to taste

▆ Directions

1. Heat oil in a large skillet or deep fryer to 375 degrees.
2. Deep fry chicken wings in oil until done (about ten minutes).
3. Remove chicken from skillet or deep fryer, and drain on paper towels.
4. Melt butter in a large skillet.
5. Stir in vinegar and hot pepper sauce into melted butter.
6. Season mixture with salt and pepper to taste.
7. Add fried chicken to sauce, and stir over low heat to coat.
8. Serve warm.

▆ Freezing Instructions

Allow wings to cool completely prior to freezing. Place portions in an airtight
freezer container. Freeze. Allow wings to thaw overnight in refrigerator prior to
reheating. To reheat, preheat oven to 350 degrees. Place wings on greased baking
sheet, and bake for 30 to 45 minutes.

CHAPTER

Soups and Sauces

NINE

Any of the soups or sauces in this section can be frozen or canned. If you plan on freezing the soups or sauces, allow them to cool, and place them in an airtight container to freeze. They may be reheated on the stovetop or in a microwave oven directly from the freezer. It is recommended that the noodles and cheese in the recipes be added when the dishes are reheated, though you may freeze them in the soup if you desire.

If you plan on canning the soups and/or sauces, read the section on canning very carefully. *You can find more information on canning in appendices B and C.* For the meat-based recipes, you will need a pressure canner to make sure that the temperature gets hot enough to kill any bacteria.

If you plan to can the vegetable- or tomato-based soups or sauces, such as salsa, you may do so using the boiling water canning method. In any case, read the section on canning in the Appendix instructions very carefully.

Vegetable Broth

Serving size: 1 cup

■ Ingredients

12 ½ pounds (36 cups) celery

18 ¾ pounds (56 cups) sweet onions

12 ½ pounds (36 cups) carrots, chopped

12 ½ pounds (18 cups) tomatoes, cored

12 ½ pounds (36 cups) green bell peppers, chopped

6 ¼ pounds (18 cups) turnips, cubed

½ pound (1 ½ cups 1 tablespoon) olive oil

37 ½ garlic cloves

37 ½ whole cloves

12 bay leaves

75 whole black peppercorns

½ pound (12 ½ bunches) fresh parsley, chopped

96 pounds (12 ½ gallons water)

■ Directions

1. Preheat oven to 450 degrees.

2. Remove leaves and tender inner parts of celery, and set aside.

3. Toss onions, carrots, tomatoes, bell peppers, and turnips with olive oil.

4. Place vegetables in a roasting pan, and place them in the preheated oven.

5. Stir the vegetables every 15 minutes.

6. Roast until all vegetables have browned and the onions start to caramelize. (This should take about an hour.)

7. Put the browned vegetables, celery, garlic, cloves, bay leaf, peppercorns, parsley, and water into a large stockpot.

8. Bring the mixture to a full boil.

9. Reduce heat to simmer.

10. Cook the mixture uncovered until the liquid is reduced by half. (This should take about two hours.)

11. Pour the broth through a sieve, catching the broth in a large bowl or pot.

12. The liquid in the bowl or pot is vegetable broth. It can be used immediately or stored for later use.

■ Freezing Instructions

Allow food to cool completely prior to freezing. Place in an airtight container. Freeze. Reheat over a medium high heat on the stovetop or in a microwave oven for three to five minutes, stirring occasionally.

Chicken Broth

Serving size: 1 cup

■ Ingredients

42 pounds chicken, bones and pieces

10 pounds (30 cups) celery, chopped

10 pounds (30 cups) carrots, chopped

10 pounds (30 cups) onions, quartered

33 bay leaves

3 tablespoons (⅔ ounce) dried rosemary

3 tablespoons (⅓ ounce) dried thyme

133 whole black peppercorns

64 pounds (8 ½ gallons) water

■ Directions

1. Place all ingredients in a large pot or Dutch oven.

2. Place on a medium heat, and bring to a boil.

3. Reduce heat to simmer.

4. Skim foam off the surface of the mixture.

5. Cover, and simmer for two hours.

6. Remove chicken from the pot, and set chicken aside until cool enough to handle.

7. Remove chicken meat from bones and discard bones. Save meat for another use.

8. Pour the broth through a sieve, catching the broth in a large bowl or pot.

9. Refrigerate for eight hours or overnight. Skim fat from surface.

■ Freezing Instructions

Allow broth to cool completely prior to freezing. Place in an airtight container. Freeze. Reheat over a medium high heat on the stovetop or in a microwave oven for three to five minutes, stirring occasionally.

Beef or Ham Stock

Serving size: 1 cup

■ Ingredients

42 pounds beef or ham, bones and meat

10 pounds (30 cups) celery, chopped

10 pounds (30 cups) carrots, chopped

10 pounds (30 cups) onions, quartered

33 bay leaves

⅔ ounce (3 tablespoons) dried rosemary

⅓ ounce (3 tablespoons) dried thyme

133 whole black peppercorns

64 pounds (8 ½ gallons) water

■ Directions

1. Preheat convection oven to 375 degrees (400 degrees for a conventional oven).

2. Remove leaves and tender inner parts of celery, and set aside.

3. Toss beef, bones, onions, carrots, tomatoes, bell peppers, and turnips with olive oil.

4. Place beef and vegetables in a roasting pan, and place them in the preheated oven.

5. Roast for 45 minutes, stirring every 15 minutes.

6. Put the browned vegetables, celery, garlic, cloves, bay leaf, peppercorns, parsley, and water into a large stockpot.

7. Place the roasting pan on the stovetop on low heat (this will cover two burners), pour ½ cup to 1 cup of hot water over the pan, and use a metal spatula to scrape up all of the browned bits stuck to the bottom of the pan.

8. Pour the browned bits and water into the stockpot.

9. Bring the mixture to a full boil over a medium high heat.

10. Reduce heat to simmer.

11. Cook uncovered for three to six hours, stirring occasionally.

12. Remove from heat, and allow to cool slightly.

13. Pour the broth through a sieve, catching the broth in a large bowl or pot.

14. Refrigerate for eight hours or overnight. Skim fat from surface.

■ Freezing Instructions

Allow broth to cool completely prior to freezing. Place in an airtight container. Freeze. Reheat over a medium high heat on the stovetop or in a microwave oven for three to five minutes, stirring occasionally.

Bean Soup with Smoked, Cured Ham Hocks

Serving size: 1 cup

■ Ingredients

6¼ pounds (3 quarts 2 cups) dried white beans

16¾ pounds (2 gallons) cold water

5 gallons ham broth (*see recipe earlier in this chapter*)

2½ pounds frozen pork hocks, cured and smoked

1 pound (1 quart ⅛ cup) fresh shredded carrots

2 pounds (1 quart 1⅝ cups) fresh chopped onions

⅛ ounce (⅓ teaspoon) ground black pepper

13¼ ounces (3 cups) general-purpose wheat flour

2⅛ pounds (1 quart) cold water (this is in addition to the water listed previously)

■ Directions

1. Pick over beans, removing discolored beans and foreign matter.

2. Wash beans thoroughly in cold water.

3. Cover with cold water, bring to a boil, and boil for two minutes. Turn off heat, cover the dish, and let it stand for one hour.

4. Prepare stock according to recipe found earlier in this chapter. Add to beans, bring to a boil, cover, and simmer for two hours or until beans are tender.

5. Place thawed, smoked, cured pork hocks in water to cover. Simmer for one hour, remove from heat, and cool. Remove lean meat, and chop into small pieces.

6. Add carrots, onions, pepper, and chopped ham hocks to bean mixture. Simmer for 30 minutes.

7. Blend flour and water to form a smooth paste. Stir into soup, and cook for ten minutes.

8. Internal temperature must reach 165 degrees or higher for 15 seconds.

Freezing Instructions

Allow food to cool completely prior to freezing. Place in an airtight container. Freeze. Reheat over a medium high heat on the stovetop or in a microwave oven for three to five minutes, stirring occasionally.

Beef Barley Soup

Serving size: 1 cup

Ingredients

1 ½ pounds raw lean beef, diced

58 ½ pounds (7 gallons) beef broth

1 pound (3 ½ cups) frozen carrots, sliced

12 ⅛ ounce (2 ⅞ cups) fresh celery, chopped

1 pound (2 ⅞ cups) fresh onions, chopped

⅛ ounce (⅓ teaspoon) ground black pepper

⅛ ounce (3 leaves) whole dried bay leaf

2 ⅔ pounds (1 quart 2 cups) uncooked barley

Directions

1. Cook beef in a steam-jacketed kettle for five minutes. Dice beef into ½-inch pieces.
2. Prepare beef broth according to package directions.
3. Add beef broth, beef, carrots, celery, onions, pepper, and bay leaves to steam jacketed kettle or stockpot. Cover, and bring to a boil.
4. Add barley. Cover, and simmer 25 to 30 minutes, stirring occasionally until barley is tender. Remove bay leaves.
5. Internal temperature must reach 165 degrees or higher for 15 seconds.

■ Freezing Instructions

Allow food to cool completely prior to freezing. Place in an airtight container. Freeze. Reheat over a medium high heat on the stovetop or in a microwave oven for three to five minutes, stirring occasionally.

Carrot Soup

Serving size: 1 cup

■ Ingredients

2 ounces (¼ cup ⅓ tablespoon) nonstick cooking spray

5 pounds (1 gallon ⅞ quart) fresh chopped onions

12 pounds (2 gallons 2 ⅝ quarts) fresh chopped carrots

2 pounds fresh (6 cups), sliced celery

50 pounds (6 gallons vegetable broth)

¼ ounce (1 tablespoon) ground black pepper

4 pounds (12 cups) jasmine rice

■ Directions

1. Spray steam-jacketed kettle with nonstick cooking spray.

2. Add onions, celery, and carrots. Cook for ten minutes, stirring frequently.

3. Prepare vegetable broth according to manufacturer's instructions. Add to onions, celery, and carrots. Add black pepper, and bring to a boil. Add rice.

4. Simmer for 30 minutes. Stir vigorously with a wire whip to break up rice.

5. Bring the temperature to 165 degrees for 15 seconds.

6. Hold for service at 140 degrees or higher.

■ **Freezing Instructions**

Allow food to cool completely prior to freezing. Place in an airtight container. Freeze. Reheat over a medium high heat on the stovetop or in a microwave oven for three to five minutes, stirring occasionally.

Chicken Noodle Soup

Serving size: 1 cup

■ **Ingredients**

59 pounds (7 gallons 2 quarts) chicken broth

1 ½ pounds cooked chicken, diced

1 pound (3 ½ cups) frozen carrots, sliced

12 ⅔ ounces (3 cups) fresh celery, chopped

1 pound (3 ½ cups) frozen onions

⅛ ounce (⅓ teaspoon) ground black pepper

⅛ ounce (2 leaves) whole bay leaf, dried

1 pound (1 quart ⅜ cup) dry egg noodles

■ **Directions**

1. Prepare chicken broth according to directions found earlier in this chapter.

2. Combine chicken broth, diced chicken, carrots, celery, onions, pepper, and bay leaves in a steam-jacketed kettle or stockpot. Cover, and bring to a boil.

3. Add noodles, and stir. Cover, bring to a boil, and reduce heat. Allow the mixture to simmer for 15 to 20 minutes, stirring occasionally until chicken is cooked and noodles and vegetables are tender. Remove bay leaves.

4. Internal temperature must reach 165 degrees or higher for 15 seconds.

5. Hold for service at 140 degrees or higher.

■ Freezing Instructions

Allow food to cool completely prior to freezing. Place in an airtight container. Freeze. Reheat over a medium high heat on the stovetop or in a microwave oven for three to five minutes, stirring occasionally.

■ Note

If you plan on freezing this dish, it is best frozen without the noodles. Cook the noodles fresh prior to serving.

Chicken Vegetable Soup

Serving size: 1 cup

■ Ingredients

1 pound (2 ⅞ cups) fresh onions, chopped

1 ⅓ pound (1 quart) fresh green peppers, chopped

6 ounces (¾ cup) butter

13 ¼ ounces (3 cups) general-purpose wheat flour

42 pounds (5 gallons 2 quarts) chicken broth

1 ½ pounds cooked chicken, diced

6 ⅝ pounds (3 quarts) canned crushed tomatoes, including liquids

1 pound (3 ½ cups) fresh carrots, chopped

1 pound (3 ¾ cups) fresh celery, chopped

1 ½ pounds (1 quart 1 ½ cups) fresh apples, peeled and sliced

⅔ ounces (3 tablespoons) curry powder

Less than ¹⁄₁₆ ounce (⅛ teaspoon) ground cloves

⅛ ounce (⅓ teaspoon) ground black pepper

■ Directions

1. Sauté onions and peppers in butter or margarine until tender. Remove from fat; set aside for use in Step 5. Reserve fat for use in Step 2.
2. Blend fat and flour to form a roux (a thick sauce).

3. Prepare broth according to recipe found earlier in this chapter.

4. Add broth to roux, stirring constantly. Cook until blended.

5. Add chicken, sautéed onions and peppers, tomatoes, carrots, celery, apples, curry powder, cloves, and pepper.

6. Simmer for 45 minutes or until vegetables are tender.

7. Allow the temperature to reach 165 degrees or higher for 15 seconds.

8. Hold for service at 140 degrees or higher.

■ Freezing Instructions

Allow food to cool completely prior to freezing. Place in an airtight container. Freeze. Reheat over a medium high heat on the stovetop or in a microwave oven for three to five minutes, stirring occasionally.

French Onion Soup

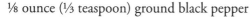

Serving size: 1 cup

■ Ingredients

11⅜ pounds (2 gallon 3¼ quarts) fresh sliced onions

1½ pounds (3⅜ cups) melted vegetable shortening

8⅞ ounces (2 cups) general-purpose wheat flour

⅛ ounce (⅓ teaspoon) ground black pepper

2⅛ ounce (¼ cup ⅓ tablespoon) Worcestershire sauce

42 pounds (5 gallons 1 quart) beef broth

2 pounds (1 gallon 2½ quarts) stale white bread, sliced

12 ounces (1½ cups) melted butter

5¼ ounces (1½ cups) grated Parmesan cheese

■ Directions

1. Sauté onions in shortening or salad oil until lightly browned.

2. Blend flour, pepper, and Worcestershire sauce with sautéed onions.

3. Prepare beef broth according to recipe found earlier in this chapter.

4. Add onion mixture, and stir well. Simmer for 15 minutes.

5. Prepare Parmesan croutons.

   Trim crusts from bread and cut bread into ½-inch cubes. Place bread cubes on sheet pans. Brown lightly in 325 degree oven for 20 to 25 minutes or in 375 degree convection oven for six minutes on high fan, open vent. Melt butter or margarine, and blend in grated Parmesan cheese. Pour mixture over lightly browned croutons in steam table pans, and toss lightly.

6. Place eight croutons in each soup bowl, and pour soup over croutons.

7. Allow the temperature to reach 165 degrees or higher for 15 seconds.

8. Hold for service at 140 degrees or higher.

■ Freezing Instructions

Freeze after step 4, allowing food to cool completely prior to freezing. Place in an airtight container. Freeze. To reheat, do so over a medium high heat on the stovetop or in a microwave oven for three to five minutes, stirring occasionally. Then continue from Step 5.

■ Notes

In Step 5, 2 pounds bread will yield about 1 gallon lightly browned croutons.

Barbecue Sauce

Serving size: ¼ cup

■ Ingredients

1 ⅓ pounds (2 ½ cups) distilled vinegar

3 ½ pounds (1 quart 2 cups) canned tomato paste

3 ⅔ pounds (1 quart 3 cups) ketchup

3 ⅔ pounds (1 quart 3 cups) water

1 pound (3 ¼ cups) packed brown sugar

1 ⅞ ounces (3 tablespoons) salt

8 ⅞ ounces (1 cup) prepared mustard

¼ ounce (1 tablespoon) red ground pepper

1 pound (2 ⅞ cups) fresh onion, chopped

1 pound (3 ¾ cups) fresh celery, chopped

1 ⅝ ounce (¼ cup 1 ⅔ tablespoons) garlic powder

¼ ounce (1 tablespoon) dark ground chili powder

1 ⅞ ounce (3 tablespoons) liquid smoke

■ Directions

1. Combine vinegar, tomato paste, ketchup, water, sugar, salt, mustard, red pepper, onions, celery, garlic, chili powder, and liquid smoke (optional).

2. Bring to a boil, reduce heat, cover, and simmer for 40 minutes or until sauce is blended.

3. Allow temperature to reach 145 degrees or higher for 15 seconds.

4. Hold for service at 140 degrees or higher.

■ Freezing Instructions

Allow food to cool completely prior to freezing. Place in an airtight container. Freeze. Reheat over a medium high heat on the stovetop or in a microwave oven for three to five minutes, stirring occasionally.

Marinara Sauce

Serving size: ¾ cup

■ Ingredients

⅞ ounces (3 tablespoons) garlic powder

3 ⅛ pounds (2 quarts 1 cup) fresh onions, chopped

1 ¾ ounces (¼ cup ⅓ tablespoon) melted vegetable shortening

26 ½ pounds (3 gallons) canned crushed tomatoes, including liquid

10 pounds (1 gallon ⅓ quarts) canned tomato paste

8 ⅓ pounds (1 gallon) water

¼ ounce (6 leaves) whole bay leaf, dried

⅓ ounce (2 tablespoons) crushed oregano

⅓ ounce (2 tablespoon) dried basil, crushed

3 ⅜ ounces (¼ cup 1 ⅔ tablespoons) salt

5 ¼ ounces (¾ cup) granulated sugar

⅓ ounce (2 tablespoons) ground thyme

■ Directions

1. Sauté garlic and onions in shortening, salad oil, or olive oil until tender.
2. Combine sautéed onions and garlic with tomatoes, tomato paste, water, bay leaves, oregano, basil, salt, sugar, and thyme. Mix well.
3. Bring to a boil, reduce heat, and simmer one hour or until thickened, stirring occasionally. Remove bay leaves before serving.
4. Allow temperature to reach 145 degrees or higher for 15 seconds.
5. Hold for service at 140 degrees or higher.

■ Freezing Instructions

Allow food to cool completely prior to freezing. Place in an airtight container. Freeze. Reheat over a medium high heat on the stovetop or in a microwave oven for three to five minutes, stirring occasionally. You may also allow to thaw for six to eight hours in the refrigerator before using in your favorite recipe.

Pizza Sauce

Serving size: 2 ½ tablespoons

■ Ingredients

½ ounce (1 tablespoon) salad oil

12 ⅔ ounces (2 ¼ cups) fresh onions, chopped

8 ¼ pounds (3 quarts 3 cups) canned crushed tomatoes, including liquids

1 ½ pounds (2 ⅝ cups) canned tomato paste

1 ¾ ounce (¼ cup ⅓ tablespoon) granulated sugar

1 ounce (1 tablespoon) salt

⅛ ounce (⅛ teaspoon) ground black pepper

⅓ ounce (2 tablespoons) dried basil, crushed

⅛ ounce (3 leaves) whole bay leaf, dried

⅛ ounce (⅛ teaspoon) garlic powder

⅓ ounce (2 tablespoons) crushed oregano

■ Directions

1. Sauté onions in shortening, salad, or olive oil until tender.
2. Add tomatoes, tomato paste, sugar, salt, pepper, basil, bay leaves, garlic, and oregano. Bring to a boil, reduce heat, and simmer for one hour. Remove bay leaves.
3. Allow temperature to reach 145 degrees or higher for 15 seconds.

■ Freezing Instructions

Allow sauce to cool completely prior to freezing. Place in an airtight container. Freeze. Reheat over a medium high heat on the stovetop or in a microwave oven for three to five minutes, stirring occasionally. You may also allow the sauce to thaw for six to eight hours in the refrigerator before using in your favorite recipe.

Creole Sauce

Serving size: ⅓ cup

■ Ingredients

1 ½ pounds (1 quart ¼ cup) fresh onions, chopped

1 ½ pounds (1 quart ½ cup) fresh green peppers, chopped

1 ½ pounds (1 quart 1 ⅝ cups) fresh celery, chopped

3 ⅝ ounces (½ cup) vegetable shortening, melted

14 ⅞ pounds (1 gallon 2 ¾ quarts) crushed canned tomatoes, including liquids

1 ounce (1 tablespoon) salt

⅓ ounce (1 tablespoon) ground black pepper

⅛ ounce (⅓ teaspoon) ground red pepper

⅜ ounce (2 ⅔ tablespoon) crushed oregano

⅜ ounce (2 ⅔ tablespoon) whole sweet basil, crushed

⅜ ounce (2 ⅔ tablespoon) ground thyme

⅓ ounce (1 tablespoon) garlic powder

¼ ounce (1 tablespoon) ground paprika

1 ¾ ounce (¼ cup ⅓ tablespoon) granulated sugar

1 ounce (2 tablespoons) Worcestershire sauce

4 ⅜ ounces (1 cup) general-purpose wheat flour

8 ⅓ ounces (1 cup) water

■ Directions

1. Sauté onions, peppers, and celery in shortening, salad oil, or olive oil for ten minutes or until tender.

2. Add tomatoes, salt, black pepper, red pepper, oregano, basil, thyme, garlic powder, paprika, sugar, and Worcestershire sauce to vegetables. Bring to a boil, and reduce heat; cover, and simmer for ten minutes.

3. Blend flour and water to make a smooth paste, and add to sauce. Stir to combine. Simmer for five minutes or until thickened, stirring constantly.

4. Internal temperature must reach 145 degrees or higher for 15 seconds.

5. Hold at 140 degrees or higher for service.

■ Freezing Instructions

Allow sauce to cool completely prior to freezing. Place in an airtight container. Freeze. Reheat over a medium high heat on the stovetop or in a microwave oven for three to five minutes, stirring occasionally. You may also allow to thaw for six to eight hours in the refrigerator before using in your favorite recipe.

Salsa

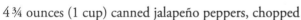

Serving size: 2 tablespoons

■ Ingredients

7 ⅛ pounds (3 quarts 1 cup) diced canned tomatoes, drained

8 /12 ounces (1 ½ cups) fresh onions, chopped

4 ¾ ounces (1 cup) canned jalapeño peppers, chopped

1 ½ ounces (2 ⅓ tablespoon) salt

⅞ ounce (2 tablespoons) granulated sugar

■ Directions

1. Combine coarsely chopped canned tomatoes or finely chopped fresh tomatoes with onions, peppers, salt, and sugar. Blend well.

2. Cover and refrigerate at 41 degrees or lower at least one hour before serving.

■ Freezing Instructions

Allow food to cool completely prior to freezing. Place in an airtight container. Freeze. Reheat over a medium high heat on the stovetop or in a microwave oven for three to five minutes, stirring occasionally. You may also allow to thaw for six to eight hours in the refrigerator before using in your favorite recipe.

■ Notes

To make a green salsa, cut the amount of tomatoes in half and replace them with fresh tomatillos.

CHAPTER

Side Dishes

TEN

Boston Baked Beans

Serving size: ½ cup

■ Ingredients

8 ⅞ pounds (1 gallon 1 ½ quarts) dry kidney beans

46 pounds (5 gallons 2 quarts) cold water

1 pound raw bacon

1 ½ ounces (2 ⅓ tablespoons) salt

2 ½ ounces (¼ cup 2 ⅔ tablespoons) dry mustard

10 ⅞ ounces (2 ⅛ cups) packed brown sugar

2 ⅛ ounces (¼ cup ⅓ tablespoon) distilled vinegar

1 ½ pounds (2 cups) molasses

2 ounces (¼ cup ⅓ tablespoon) nonstick cooking spray

■ Directions

1. Pick over beans, removing discolored beans and foreign matter. Wash beans thoroughly. Cover, and let soak for one hour.

2. Cover with water. Bring beans to a boil, and add more water if necessary to keep beans covered. Turn down heat, simmer 1 ½ hours or until tender but not mushy. Drain beans. Reserve liquid and beans for use in Step 4.

3. Cook bacon by arranging slices in rows down the length of 18 by 26 sheet pan, with fat edges slightly overlapping lean edges. Using a convection oven, bake 25 minutes at 325 degrees on high fan, open vent. If you are using a standard oven, bake at 350 degrees. Drain excess fat. Bake an additional five to ten minutes or until bacon is slightly crisp. Do not overcook. Drain thoroughly, and chop finely.

4. Take reserved bean liquid, and add water to equal 1 gallon and combine with salt, mustard, brown sugar, vinegar, molasses, and chopped bacon. Add to beans, and mix well.

5. Lightly spray pans with nonstick cooking spray. Pour 20 pounds or 7 ½ quarts bean mixture into each lightly sprayed pan and cover. Using a convection oven, bake at 325 degrees for one hour to one hour 15 minutes, or until sauce is just below surface of beans, on high fan, closed vent. If you are using a standard oven, bake at 350 degrees. Uncover, stir, and bake additional 15 minutes or until set, on low fan.

6. Heat to 145 degrees or higher for 15 seconds.

7. Hold at 140 degrees or higher for service.

■ Freezing Instructions

Allow food to cool completely prior to freezing. Place in an airtight container. Freeze. Reheat over a medium high heat on the stovetop or in a microwave oven for three to five minutes, stirring occasionally.

Spanish Style Beans

Serving size: ½ cup

■ Ingredients

8 ½ pounds (1 gallon 1 quart) dry pinto beans

41 ¾ pounds (5 gallons) cold water

3 ¾ ounces (¼ cup 2 ⅓ tablespoons) salt

1 pound (3 cups) fresh onions, chopped

6 ⅝ pounds (3 quarts) canned crushed tomatoes, including liquids

1 pound (2 ¼ cups) granulated sugar

Less than ¹⁄₁₆ ounce (⅛ teaspoon) ground cloves

⅛ ounce (⅛ teaspoon) ground black pepper

¾ ounce (2 tablespoons) dry mustard

■ Directions

1. Pick over beans, removing discolored beans and foreign matter. Wash beans thoroughly.

2. Cover with water, and let the beans soak for one hour.

3. Add salt. Bring to a boil in steam-jacketed kettle, and boil for two minutes.

4. Add onions, tomatoes, sugar, mustard, cloves, and pepper. Reduce heat, and add more water to cover beans. Simmer for one hour or until beans are just tender.

5. Heat to 145 degrees or higher for 15 seconds.

6. Hold at 140 degrees or higher for service.

■ Freezing Instructions

Allow food to cool completely prior to freezing. Place in an airtight container. Freeze. Reheat over a medium high heat on the stovetop or in a microwave oven for three to five minutes, stirring occasionally.

Creole Green Beans

Serving size: ½ cup

■ Ingredients

16 pounds (3 gallons 2 ⅝ quarts) whole green beans, frozen

⅝ ounce (1 tablespoon) salt

12 ½ pounds (1 gallon 2 quarts) water

1 gallon 2 quarts Creole sauce

■ Directions

1. Add beans to salted water.
2. Bring to a boil, cover, and simmer five to eight minutes or until beans are tender. Drain and reserve 1 quart liquid.
3. Heat to 145 degrees or higher for 15 seconds.
4. Hold for service at 140 degrees or higher.
5. Add Creole sauce (*see recipe in Chapter 9*) to drained beans.

■ Freezing Instructions

Allow food to cool completely prior to freezing. Place in an airtight container. Freeze. Reheat over a medium high heat on the stovetop or in a microwave oven for three to five minutes, stirring occasionally.

Southern Style Green Beans

Serving size: ½ cup

■ Ingredients

1 pound bacon, raw

3 ⅝ ounces (½ cup) bacon fat, rendered

16 pounds (3 gallons 2 ⅝ quarts) whole green beans

12 ½ pounds (1 gallon 2 quarts) boiling water

Less than ¹⁄₁₆ ounce (⅛ teaspoon) ground black pepper

■ Directions

1. Cook bacon until crisp. Drain, crumble bacon, and reserve bacon fat.

2. Add bacon fat to beans and water. Bring to a boil, cover, and simmer five to eight minutes or until beans are tender. Drain and reserve 1 quart liquid.

3. Add reserved bean liquid, crumbled bacon, and black pepper to beans.

4. Mix lightly.

5. Heat to 145 degrees or higher for 15 seconds.

■ Freezing Instructions

Allow food to cool completely prior to freezing. Place in an airtight container. Freeze. Reheat over a medium-high heat on the stovetop or in a microwave oven for three to five minutes, stirring occasionally.

Refried Beans

Serving size: ½ cup

■ Ingredients

8 ¼ pounds (12 cups) dried pinto beans, rinsed

1 cup 1 tablespoon minced garlic

6⅝ pounds (3 quarts) fresh tomato, diced

3½ ounces (1 cup 1 tablespoon) ground cumin

1 ounce (½ cup 1 teaspoon) chili powder

½ pound (1 cup 1 tablespoon) olive oil

Salt, to taste

■ Directions

1. Place the beans in a large pot, and cover with water.

2. Place pot on a high heat, and bring to a boil.

3. When the beans have come to a boil, drain, and return them to the same pot.

4. Cover the beans with water, and stir in half the garlic, tomatoes, cumin, and chili powder.

5. Bring to a boil over high heat, reduce heat to low, and simmer until the beans are very soft (which should take about four hours), adding water as needed.

6. Once the beans have cooked, mash them with the remaining garlic, the oil, and salt to taste. Use additional water as needed to achieve desired consistency.

7. Place over low heat for 30 minutes, stirring occasionally.

■ Freezing Instructions

Allow food to cool completely prior to freezing. Place in an airtight container. Freeze. Reheat over a medium-high heat on the stovetop or in a microwave oven for three to five minutes, stirring occasionally.

Hot Spiced Beets

Serving size: ¾ cup

■ Ingredients

39 pounds (4 gallons 2 quarts) canned
  beets, sliced, including liquid

6 ¼ pounds (3 quarts) distilled vinegar

⅓ ounce (1 tablespoon) ground cinnamon

⅔ ounce (3 tablespoons) ground cloves

⅝ ounce (1 tablespoon) salt

¼ ounce (1 tablespoon) ground black pepper

1 ⅓ pounds (3 cups) granulated sugar

2 pounds (1 quart 2 ⅜ cups) packed brown sugar

8 ounces (1 cup) margarine

■ Directions

1. Drain beets. Reserve liquid for use in Step 2 and beets for use in Step 4.

2. Take 4 ½ quarts (18 cups) reserved beet liquid, and add 57 cups water (to equal 75 cups liquid), and add to vinegar, cinnamon, cloves, salt, pepper, and sugars. Mix well.

3. Bring to a boil, reduce heat, and simmer for ten minutes.

4. Add beets and margarine or butter.

5. Heat to 145 degrees or higher for 15 seconds.

6. Hold at 140 degrees or higher for service.

■ Freezing Instructions

Allow food to cool completely prior to freezing. Place in an airtight container. Freeze. Reheat over a medium-high heat on the stovetop or in a microwave oven for three to five minutes, stirring occasionally.

Broccoli

Serving size: 3 stalks

■ Ingredients

37 ⅝ pounds (4 gallons 2 quarts) water

⅝ ounce (1 tablespoon) salt

30 pounds fresh broccoli, fresh

■ Method

1. Bring water to a boil in steam-jacketed kettle or stockpot.
2. Add salt.
3. Add broccoli, and bring water back to a boil. Cover, and cook for ten to 15 minutes.
4. Place broccoli in serving pans.
5. Heat to 145 degrees or higher for 15 seconds for service.
6. Hold for service at 140 degrees or higher.

■ Freezing Instructions

See notes in Chapter 2 on freezing about blanching and freezing vegetables.

Herbed Broccoli

Serving size: ⅓ cup

■ Ingredients

10 ½ pounds (1 gallon 1 quart) water

20 pounds (3 gallons 2 ½ quarts) fresh broccoli, cut

7 ounces (1 ¼ cup) fresh onions, chopped

¼ ounce (¼ cup ⅓ tablespoon) ground sweet marjoram

½ ounce (3 tablespoons) dried basil, crushed

■ Direction

1. Bring water to a boil.
2. Add broccoli, onions, marjoram, and basil to boiling water.
3. Return to boil, and cover.
4. Reduce heat, and cook for ten minutes or until tender.
5. Drain, reserving 1 quart of liquid to pour over vegetables.
6. Hold at 140 degrees or higher for service.

■ Freezing Instructions

See notes in Chapter 2 on freezing about blanching and freezing vegetables.

Glazed Carrots

Serving size: ½ cup

■ Ingredients

18 pounds fresh carrots, sliced

18 ¾ pounds (2 gallons 1 quart) boiling water

⅝ ounce (1 tablespoon) salt

8 ounces (1 cup) butter

⅝ ounce (3 tablespoons) ground ginger

1 ¼ pounds (2 ¾ cups) granulated sugar

⅜ ounce (⅓ teaspoon) salt

■ Directions

1. Cook carrots ten to 13 minutes.
2. Drain, and reserve carrots for use in Step 5.
3. Melt butter in a steam-jacketed kettle or tilting frying pan. Add ginger, and stir until well blended.
4. Add sugar, and stir. The mixture will resemble a thick roux.

5. Toss carrots in sauce until well coated. Cook for five minutes, tossing occasionally.

6. Heat to 145 degrees or higher for 15 seconds.

■ Freezing Instructions

Allow food to cool completely prior to freezing. Place in an airtight container. Freeze. Reheat over a medium high heat on the stovetop or in a microwave oven for three to five minutes, stirring occasionally.

Orange Carrots Amandine

Serving size: ½ cup

■ Ingredients

16 pounds (3 gallons 2⅛ quarts) fresh carrots, sliced

⅜ ounce (⅓ teaspoon) salt

16¾ pounds (2 gallons) boiling water

10 ounces (1¼ cup) melted margarine

5⅛ ounces (1 cup) packed brown sugar

10⅛ ounces (3 cups) fresh orange peel, grated

2⅞ ounce (¼ cup 1⅔ tablespoon) orange juice

11⅜ ounces (3 cups) slivered almonds

■ Directions

1. Cook carrots ten to 13 minutes. Add carrots to salted boiling water. Return to a boil, reduce heat, and simmer 15 minutes or until tender. Drain.

2. Add brown sugar, orange rind, orange juice, and almonds to melted butter or margarine. Blend well.

3. Add glaze to carrots. Mix until carrots are well coated.

4. Heat to 145 degrees or higher for 15 seconds.

■ Freezing Instructions

Allow food to cool completely prior to freezing. Place in an airtight container. Freeze. Reheat over a medium high heat on the stovetop or in a microwave oven for three to five minutes, stirring occasionally.

Calico Corn

Serving size: ¾ cup

■ Ingredients

1 pound raw bacon

28 ⅞ pounds (5 gallons) canned whole kernel corn, drained

⅛ ounce (⅜ teaspoon) ground black pepper

7 ⅝ ounces (1 ⅛ cups) chopped canned pimiento, drained

■ Directions

1. Cook bacon until crisp, and drain. Set bacon aside for use in Step 2.
2. Drain corn, and mix with pepper and pimientos. Crumble bacon. Add to corn mixture. Mix well.
3. Heat at medium heat until hot, stirring constantly.
4. Heat to 145 degrees or higher for 15 seconds.

■ Freezing Instructions

Allow food to cool completely prior to freezing. Place in an airtight container. Freeze. Reheat over a medium high heat on the stovetop or in a microwave oven for three to five minutes, stirring occasionally.

Corn on the Cob

Serving size: 1 ear

■ Ingredients

50 ⅛ pounds (6 gallons) water

⅝ ounce (1 tablespoon) salt

55 pounds fresh corn on the cob

■ Directions

1. Bring water to a boil in steam-jacketed kettle or stockpot.
2. Add salt.
3. Add corn, and bring water back to a boil. Cover corn, and allow it to cook five to ten minutes.
4. Heat to 145 degrees or higher for 15 seconds.
5. Place corn in serving pans.

■ Freezing Instructions

Corn on the cob should be blanched before freezing.

Blanching times for corn on the cob:

▸ Small ears (1 ¼ inches or less in diameter) seven minutes

▸ Medium ears (1 ¼ to 1 ½ inches in diameter) nine minutes

▸ Large ears (more than 1 ½ inches in diameter) 11 minutes

After blanching, put the cobs directly into an ice water bath to stop the cooking process. The corn should be kept in the ice water for the same amount of time that it blanched.

Drain the corn, and place in freezer bags. Remove as much air from the freezer bags as possible. Freeze. To reheat the corn directly from the freezer, you may microwave it for three to four minutes or reheat in a pot of boiling water for five to six minutes.

Collard Greens

Serving size: ¾ cup

■ Ingredients

25 ⅛ pounds (3 gallons) water

⅝ ounce (1 tablespoon) salt

30 pounds fresh collard greens

■ Directions

1. Bring water to a boil in steam-jacketed kettle or stockpot.
2. Add salt.
3. Add greens, and bring water back to a boil. Cover, and cook greens 20 to 30 minutes.
4. Heat greens to 145 degrees or higher for 15 seconds.
5. Place greens in serving pans. Garnish if desired.

■ Freezing Instructions

Read instructions in Chapter 2 regarding blanching vegetables. Collard greens should be blanched for two minutes prior to freezing. After blanching, place greens in a single layer on a cookie sheet, and freeze. Once the greens are frozen, place them in a freezer bag, and return to freezer. Reheat in microwave for two minutes or in a steamer until hot.

Southern Style Greens

Serving size: ¾ cup

■ Ingredients

10 pounds frozen pork hocks, cured and smoked

33 ½ pounds (4 gallons) boiling water

171

1 ⅝ pounds (1 quart ½ cup) fresh onions, chopped

¼ ounce (1 tablespoon) black ground pepper

33 ½ pounds (4 gallons) water

20 pounds (2 gallons 3 ⅞ quarts) fresh collard greens

■ Directions

1. Add water to steam-jacketed kettle or stockpot. Add pork hocks and onions to water. Cover, and simmer 2½ hours or until tender. Remove hocks and onions, and trim meat and fat from bones. Cut meat into small pieces. Add meat and bones to stock.

2. Add greens, pepper, and water to stock. Bring to a boil, and stir immediately.

3. Simmer for one hour uncovered, or until greens are tender, stirring occasionally.

4. Heat to 145 degrees or higher for 15 seconds. Remove bones, and serve greens with cooking liquid.

■ Notes

In Step 1, 2 pounds raw bacon may be used for pork hocks per 100 portions.

■ Freezing Instructions

Read instructions in Chapter 2 regarding blanching vegetables. Greens should be blanched for two minutes prior to freezing. After blanching, place greens in a single layer on a cookie sheet and freeze. Once the greens are frozen, place them in a freezer bag, and return to freezer. Reheat in microwave for two minutes or in a steamer until hot.

This recipe can be made with collard greens frozen as described in the previous recipe.

Okra and Tomato Gumbo

Serving size: ½ cup

■ Ingredients

2 ⅛ pounds (1 quart 2 cups) fresh onions, chopped

1 pound raw bacon

10 pounds cut okra, frozen or fresh

4 ⅜ ounces (1 cup) general-purpose wheat flour

1 ¾ ounce (¼ cup ⅓ tablespoon) granulated sugar

1 ⅞ ounce (3 tablespoons) salt

1 ounce (¼ cup ⅓ tablespoon) dark ground chili powder

⅛ ounce (⅛ teaspoon) ground black pepper

13 ¼ pounds (1 gallon 2 quarts) canned crushed tomatoes, including liquids

3 ⅛ pounds (1 quart 2 cups) boiling water

2 pounds (1 gallon 2 ½ quarts) stale white bread, sliced

12 ounces (1 ½ cups) melted butter

⅛ ounce (¼ teaspoon) fresh garlic cloves, minced

■ Directions

1. Sauté onions and bacon until onions are tender and bacon is crisp.
2. Add okra to onions and bacon. Cook for five minutes, stirring frequently.
3. Add flour, sugar, salt, chili powder, and pepper. Stir until blended.
4. Add tomatoes and water; mix well.
5. Bring to a boil. Reduce heat, and simmer for 15 minutes or until okra is tender.
6. Heat to 145 degrees or higher for 15 seconds.
7. Prepare garlic croutons.

   Trim crusts from bread; cut bread into ½-inch cubes. Place bread cubes on sheet pans. Brown lightly in 325 degree oven, about 20 to 25 minutes, or in 375 degrees convection oven for about six minutes on high fan, open vent. Melt butter or margarine, and blend in minced garlic. Pour mixture evenly over lightly browned croutons in steam table pans and toss lightly.

Notes

In Step 1, 2 pounds bread will yield about 1 gallon lightly browned croutons.

Freezing Instructions

Freeze in airtight container after dish cools following Step 6 above. Reheat in microwave or on stovetop directly from freezer before proceeding to Step 8.

Sweet Potatoes

Serving size: 3 pieces

Ingredients

34 ½ pounds fresh sweet potatoes

37 ⅝ pounds (4 gallons 2 quarts) water

⅝ ounce (1 tablespoon) salt

Directions

1. Cut sweet potatoes into 1-inch pieces.
2. Add salt to water. Bring water to a boil in steam-jacketed kettle or stockpot.
3. Add sweet potatoes, and bring water back to a boil. Cover, and cook 25 to 35 minutes.
4. Heat to 145 degrees or higher for 15 seconds.
5. Place sweet potatoes in serving pans and garnish as desired.

Freezing Instructions

Allow cooked sweet potatoes to cool. Place sweet potatoes in freezer bags. Freeze. Though you may microwave sweet potatoes to reheat, the preferred method of reheating frozen sweet potatoes is to steam them until they are hot.

Mashed Sweet Potatoes

Serving size: ½ cup

▪ Ingredients

3 ⅝ ounces (1 ½ cups) nonfat dry milk

4 ½ pounds (2 quarts ½ cup) warm water

31 ⅛ pounds (3 gallons 3 ½ quarts) cooked sweet potatoes

1 ¼ ounce (2 tablespoons) salt

8 ounces (1 cup) melted butter

7 ounces (1 cup) granulated sugar

2 ounces (¼ cup ⅓ tablespoon) nonstick cooking spray

▪ Directions

1. Reconstitute milk in mixer bowl.

2. Add sweet potatoes, and beat at low speed for two minutes or until smooth.

3. Add salt, melted butter or margarine, and sugar, and blend at medium speed.

4. Scrape the sides of the bowl, and beat at medium speed for two minutes.

5. Lightly spray each steam table pan with nonstick cooking spray. Place 7 ½ quarts potatoes in each sprayed pan, and cover the pan.

6. Using a convection oven, bake at 325 degrees for 30 minutes on high fan, closed vent or until heated thoroughly. Using a standard oven, bake at 350 degrees.

7. Internal temperature must reach 145 degrees or higher for 15 seconds.

▪ Freezing Instructions

Place individual portions in freezer bags to freeze. Reheat on stovetop over medium high heat. You can use a microwave to reheat by placing desired portion in a microwave safe dish and covering with a paper towel. Microwave for two to three minutes.

Potatoes

Serving size: 3 pieces

■ Ingredients

37 ⅝ pounds (4 gallons 2 quarts) water

⅝ ounce (1 tablespoon) salt

35 pounds fresh white potatoes, quartered
  or cubed

■ Directions

1. Bring water to a boil in steam-jacketed kettle or stockpot.

2. Add salt.

3. Add potatoes, and bring water back to a boil. Cover, and cook potatoes
   20 to 25 minutes.

4. Heat to 145 degrees or higher for 15 seconds.

5. Place potatoes in serving pans, and garnish as desired.

■ Freezing Instructions

Allow cooked potatoes to cool. Place potatoes in freezer bags. Freeze. Though
you may microwave potatoes to reheat, the preferred method of reheating frozen
potatoes is to steam them until they are hot.

Mashed Potatoes

Serving size: ½ cup

■ Ingredient

22 pounds fresh potatoes, peeled and cubed

12 ½ pounds (1 gallon 2 quarts) water

1 ¼ ounce (2 tablespoons) salt

8 ounces (1 cup) softened margarine

⅛ ounce (¼ teaspoon) white ground pepper

2 ⅔ ounces (1 ⅛ cup) nonfat dry milk

3 pounds (1 quart ¾ cup) warm water

■ Directions

1. Cover potatoes with salted water, and bring to a boil. Reduce heat, and simmer 25 minutes or until tender. Drain well.

2. Beat potatoes in mixer bowl at low speed until broken into smaller pieces, which should take about one minute.

3. Add butter or margarine and pepper. Beat at high speed three to five minutes or until smooth.

4. Reconstitute milk with 1 quart ¾ cup water, heat to a simmer, and blend into potatoes at low speed. Beat at high speed for two minutes or until light and fluffy.

5. Internal temperature must reach 145 degrees or higher for 15 seconds.

■ Freezing Instructions

Place individual portions in freezer bags to freeze. Reheat on stovetop over medium high heat. You can use a microwave to reheat by placing desired portion in a microwave safe dish and covering with a paper towel. Microwave for two to three minutes.

Latkes (Potato Pancakes)

Serving size: 2 latkes

■ Ingredients

22 pounds (about 66) potatoes

5 pounds (15 cups) yellow onions

2 pounds (16) fresh eggs, beaten

2 ounces (⅓ cup 1 teaspoon) salt

½ pound (2 cups 1 tablespoon) general-purpose wheat flour

Ground black pepper, to taste

Vegetable oil, for frying

■ Directions

1. Finely grate potatoes with onion into a large bowl.
2. Drain off excess liquid.
3. Mix beaten egg, salt, and black pepper into the potato/onion mixture.
4. Add flour, ¼ cup at a time, until mixture is thick.
5. Preheat oven to 200 degrees (same for convection and conventional).
6. Heat ¼ inch oil in the bottom of a heavy skillet over medium high heat.
7. Drop ¼ cup mounds of potato mixture into hot oil, and flatten to make ½-inch thick pancakes.
8. Fry pancakes, turning once, until golden brown.
9. Transfer to paper towel lined plates to drain, and keep warm in low oven until serving.
10. Repeat until all potato mixture is used.

■ Freezing Instructions

Wrap individual portions in wax paper. Place wrapped portions in freezer bags. Freeze. Reheat in lightly greased frying pan over a medium heat.

Perogies

Serving size: 3 perogies

■ Ingredients

6 ½ pounds (22 ½ cups) general-purpose wheat flour

1 ½ ounces (3 tablespoons and 1 teaspoon) salt

¼ pound (½ cup and 2 tablespoons) butter, melted

2 ½ pounds (10 cups) sour cream

1 ½ pounds (10) fresh eggs, whole

5 egg yolks

¼ pound (½ cup 2 tablespoons) vegetable oil

15 pounds (40) baking potatoes, peeled and cubed

1 ½ pounds (5 cups) shredded cheddar cheese

Seasoned salt to taste (optional)

Ground black pepper, to taste

■ Directions

1. Sift together the flour and salt into a large bowl.
2. In a separate bowl, whisk together the butter, sour cream, eggs, egg yolk, and oil.
3. Stir the wet ingredients into the flour until well blended.
4. Cover the bowl with a towel, and let stand for 15 to 20 minutes.
5. Place potatoes into a pot, and cover with water.
6. Bring potatoes to a boil, and cook until tender, about 15 minutes.
7. Drain potatoes, and mash with shredded cheese while still hot.
8. Add seasoned salt and pepper to taste.
9. Set aside to cool.
10. Separate the perogie dough into balls about the size of a grapefruit.
11. Roll out one piece at a time on a lightly floured surface until it is thin enough to work with, but not so thin that it tears.
12. Cut into circles using a cookie cutter, perogie cutter, or a glass.

13. Brush a little water around the edges of the circles, and spoon some filling into the center.

14. Fold the circles over into half circles, and press to seal the edges.

15. Place perogies on a cookie sheet, and freeze. Once frozen, transfer to freezer storage bags or containers.

16. To cook perogies: Bring a large pot of lightly salted water to a boil. Drop perogies in one at a time. They are done when they float to the top. Do not boil too long, or they will be soggy. Remove with a slotted spoon.

■ Freezing Instructions

Place individual portions in freezer bags. Freeze. Reheat in microwave, steamer, or lightly greased frying pan until interior temperature reaches 165 degrees. Test temperature with an instant read thermometer.

CHAPTER

Dinner Main Dishes

ELEVEN

Pot Pies

Note: The following two recipes describe two different styles of pot pies. You may prepare the beef pot pie in the style described in the chicken pot pie recipe and vice versa.

Beef Pot Pie

Serving size: 1 cup

■ Ingredients

30 pounds lean raw beef, diced

3 ½ pounds (2 quarts 2 cups) fresh onions, chopped

25 ⅛ pounds (3 gallons) water

12 ⅓ pounds (1 gallon 1 ¾ quarts) canned tomato juice

1 ⅞ ounces (3 tablespoons) salt

½ ounce (2 tablespoons) ground black pepper

6 pounds (1 gallon 1 ⅓ quarts) fresh sliced carrots

9 pounds (1 gallon 2 ⅝ quarts) fresh potatoes, chopped

11 ounces (2 quarts 2 cups) general-purpose wheat flour

2 ⅛ pounds (1 quart) water

100 baking powder biscuits (*see Chapter 5 for recipe*)

■ Directions

1. Cook beef and onions in a steam-jacketed kettle about five minutes.

2. Add water, tomato juice, salt, and pepper to meat. Bring to a boil, reduce heat, cover, and simmer one hour 15 minutes.

3. Add carrots. Cover and simmer for ten minutes.

4. Add potatoes. Cover and simmer 20 minutes or until vegetables are tender.

5. Combine flour and water, add to meat and vegetable mixture while stirring, and simmer for five minutes or until thickened, stirring constantly.

6. Place 7 quarts mixture in each steam table pan.

7. Prepare baking powder biscuits (*see Chapter 5 for recipe*)

8. Place 25 biscuits on top of hot mixture in each pan.

9. Using a convection oven, bake at 400 degrees (425 degrees in a conventional oven) for ten to 15 minutes or until biscuits are lightly browned.

■ Freezing Instructions

The two basic components of this recipe should be frozen separately. Freeze the beef filling in airtight containers. Freeze the biscuits as per the freezing instructions for biscuits in Chapter 5. To reheat, allow biscuits to thaw overnight at room temperature. Thaw filling in microwave for two to three minutes. After components are thawed, proceed with recipe from Step 9 allowing for size of servings.

Chicken Pot Pie

Serving size: 1 cup

■ Ingredients

⅛ ounce (⅛ teaspoon) nonstick cooking spray

2 pounds (1 quart 1 ⅝ cups) fresh onions, chopped

¼ ounce (1 tablespoon) ground black pepper

⅛ ounce (1 tablespoon) ground thyme

⅓ ounce (9 leaves) whole bay leaf, dried

2 gallons chicken broth

8 pounds (1 gallon 1 ⅞ quarts) fresh potatoes, peeled and cubed

8 pounds (1 gallon 3 ⅛ quarts) fresh carrots, chopped

2 pounds (1 quart 3 ½ cups) fresh celery, chopped

4 ⅛ pounds (2 quarts) cold water

2 ⅓ pounds (2 quarts ½ cup) general-purpose wheat flour

18 pounds cooked chicken, diced

5 ¾ pounds (1 gallon ½ quart) green peas, frozen

3 ⅓ pounds (3 quarts) general-purpose wheat flour (this is in addition to the flour previously listed)

2 ⅓ ounces (¼ cup 1 ⅔ tablespoon) granulated sugar

2 ⅜ ounces (¼ cup 1 ⅓ tablespoon) baking powder

⅝ ounces (1 tablespoon) salt

4 ⅞ pounds (2 quarts 1 ⅜ cups) warm water

4 ¾ ounces (2 cups) nonfat dry milk

2 ⅛ pounds (1 quart) egg whites

4 ounces (½ cup) melted margarine

■ Directions

1. Lightly spray steam-jacketed kettle or stockpot with nonstick spray. Add onions, pepper, thyme, and bay leaves. Stir, and cook five minutes until onions are tender.

2. Add broth, potatoes, carrots, and celery. Bring to a boil. Cover, reduce heat, simmer 15 minutes or until potatoes are almost tender. Remove bay leaves.

3. Blend flour and cold water together, and stir to make a thick sauce. Add thick sauce to vegetable mixture stirring constantly. Bring to boil. Cover, reduce heat, and simmer eight to ten minutes or until thickened, stirring frequently to prevent sticking.

4. Fold in chicken and peas, and bring to a boil. Cover, reduce heat, and simmer five to ten minutes.

5. Pour 1 ⅓ gallons of mixture into each ungreased pan.

6. For batter topping, sift together flour, sugar, baking powder, and salt into mixer bowl.

7. Reconstitute milk in warm water. Combine milk, egg whites, and margarine or butter. Add to dry ingredients and mix at low speed until dry ingredients are moistened, which should take about 30 seconds. Do not overmix.

8. Pour 3 ¼ cups of batter evenly over top of chicken mixture in each pan.

9. Using a convection oven, bake 20 to 25 minutes at 400 degrees or until lightly browned on low fan, open vent. If using a standard oven, bake at 425 degrees.

10. Internal temperature must reach 165 degrees or higher for 15 seconds.

11. Cut three rows of six pieces each.

■ Notes

In Step 3, 8 pounds 8 ounces drained, sliced carrots or 8 pounds frozen carrots may be used per 100 portions. Add carrots to sauce in Step 5.

In Step 9, batter will be very thin. Do not add additional flour. If prepared in advance, refrigerate at 41 degrees or lower until ready to use.

Freezing Instructions

Freeze individual portions in airtight containers. To reheat, bake for 20 to 30 minutes, covered, in a 350 degree oven. You may also microwave, covered, for five minutes.

Braised Beef and Noodles

Serving size: 1 ¼ cups

Ingredients

30 pounds lean raw beef, diced

14 ⅝ pounds (1 gallon 3 quarts) water

4 pounds (1 gallon) fresh onions, sliced

2 ⅛ pounds (1 quart) ketchup

⅔ ounce (3 tablespoons) ground black pepper

½ ounce (3 tablespoons) ground thyme

⅜ ounce (1 tablespoon) garlic powder

¼ ounce (6 leaves) whole bay leaf, dried

3 ⅜ ounces (¼ cup 1 ⅔ tablespoon) salt

3 ½ pounds (2 gallons 2 ½ quarts) egg noodles

58 ½ pounds (7 gallons) boiling water

1 ½ ounces (2 ⅓ tablespoons) salt

1 ½ pounds (1 quart 1 ½ cups) general-purpose wheat flour

3 ⅛ pounds (1 quart 2 cups) cold water

Directions

1. Place beef, water, onions, ketchup, pepper, thyme, garlic powder, bay leaves, and salt in steam-jacketed kettle or stockpot. Bring to a boil, reduce heat, cover, and simmer about two hours or until tender. Skim off excess fat, and remove bay leaves.

2. Add noodles to boiling salted water, return to a boil, and cook eight to ten minutes or until tender. Drain thoroughly.

3. Combine flour and water to make smooth mixture, and stir into beef mixture. Blend well, and return to boil. Reduce heat, and cook ten minutes or until thickened.

4. Internal temperature must reach 145 degrees or higher for 15 seconds.

5. Add cooked noodles to beef mixture, and stir well.

■ Freezing Instructions

Freeze in airtight containers. You may freeze with the noodles, though it is suggested that the noodles be prepared separately just prior to serving. Reheat beef in microwave or on stovetop.

Mexican Pepper Steak

Serving size: ¾ cup

■ Ingredients

7 ⅔ ounces (1 cup) salad oil

⅞ ounce (¼ cup ⅓ tablespoon) ground cumin

25 pounds beef strips

8 pounds (1 gallon 2 ⅛ quarts) fresh green peppers, julienned

8 pounds fresh onions, diced

8 ⅝ pounds (1 gallon) salsa sauce

■ Directions

1. Combine oil and cumin. Mix well. Add fajita strips, and mix so that all strips are coated.

2. Cook fajita strips on a 400 degree griddle on medium high for five minutes, turning frequently.

3. Bring the internal temperature to reach 145 degrees for 15 seconds.

4. Divide fajita strips evenly between two steam table pans. Do not scrape griddle.

5. Add peppers and diced onions to griddle, and cook about five minutes or until onions are tender. Divide peppers and onions equally between the pans of beef. Mix well.

6. Heat salsa. Add 2 quarts heated salsa to each pan. Mix well.

■ Freezing Instructions

Freeze the cooked beef and vegetables in airtight containers. Reheat on a lightly oiled medium heat griddle or frying pan.

The salsa should be frozen or canned separately. *See instructions for doing this in Chapter 2.* Reheat salsa in covered microwavable dish or on stovetop.

Meatloaf

Serving size: 6 oz.

■ Ingredients

30 pounds raw ground beef

3¾ pounds (1 gallon) breadcrumbs

3¾ ounces (¼ cup 2⅓ tablespoon) salt

¼ ounce (1 tablespoon) ground black pepper

⅓ ounce (1 tablespoon) garlic powder

2⅜ ounces (1 cup) nonfat dry milk

2⅞ pounds (1 quart 1½ cups) water

1 pound (3¾ cups) fresh celery, chopped

1 pound (2⅞ cups) fresh chopped onions

1 pound (3 cups) fresh green peppers, chopped

2⅜ pounds (1 quart ½ cup) whole fresh eggs

3⅛ pounds (1 quart 1¾ cups) canned tomato juice

■ Directions

1. Combine beef with breadcrumbs, salt, pepper, and garlic. Mix until well blended.

2. Reconstitute milk.

3. Add milk, celery, onions, sweet peppers, eggs, and tomato juice. Mix lightly but thoroughly. Do not overmix.

4. Place 11 pounds 6 ounces meat mixture into each steam table pan and divide into two loaves per pan.

5. Using a convection oven, bake one hour 15 minutes at 300 degrees. Bake at 325 degrees in a conventional oven.

6. Internal temperature must reach 155 degrees or higher for 15 seconds.

7. Skim off excess fat and liquid during cooking.

8. Let stand 20 minutes before slicing. Cut 13 slices per loaf.

■ Freezing Instructions

Meatloaf can be frozen after Step 4, before cooking. To bake a frozen loaf, proceed from Step 5 but bake oen and a half to two times longer. Check for doneness with a meat thermometer. The temperature should reach 155 degrees.

Whole meat loaves can also be frozen after Step 7. Allow to cool to room temperature, wrap in foil, place in a freezer bag, and store in the freezer up to six months. Allow meatloaf to thaw overnight in refrigerator. Reheat to 155 degrees in an oven preheated to 350 degrees (about one and a half hours).

Enchiladas

Serving size: 2 enchiladas

■ Ingredients

1 ¼ pounds (1 quart ½ cup) general-purpose wheat flour

1 pound (2 ¼ cups) shortening

2 ¼ pounds (3 ⅞ cups) canned tomato paste

4 ½ ounces (1 cup) ground dark chili powder

1 ounce (¼ cup ⅔ tablespoon) ground cumin

2 quarts 1 ¼ cup beef broth

Less than ⅟₁₆ ounce (⅛ teaspoon) ground black pepper

18 pounds raw ground beef

2 ½ pounds (1 quart 3 ⅛ cups) fresh onions, chopped

4 ¼ ounces (1 cup) dark ground chili powder

1 ⅞ ounces (3 tablespoons) salt

½ ounce (2 ⅔ tablespoons) ground red pepper

⅓ ounce (1 tablespoon) garlic powder

11 ½ pounds (200 count) 6-inch corn tortillas

4 pounds (1 gallon) cheddar cheese, shredded

1 ⅞ pounds (1 quart 1 ⅜ cups) fresh onion, chopped

■ Directions

1. Blend together melted shortening or salad oil and sifted general-purpose flour until smooth to make a roux. Cook at low heat two minutes. Add canned tomato paste, chili powder, and ground cumin, and blend well.

2. Prepare beef broth following package directions. Add stock to roux, stirring constantly. Bring to a boil, reduce heat, and simmer for ten minutes or until thickened, stirring constantly. Add pepper, and stir to blend.

3. Cook beef until beef loses its pink color, stirring to break apart. Drain or skim off excess fat.

4. Add 2 quarts gravy, onions, chili powder, salt, red pepper, and garlic powder to beef. Blend well.

5. Hold at 140 degrees or higher for use in Step 8.

6. Spread 2 cups gravy in each pan.

7. Wrap tortillas in foil, and place in 150 degree oven or in a warmer for 15 minutes or until warm and pliable.

8. Place 3 tablespoons meat filling in center of each tortilla. Roll tightly around filling, and place seam side down in pan, 50 per pan.

9. Pour 1 ¼ quarts gravy evenly over enchiladas in each pan.

10. Using a convection oven, bake 18 to 20 minutes in 325 degree oven or until thoroughly heated. If using a standard oven, bake at 350 degrees.

11. Internal temperature must reach 155 degrees or higher for 15 seconds. Remove from oven.

12. Sprinkle 1 quart cheese and 1 ⅓ cups onions over enchiladas in each pan.

13. Heat in oven three minutes to melt cheese.

■ Freezing Instructions

Wrap individual portions in wax paper, and place wrapped portions in freezer bags. Freeze. Reheat in microwave directly from freezer. Remove from freezer bag and wax paper. Place in covered microwave dish, and microwave for about five minutes. May also be reheated in oven preheated to 350 degrees and baked for about 20 minutes.

Lasagna

Serving size: 9.5 oz

■ Ingredients

12 pounds raw ground beef

5 pounds (2 quarts 1 cup) canned diced tomatoes, drained

7 ¾ pounds (3 quarts 1 ½ cups) canned tomato paste

5 ¼ pounds (2 quarts 2 cups) water

4 ¼ pounds (3 quarts) fresh onions, chopped

5 ¼ ounces (¾ cup) granulated sugar

1 ⅞ ounces (3 tablespoons) salt

⅞ ounce (¼ cup 1 ⅔ tablespoons) whole sweet basil, crushed

⅝ ounce (2 tablespoons) garlic powder

⅞ ounce (¼ cup 1 ⅔ tablespoon) crushed oregano

⅓ ounce (2 tablespoons) ground thyme

¼ ounce (1 tablespoon) ground black pepper

Less than ¹⁄₁₆ ounce (⅛ teaspoon) ground red pepper

3 ⅝ pounds (1 quart 2 ¾ cups) whole fresh eggs

11 pounds (1 gallon 1 ½ quarts) low-fat cottage cheese

3 ¾ pounds (3 quarts 3 cups) part skim mozzarella cheese, shredded

14 ⅛ ounces (1 quart) Parmesan cheese, grated

¼ ounce (¼ cup 2 ⅓ tablespoons) dehydrated flaked parsley

6 pounds (1 gallon 2 ½ quarts) no-cook lasagna noodles

5 ¼ ounces (1 ½ cups) grated Parmesan cheese

■ Directions

1. Cook beef until beef loses its pink color, stirring to break apart. Drain or skim off excess fat.

2. Add tomatoes, tomato paste, water, onions, sugar, salt, basil, garlic powder, oregano, thyme, black pepper, and red pepper. Blend well, and simmer for one hour.

3. Combine eggs, cheeses, and parsley. Mix well, place in pans, and cover.

4. Arrange in layers in each pan. During panning, remove small amounts of filling from your fridge at a time. Ensure entire panning procedure does not exceed four hours total time between temperatures of 40 and 140 degrees. Preparing progressively, and cooking the product immediately will ensure food safety. Layer the ingredients as follows:

   - 2 ½ cups meat sauce
   - Noodles, flat and in rows
   - 3 ½ cups chilled filling
   - 1 quart meat sauce
   - Noodles, flat and in rows
   - 3 ½ cups chilled filling
   - 1 quart meat sauce
   - Noodles, flat and in rows
   - 1 ¼ quart meat sauce
   - Sprinkle with parmesan cheese

5. Cover. Using a convection oven, bake at 300 degrees for 55 minutes on high fan, closed vent. (Bake at 325 degrees in a conventional oven). Uncover, and bake for five minutes.

6. Internal temperature must reach 155 degrees or higher for 15 seconds.

7. Let stand ten to 15 minutes before cutting to allow cheeses to firm. Cut four pieces in five rows.

■ Notes

Make sure to choose no-cook lasagna noodles. If you choose noodles that need to be pre-cooked, you may use the same amount and follow the package directions for cooking prior to panning your lasagna.

You may substitute the same amount of ricotta cheese for the cottage cheese.

▪ Freezing Instructions

Wrap individual portions in wax paper. Place wrapped portions in freezer bags. Freeze. Reheat in microwave directly from freezer. Remove from freezer bag and wax paper. Place in covered microwave dish. Microwave for about five minutes. May also be reheated in oven preheated to 350 degrees and baked for about 20 minutes.

Spaghetti and Meatballs

Serving size: 3 meatballs, ¾ cup sauce,
1 cup spaghetti

▪ Ingredients

26½ pounds (2 gallons 3½ quarts) canned
  diced tomatoes, including liquids

9¼ pounds (1 gallon) tomato paste, canned

8⅓ pounds (1 gallon) water

3⅛ pounds (2 quarts 1 cup) fresh onions, chopped

7 ounces (1 cup) granulated sugar

2½ ounces (¼ cup ⅓ tablespoon) salt

1 ounce (3⅓ tablespoons) garlic powder

⅝ ounce (¼ cup ⅓ tablespoon) whole sweet basil, crushed

⅓ ounce (2 tablespoons) ground thyme

⅝ ounce (¼ cup ⅓ tablespoon) crushed oregano

⅛ ounce (¼ teaspoon) ground red pepper

⅜ ounce (12 leaves) whole bay leaf, dried

20 pounds raw ground beef

2⅓ pounds (1 quart 2⅝ cups) fresh onions, chopped

2⅛ pounds (2 quarts 1 cup) breadcrumbs

12⅞ ounces (1½ cups) whole fresh eggs

3 ounces (¼ cup 1 tablespoon) salt

¼ ounce (1 tablespoon) ground black pepper

66 ⅞ pounds (8 gallons) boiling water

2 ½ ounces (¼ cup ⅓ tablespoon) salt

12 pounds (3 gallons 1 quart) dry spaghetti noodle

■ Directions

1. Combine tomatoes, tomato paste, water, onions, sugar, salt, garlic powder, basil, thyme, oregano, red pepper, and bay leaves. Mix well.

2. Bring to a boil, reduce heat, and simmer one hour or until thickened, stirring occasionally. Remove bay leaves.

3. Combine beef, onions, breadcrumbs, eggs, salt, and pepper. Mix lightly but thoroughly.

4. Shape into 300 1 ⅓ ounce balls. Place 100 balls on each pan.

5. Using a convection oven, bake ten to 12 minutes at 350 degrees on high fan, closed vent or until browned. Bake at 375 degrees in a conventional oven.

6. Internal temperature must reach 155 degrees or higher for 15 seconds. Discard fat. Remove to serving pan.

7. Add salt to boiling water. Slowly add spaghetti while stirring constantly until water boils again. Cook about ten to 12 minutes or until tender, stirring occasionally. Do not overcook. Drain thoroughly.

■ Notes

You can preserve the component parts of this dish in a variety of ways. The sauce can be canned or frozen. *See instructions for canning or freezing spaghetti sauce in the section on canning in the Appendix.* Spaghetti sauce can also be frozen in an airtight container. Whether you can or freeze the sauce, it can be reheated in a covered microwave safe container or in a pan over a medium heat on the stovetop.

Meatballs can be frozen prior to cooking or after they are cooked. If you freeze them before cooking them, allow them to thaw overnight in the refrigerator before proceeding to Step 5 above. If you freeze the meatballs after you cook them, you can reheat them in a covered microwave bowl directly from the freezer, or you can put them in the sauce as you heat the sauce in the microwave or on the stovetop.

Cook the spaghetti fresh just prior to serving.

Beef Stew

Serving size: 1 ¼ cups

■ Ingredients

30 pounds raw lean beef, diced

16 ¾ pounds (2 gallons) water

6 ⅝ pounds (3 quarts) canned diced tomatoes, drained

4 ¼ ounces (¼ cup 3 tablespoons) salt

½ ounce (2 tablespoons) ground black pepper

⅝ ounce (2 tablespoons) garlic powder

¼ ounce (1 tablespoon) ground thyme

⅛ ounce (4 leaves) whole bay leaf, dried

8 pounds (1 gallon 3 ⅛ quarts) fresh sliced carrots

4 ¼ pounds (1 gallon) fresh celery, sliced

3 pounds (2 quarts 3 ⅞ cups) fresh onions, quartered

10 ⅓ pounds (1 gallon 3 ½ quarts) fresh potatoes, chopped

1 ¼ pounds (1 quart ½ cup) general-purpose wheat flour

3 ⅛ pounds (1 quart 2 cups) cold water

■ Directions

1. Place beef, water, tomatoes, salt, pepper, garlic, thyme, and bay leaves in steam-jacketed kettle or stockpot. Bring to a boil, reduce heat, and cover. Simmer one hour 40 minutes or until tender.

2. Add carrots to beef mixture. Cover, and simmer 15 minutes.

3. Add celery, onions, and potatoes, and stir. Cover, and simmer 20 minutes or until vegetables are tender.

4. Remove bay leaves. Combine flour and water. Add to stew while stirring. Cook for five minutes or until thickened.

5. Internal temperature must reach 145 degrees or higher for 15 seconds.

■ Notes

In Step 2, two No. 10 canned carrots, drained, or 8 pounds frozen carrots may be used per 100 servings.

■ Freezing Instructions

Freeze individual portions in airtight containers. Reheat in covered microwave dish directly from the freezer or in a saucepan over a medium heat on the stovetop.

Pork Adobo

Serving size: 5 ounces

■ Ingredients

32 pounds raw pork, cubed

1 pound (1 ½ cups) soy sauce

2 ⅛ pounds (1 quart) distilled vinegar

⅛ ounce (⅛ teaspoon) garlic powder

¾ ounce (¼ cup ⅓ tablespoon) ground ginger

⅛ ounce (4 leaves) fresh bay leaf

½ ounce (2 tablespoons) ground black pepper

11 ¼ ounces (2 ½ cups) cornstarch

2 ⅛ pounds (1 quart) cold water

3 pounds (2 quarts 3 ⅞ cups) fresh onions, sliced

4 pounds (3 quarts ⅛ cup) fresh green peppers, thinly sliced

■ Directions

1. Place pork in steam-jacketed kettle or stockpot.

2. Combine soy sauce, vinegar, garlic, ginger, bay leaves, and pepper. Pour over pork, and mix well. Cover, bring to a boil, reduce heat, and simmer for 30 minutes. Skim off excess fat, and remove bay leaves.

3. Dissolve cornstarch in water, and stir into pork mixture. Bring to a boil, reduce heat, and cook five minutes or until thickened.

4. Add onions and peppers to pork mixture, cook until tender, about 20 minutes.

5. Internal temperature of pork must reach 145 degrees or higher for 15 seconds.

■ Freezing Instructions

Freeze individual portions in airtight containers. Reheat in covered microwave dish directly from the freezer or in a saucepan over a medium heat on the stovetop.

Glazed Ham Loaf

Serving size: 5 ounces

■ Ingredients

3 ounces (1 ¼ cups) dry nonfat milk

3 ½ pounds (1 quart 2 ⅝ cups) water

1 ½ pounds (1 gallon 1 quart) white bread, sliced

1 ⅓ pounds (3 ¾ cups) fresh onions, chopped

1 ¾ pounds (2 ¼ cups) whole fresh eggs

18 pounds (3 gallons ⅜ quart) ground cured ham

12 pounds raw ground pork

¼ ounce (1 tablespoon) ground black pepper

10 ⅞ ounces (2 ⅛ cups) packed brown sugar

3 ⅛ ounces (½ cup) dry mustard

12 ½ ounces (1 ½ cups) distilled vinegar

■ Directions

1. Reconstitute milk in mixer bowl.

2. Add bread, and mix to moisten. Let mixture stand for five minutes, and then mix until smooth.

3. Add onions, eggs, ham, pork, and pepper. Mix at medium speed until well blended.

4. Shape into eight 4-pound 14-ounce loaves. Place four loaves, crosswise, in each roasting pan.

5. Combine brown sugar, dry mustard, and vinegar. Blend well. Spoon 6 tablespoons mixture over each loaf.

6. Bake oen and a half hours at 350 degrees. (Bake at 375 degrees in a conventional oven.) Baste each loaf with brown sugar mixture at least twice during a cooking period.

7. Internal temperature must reach 145 degrees or higher for 15 seconds.

8. Remove excess liquid, and cool slightly. Cut 13 slices per loaf.

■ Freezing Instructions

Ham loaf can be frozen after Step 5, before cooking. To bake a frozen loaf, proceed from Step 6 but bake one a half to two times longer. Check for doneness with a meat thermometer. Temperature should reach 145 degrees.

Whole loaves can also be frozen after Step 7. Allow to cool to room temperature, wrap in foil, place in a freezer bag, and store in the freezer up to six months. Allow loaf to thaw overnight in refrigerator. Reheat each loaf to 145 degrees in an oven preheated to 350 degrees (this should take about one and a half hours).

Chalupa

Serving size: 1 cup

■ Ingredients

8 ½ pounds (1 gallon 1 quart) dry pinto beans

25 ⅛ pounds (3 gallons) cold water

32 pounds raw pork cubes

41 ¾ pounds (5 gallons) water

1 ¾ pounds (1 quart 1 cup) fresh onions, chopped

½ ounce (1 tablespoon) garlic powder

3 ¾ ounce (¼ cup 2 ⅓ tablespoon) salt

5 ¼ ounces (1 ¼ cups) ground dark chili powder

2 ¼ ounces (½ cup 2 ⅔ tablespoons) ground cumin

3 ¾ ounces (1 ½ cups) crushed oregano

2 ⅔ ounces (½ cup 1 tablespoon) canned jalapeno peppers, chopped

■ Directions

1. Pick over beans, removing discolored beans and foreign matter. Wash beans thoroughly.

2. Cover with water, bring to a boil, boil two minutes, and turn off heat.

3. Cover, and let the beans soak for one hour. Drain beans.

4. Combine pork, water, onions, garlic, salt, chili powder, cumin, oregano, and jalapeno peppers with beans in steam-jacketed kettle or stockpot. Simmer one and a half to two hours or until beans are tender. Do not cover. Stir occasionally.

5. Internal temperature must reach 145 degrees or higher for 15 seconds.

6. Hold at 140 degrees or higher for service.

■ Notes

Chalupas can be served with shredded lettuce, chopped onions, chopped tomatoes, or sour cream.

■ Freezing Instructions

Freeze individual portions in airtight containers. Reheat in covered microwave dish directly from the freezer for five minutes or in a saucepan over a medium heat on the stovetop.

White Bean Chicken Chili

Serving size: 1½ cups

■ Ingredients

33⅛ pounds (3 gallon 2⅔ quarts) canned cannellini beans, drained

1½ ounces (3 tablespoons) nonstick cooking spray

6 pounds (1 gallon ¼ quart) fresh onions, chopped

4⅞ pounds (3 quarts 2⅞ cups) fresh green peppers, chopped

4⅞ pounds (3 quarts 2⅞ cups) fresh red peppers, chopped

4⅝ ounces (1⅜ cups) chili seasoning

19 pounds (2 gallons 1 quart) chicken stock

18 pounds cooked chicken, diced

10⅓ pounds (1 gallon ½ quart) canned diced tomatoes, including liquids

1¼ ounces (½ cup) crushed oregano

1 pound (3⅝ cups) general-purpose wheat flour

2⅛ pounds (1 quart) cold water

■ Directions

1. Rinse cannellini beans in cold water, and drain well. Set aside for use in Step 3.

2. Stir-cook (stir as you cook) onions and peppers in a lightly sprayed steam-jacketed kettle or stockpot for eight to ten minutes or until tender, stirring constantly. Add the chili seasoning. Stir-cook for one minute to release the volatile oils.

3. Add the cannellini beans, chicken broth, chicken, tomatoes, and oregano to cooked onion and pepper mixture. Bring to a boil. Cover, and reduce heat. Allow the mixture to simmer 15 minutes.

4. Blend flour and cold water together, and stir to make a smooth slurry. Add slurry to white bean chicken chili, stirring constantly. Bring to a boil. Cover, reduce heat, and simmer for ten minutes or until thickened, stirring frequently to prevent sticking.

5. Internal temperature must reach 165 degrees or higher for 15 seconds.

6. Pour 3 gallons white bean chicken chili into each ungreased pan.

■ Freezing Instructions

Freeze individual portions in airtight containers. Reheat in covered microwave dish directly from the freezer or in a saucepan over a medium heat on the stovetop.

Hunter Style Turkey Stew

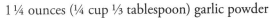

Serving size: 1 ½ cups

■ Ingredient

25 pounds cooked turkey breast, diced

1 ¼ ounces (2 tablespoons) salt

½ ounce (2 tablespoons) ground black pepper

1 ¼ ounces (¼ cup ⅓ tablespoon) garlic powder

1 ⅜ pounds (1 quart 1 cup) general-purpose wheat flour

11 ½ ounces (1 ½ cups) salad oil

2 pounds (1 quart 3 ½ cups) fresh celery, diced

4 pounds fresh onions, diced

2 gallons beef broth

4 ¼ pounds (2 quarts) canned vegetable juice

8 pounds fresh potatoes, chopped

2 ½ pounds (1 quart 7/8 cups) frozen peas

2½ pounds (2 quarts ⅞ cups) fresh carrots, sliced

■ Directions

1. Season diced turkey with salt, pepper, and granulated garlic powder. Flour the stew meat well.

2. Add oil to a steam-jacketed kettle, and heat for two minutes.

3. Brown turkey in oil. Once meat is well browned, add celery and onions. Cook for ten minutes, or until onions are transparent. Internal temperature must reach 140 degrees or higher for 15 seconds.

4. Prepare broth according to manufacturer's instructions. Add broth and vegetable juice to stew. Add bay leaves, and allow the mixture to simmer for five minutes.

5. Add potatoes, and cook another 20 minutes or until potatoes are done.

6. Add frozen vegetables and diced tomatoes, and simmer five minutes more.

7. Serve with rice on the side or over rice.

■ Freezing Instructions

Freeze individual portions in airtight containers. Reheat in covered microwave dish directly from the freezer for five minutes or in a saucepan over a medium heat on the stovetop.

Stuffed Green Peppers

Serving size: ½ pepper

■ Ingredients

1 gallon 2½ quarts marinara sauce

17¼ pounds (3 gallons 1⅛ quarts) fresh green peppers

8⅓ pounds (1 gallon) boiling water

1 gallon 2 quarts steamed rice

24 pounds lean ground turkey

2 ⅞ pounds (2 quarts ¼ cup) fresh onions, chopped

5 ⅛ ounces (½ cup) salt

⅛ ounce (⅓ teaspoon) ground black pepper

12 ⅔ ounces (1 ½ cups) Worcestershire sauce

2 ⅛ pounds (1 quart) water

■ Directions

1. Prepare Marinara Sauce (*see Chapter 9 for recipe*).
2. Cut each pepper in half lengthwise, and remove core.
3. Place peppers in boiling water. Return to a boil, and cook for one minute. Drain the peppers well, and set aside for use in Step 6.
4. Prepare rice according to recipe below.
5. Combine cooked rice, ground turkey, onions, salt, pepper, Worcestershire sauce, and water with 2 quarts marinara sauce. Do not overmix.
6. Fill each pepper with ¾ cup turkey mixture. Place filled peppers in roasting pans.
7. Pour 1 cup water around peppers in each pan to keep the peppers from drying out.
8. Pour remaining sauce over peppers in each pan and cover pans.
9. Bake about 1 ½ hours at 350 degrees (375 degrees in a conventional oven) or until tender.
10. Internal temperature must reach 165 degrees or higher for 15 seconds.
11. Hold at 140 degrees or higher for service.

■ Freezing Instructions

Wrap individual portions in wax paper. Place wrapped portions in freezer bags. Freeze. Reheat in microwave directly from freezer. Remove from freezer bag and wax paper. Place in covered microwave dish, and microwave for about five minutes. May also be reheated in oven preheated to 350 degrees and baked for about 20 minutes.

Steamed rice

Serving size: ¾ cup

■ Ingredients

8½ pounds (1 gallon 1¼ quart) long grain rice

23 pounds (2 gallons 3 quarts) cold water

1⅞ ounce (3 tablespoons) salt

1½ ounce (3 tablespoons) salad oil

■ Directions

1. Combine rice, water, salt, and salad oil, and bring to a boil. Stir occasionally.

2. Cover tightly, and simmer 20 to 25 minutes. Do not stir.

3. Remove from heat, and transfer to shallow serving pans.

■ Notes

In Step 2, rice may be baked in a 350 degree convection oven (375 degrees in a conventional oven) for 35 to 40 minutes on high fan, closed vent.

Stuffed Flounder Creole

Serving size: 4½ ounces

■ Ingredients

2 gallons ½ quart Creole sauce

12⅔ ounces (3 cups) fresh celery, chopped

1⅝ pounds (1 quart ½ cup) fresh onions, chopped

12 ounces (1½ cups) melted butter

5⅞ pounds (1 gallon 1¾ quarts) cracker crumbs

¼ ounce (⅜ teaspoon) ground black pepper

⅓ ounce (2 tablespoons) ground thyme

2 pounds cooked shrimp

2⅛ pounds (1 quart) water

30 pounds raw flounder/sole fillet

■ Directions

1. Prepare one portion of the Creole sauce recipe (*see Chapter 9 for recipe*) or utilize prepared Creole sauce.

2. Hold at 140 degrees or higher for use in Step 9.

3. Sauté celery and onions in melted butter or margarine until tender.

4. Combine cracker crumbs, pepper, and thyme, and add to vegetables. Add shrimp to vegetable crumb mixture.

5. Add water to vegetable-crumb-shrimp mixture. Toss mixture, but do not pack.

6. Separate fillets. Place ¼ cup vegetable-crumb-shrimp mixture on each fillet. Roll fillets using toothpicks to hold together.

7. Place 25 rolled fillets in each greased steam table pan.

8. Bake 20 minutes at 375 degrees. (Note: Do not bake in a convection oven as the fish will become very dry.) Remove from oven.

9. Cover fish in each pan with 2 quarts hot Creole sauce.

10. Bake five to ten minutes or until thoroughly heated.

11. Internal temperature must reach 165 degrees or higher for 15 seconds.

■ Notes

Can or freeze Creole sauce separately from fish to preserve this dish. Freeze individual fish portions wrapped in plastic wrap and placed in freezer bags after Step 6 above. To prepare individual portions, allow fish to thaw overnight in refrigerator. Continue with Step 7 above.

Baked Fish

Serving size: 4 ounces

▓ Ingredients

2 ounces (¼ cup ⅓ tablespoon) nonstick cooking spray

30 pounds raw flounder/sole fillet

12 ⅞ ounces (1 ½ cups) lemon juice

1 pound (2 cups) melted margarine

1 ⅞ ounces (3 tablespoons) salt

½ ounce (2 tablespoons) ground paprika

1 ounce (¼ cup) fresh parsley bunch, chopped

▓ Directions

1. Separate fillets or steaks, and cut into 4 ½ ounce portions, if necessary. Lightly spray pans with nonstick cooking spray. Arrange single layers of fish on pans.

2. Combine lemon juice, butter or margarine, salt, and paprika. Mix well. Drizzle ¾ cup mixture over fish in each pan.

3. Using a convection oven, bake for seven minutes at 325 degrees on high fan, closed vent or until lightly browned. If using a conventional oven, bake at 350 degrees.

4. Internal temperature must reach 145 degrees or higher for 15 seconds.

5. Garnish with parsley before serving.

▓ Note

You may freeze raw fish and allow it to thaw in refrigerator prior to cooking. It is not recommended to freeze cooked fish as the texture will turn to mush.

Salmon Loaf

Serving size: 4 ½ ounces
Bake in large (1 ½ quart) loaf pans

■ Ingredients

19 pounds (2 gallons 3 ⅔ quarts) canned pink salmon

1 ⅓ pounds (1 quart 1 cup) fresh celery, chopped

2 ounces (¼ cup ⅓ tablespoon) nonstick cooking
  spray

1 ⅓ pounds (3 ¾ cups) fresh onions, chopped

5 ¼ pounds (2 quarts 2 cups) reserved liquid
  (reserved from drained salmon)

3 ¾ pounds (1 gallons) breadcrumbs

2 pounds (3 ¾ cups) whole eggs, fresh

⅛ ounce (¼ cup ⅓ tablespoon) dehydrated flaked parsley

⅛ ounce (¼ teaspoon) ground black pepper

¾ ounce (1 tablespoon) nonstick cooking spray

■ Directions

1. Drain salmon, and reserve 2 ½ quarts of salmon liquid for use in Step 3. Remove and discard skin and bones from salmon. Flake salmon by pulling it apart into small pieces with a fork, and cover salmon and salmon liquid.

2. Stir-cook celery and onions in a lightly sprayed steam-jacketed kettle or stockpot about eight to ten minutes, stirring constantly.

3. Combine salmon, salmon liquid, and cooked vegetables with breadcrumbs, eggs, pepper, and parsley. Mix lightly but thoroughly. Do not overmix.

4. Lightly spray each sheet pan with nonstick cooking spray. Firmly and evenly pack 8 pound 2 ounce salmon mixture into each sheet pan. Divide into two equal loaves (about 7 inches wide) across the pan. Space evenly; smooth top and sides; cover.

5. Using a convection oven, bake 35 to 40 minutes at 325 degrees (Bake at 350 degrees in a conventional oven) or until lightly browned on high fan, closed vent.

6. Internal temperature must reach 145 degrees or higher for 15 seconds.

7. Let stand ten minutes before slicing. Cut 13 slices per loaf.

■ Freezing Instructions

Salmon loaf can be frozen after Step 4, before cooking. To bake a frozen loaf, proceed from Step 5 but bake 1 ½ to two times longer. Check for doneness with a meat thermometer.

Whole loaves can also be frozen after Step 6. Allow to cool to room temperature, wrap in foil, place in a freezer bag, and store in the freezer up to six months. Allow loaf to thaw overnight in refrigerator. Reheat to 145 degrees in an oven preheated to 350 degrees (it should take about one and a half hours).

Seafood Stew

Serving size: 1 ½ cups

■ Ingredients

1 ½ ounces (3 tablespoons) nonstick cooking spray

6 ⅛ pounds (1 gallon ⅔ quart) fresh green peppers, chopped

6 ⅛ pounds (1 gallon ⅔ quart) fresh red peppers, chopped

3 ¾ pounds (2 quarts 1 ½ cups) fresh onions, chopped

3 ⅛ ounces (¾ cups) dark ground chili powder

3 ¼ ounces Old Bay seasoning

1 ¼ ounce (¼ cup ⅓ tablespoon) garlic powder

8 ¾ pounds (1 gallon) orange juice

16 ⅞ pounds (2 gallons) chicken stock

20 ¾ pounds (2 gallons 1 quart) canned diced tomatoes, including liquids

4 ¼ pounds (3 quarts) long grain wild rice

16 pounds frozen skinless cod fillets

10 pounds frozen raw shrimp, peeled and deveined

Directions

1. Stir-cook peppers and onions in a lightly sprayed steam-jacketed kettle or stockpot eight to ten minutes or until tender, stirring constantly. Add the chili powder, Old Bay seasoning, and garlic powder. Stir-cook for one minute. Add orange juice to mixture, stir, and cover.

2. Add chicken broth, tomatoes, and rice to cooked vegetable mixture. Bring to a boil. Cover, reduce heat, and simmer 25 minutes or until rice is tender.

3. Temperature must register 165 degrees or higher for 15 seconds.

4. Add fish, and simmer gently for four minutes. Add shrimp, and simmer gently two to three minutes. Do not overcook.

5. Temperature must register 145 degrees or higher for 15 seconds.

6. Pour 2⅓ gallons into each steam table pan.

Freezing Instructions

Freeze individual portions in airtight containers. Reheat in covered microwave dish directly from the freezer for about five minutes or in a saucepan over a medium heat on the stovetop.

Jambalaya

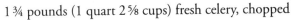

Serving size: 1½ cups

Ingredients

10 pounds raw shrimp, peeled and deveined

1½ ounces (3 tablespoons) nonstick cooking spray

12 pounds (2 gallons ½ quart) fresh onions, chopped

1¾ pounds (1 quart 2⅝ cups) fresh celery, chopped

2 pounds (1 quart 2⅛ cups) fresh green peppers, chopped

⅝ ounces (2 tablespoons) garlic powder

26½ pounds (3 gallons) canned crushed tomatoes, including liquids

1½ pounds (2½ cups) canned tomato paste

1 ⅞ ounces (3 tablespoons) salt

3 ⅛ ounces (1 ¼ cups) whole sweet basil, crushed

⅓ ounce (¼ cup 1 ⅔ tablespoons) sweet ground marjoram

⅔ ounce (½ cup) fresh thyme

⅞ ounce (¼ cup 1 ⅔ tablespoons) crushed oregano

¼ ounce (1 tablespoon) ground red pepper

¼ ounce (8 leaves) fresh bay leaf

2 gallons chicken broth

8 ½ pounds (1 gallon 1 ¼ quarts) long grain rice

13 pounds cooked boneless ham

■ Directions

1. Thoroughly rinse and drain shrimp.
2. Refrigerate at 41 degrees or lower for use in Step 5.
3. Lightly spray steam-jacketed kettle or stockpot with nonstick cooking spray. Stir-cook onions, peppers, and celery in a steam-jacketed kettle or stockpot eight to ten minutes or until tender, stirring constantly.
4. Add tomatoes, chicken broth, tomato paste, basil, salt, marjoram, thyme, oregano, garlic powder, red pepper, and bay leaves to cooked vegetables. Stir to blend. Bring to a boil. Reduce heat, and allow the mixture to simmer for ten minutes.
5. Add ham and rice to sauce mixture. Stir to blend. Bring to a boil. Cover, reduce heat, and simmer for 30 minutes or until rice is tender, stirring occasionally.
6. Internal temperature must reach 145 degrees or higher for 15 seconds.
7. Add shrimp to sauce and rice mixture. Stir to blend. Bring to a boil. Cover, reduce heat, and simmer six to eight minutes or until shrimp is just done. Do not overcook the shrimp.
8. Internal temperature of the shrimp must reach 145 degrees or higher for 15 seconds. Remove the bay leaves.

■ Freezing Instructions

Freeze individual portions in airtight containers. Reheat in covered microwave dish directly from the freezer for about five minutes or in a saucepan over a medium heat on the stovetop.

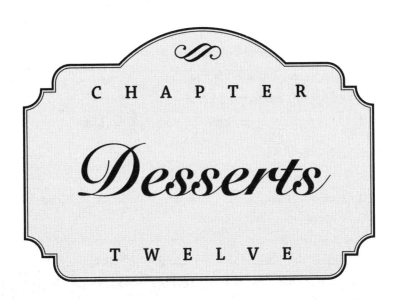

Cheesecake with Strawberries

Serving size: 1 piece
Pan size: 16 x 24 x 2 (two pans)

■ Ingredients

1 ½ pounds (3 cups) melted margarine

3 pounds graham cracker crumbs

12 ⅓ ounces (1 ¾ cups) granulated sugar

10 ¼ pounds (1 gallon 1 quart) cream
cheese, softened to room temperature

3 pounds (1 quart 2 ¾ cups) granulated sugar

4 ⅜ ounces (1 cup) general-purpose wheat flour

1 ounce (¼ cup 3 tablespoons) nonfat dry milk

¼ ounce (⅛ teaspoon) salt

2 ⅜ pounds (1 quart ½ cup) whole fresh eggs

12 ½ ounces (1 ½ cups) water

2 ⅛ ounces (¼ cup ⅓ tablespoon) lemon juice

2 ¼ ounces (¼ cup ⅓ tablespoon) orange juice

⅞ ounce (2 tablespoons) vanilla extract

⅜ ounce (2 tablespoons) grated orange rind

¼ ounce (1 tablespoon) grated lemon rind

8⅜ pounds (3 quarts 3 cups) strawberries, fresh, cut, or frozen

■ Directions

1. Grind graham crackers or crush on board with rolling pin. Combine butter or margarine, crumbs, and sugar in mixer bowl. Blend thoroughly at low speed, about one minute.

2. Press 2 quarts crumb mixture firmly in bottom of each pan. Using a convection oven, bake for three minutes on low fan, open vent at 325 degrees. If using a standard oven, bake at 350 degrees. Cool and set aside for use in Step 8.

3. Place cream cheese in mixer bowl. Whip at medium speed until fluffy, which should take about three minutes.

4. Combine sugar, flour, milk, and salt, mixing well.

5. Add to cream cheese; whip at low speed until blended, which should take about two minutes. Whip at medium speed until smooth, for about one minute.

6. Add eggs, and whip at low speed for 30 seconds. Whip at medium speed until smooth, about one minute.

7. Combine water, lemon and orange juices, vanilla, and orange and lemon rinds; add to cheese mixture. Whip at low speed until well blended, about two minutes.

8. Spread 5¼ quarts cheese filling evenly over crust in each pan.

9. Using a convection oven, bake at 325 degrees for 25 to 30 minutes on low fan, open vent or until filling is firm and lightly browned. (Bake at 350 degrees in a conventional oven.)

10. Refrigerate until ready to serve.

11. Place strawberries over each chilled pie. Cut each of the pies into rows of six by nine for 54 pieces each.

■ **Freezing Instructions**

Can be frozen in individual servings or as an entire cake. Wrap in wax paper, and place in a freezer bag after Step 9. Allow to thaw overnight in refrigerator.

Devil's Food Cake

Serving size: 1 piece
Pan size: 16 x 24 x 2 (two pans)

■ **Ingredients**

2 ¾ pounds (2 quarts 2 cups) general-purpose wheat flour

4 ⅜ pounds (2 quarts 2 cups) granulated sugar

1 ½ ounces (2 ⅓ tablespoons) salt

1 ⅝ ounces (3 ⅓ tablespoons) baking soda

1 ¼ pounds (1 quart 2 ½ cups) cocoa

4 ¼ ounces (1 ¾ cups) nonfat milk, dry

1 ¾ pounds (1 quart) shortening

2 ⅝ pounds (1 quart 1 cup) water

2 ½ pounds (1 quart ⅝ cup) whole fresh eggs

1 ⅓ pounds (2 ½ cups) water

⅞ ounce (2 tablespoons) vanilla extract

2 ounces (¼ cup ⅓ tablespoon) nonstick cooking spray

■ **Directions**

1. Sift together flour, sugar, salt, baking soda, cocoa, and milk into mixer bowl.

2. Blend shortening with dry ingredients. Add water gradually, and beat at low speed for two minutes or until blended. Beat at medium speed for two minutes, and scrape down the sides of the bowl.

3. Combine eggs, water, and vanilla, and add slowly to mixture while beating at low speed for one minute. Scrape down sides of the bowl. Beat at medium speed three minutes.

4. Lightly spray each pan with nonstick cooking spray. Pour 4½ quarts batter into each greased and floured pan. Spread evenly.

5. Using a convection oven, bake at 300 degrees for 25 to 35 minutes or until done on low fan, open vent. (Bake at 325 degrees in a conventional oven.)

6. Cool and frost cake if desired. Cut each of the cakes 6 by 9 for 54 pieces each.

■ Note

Do not freeze frosting. The consistency of the frosting will change for the worse as it thaws.

■ Freezing Instructions

Can be frozen in individual servings or as an entire cake. Wrap in wax paper, and place in a freezer bag after Step 5. Allow cake to cool before freezing. Allow cake to thaw overnight in refrigerator.

Coconut Cake

Serving size: 1 piece
Pan size: 16 x 24 x 2 (two pans)

■ Ingredients

4⅜ pounds (1 gallon) general-purpose wheat flour

4 pounds (2 quarts 1 cup) granulated sugar

1½ ounces (2⅓ tablespoons) salt

3¼ ounces (¼ cup 3 tablespoons) baking powder

3 ounces (1¼ cups) nonfat dry milk

1½ pounds (3⅜ cups) shortening

2⅓ pounds (1 quart ½ cup) water

2¼ pounds (1 quart ¼ cup) whole fresh eggs

12½ ounces (1½ cups) water (in addition to the water listed previously)

1⅞ ounces (¼ cup ⅓ tablespoon) vanilla extract

2 ounces (¼ cup ⅓ tablespoon) nonstick cooking spray

12 ounces (1 ½ cups) melted butter

13 ⅝ ounces (2 ⅝ cups) packed brown sugar

⅞ ounce (¼ cup 2 ⅓ tablespoons) nonfat dry milk

1 ⅝ pounds (2 quarts) sweetened coconut flakes

7 ⅓ ounce (¾ cups 2 tablespoons) water

■ Directions

1. Sift together flour, sugar, salt, baking powder, and milk into mixer bowl.

2. Add shortening and water to dry ingredients. Beat at low speed for one minute until blended. Scrape down sides of the bowl, and continue beating for two minutes.

3. Combine eggs, water, and vanilla. Add slowly to mixture while beating at low speed. Scrape down sides of the bowl, and beat at medium speed for three minutes.

4. Lightly spray each pan with nonstick cooking spray. Pour 3 ½ quarts of batter into each sprayed and floured 9-inch pie pan.

5. Using a convection oven, bake at 325 degrees for 25 to 30 minutes or until done on low fan, open vent. If using a standard oven, bake at 350 degrees

6. Combine melted butter or margarine, brown sugar, nonfat dry milk, prepared sweetened coconut flakes, and water. As soon as cakes are removed from oven, spread about 1 quart coconut mixture over each cake. Increase oven temperature to 400 degrees, and return to oven about seven minutes or until coconut peaks are lightly browned.

7. Cool. Cut each of the cakes into rows of six by nine for 54 pieces each.

■ Notes

Do not freeze frosting. The consistency of the frosting will change for the worse as it thaws.

■ Freezing Instructions

Can be frozen in individual servings or as an entire cake. Wrap in wax paper, and place in a freezer bag after Step 5. Allow cake to cool before freezing. Allow cake to thaw overnight in refrigerator.

Dutch Apple Cake

Serving size: 1 piece
Pan size: 16 x 24 x 2 (two pans)

■ Ingredients

4 ⅜ pounds (1 gallon) general-purpose wheat flour

4 pounds (2 quarts 1 cup) granulated sugar

1 ½ ounces (2 ⅓ tablespoons) salt

3 ¼ ounces (¼ cup 3 tablespoons) baking powder

3 ounces (1 ¼ cups) nonfat dry milk

1 ½ pounds (3 ⅜ cups) shortening

2 ⅓ pounds (1 quart ½ cup) water

2 ¼ pounds (1 quart ¼ cup) whole fresh eggs

12 ½ ounces (1 ½ cups) water

1 ⅞ ounces (¼ cup ⅓ tablespoon) vanilla extract

13 pounds (1 gallon 2 ½ quarts) prepared apple pie filling

1 gallon 2 ¾ quarts vanilla glaze (*see recipe in Chapter 4*)

■ Directions

1. Sift together flour, sugar, salt, baking powder, and milk into mixer bowl.

2. Add shortening and water to dry ingredients. Beat at low speed for one minute until blended. Scrape down the sides of the bowl, and continue beating for two minutes.

3. Combine eggs, water, and vanilla. Add slowly to mixture while beating at low speed. Scrape down the sides of the bowl, and beat at medium speed for three minutes.

4. Pour apple pie filling evenly over batter in each pan.

5. Using a convection oven, bake at 325 degrees for 25 to 30 minutes or until done on low fan, open vent. If using a standard oven, bake at 350 degrees.

6. Cool. Top each portion with ¼ cup vanilla glaze.

7. Cut each cake into rows of six by nine for 54 pieces each.

■ Notes

Do not freeze frosting. The consistency of the frosting will change for the worse as it thaws.

■ Freezing Instructions

Can be frozen in individual servings or as an entire cake. Wrap in wax paper, and place in a freezer bag after Step 5. Allow cake to cool before freezing. Allow to thaw overnight in refrigerator.

Gingerbread

Serving size: 1 piece
Pan size: 16 x 24 x 2 (two pans)

■ Ingredients

4⅜ pounds (1 gallon) general-purpose wheat flour

3 pounds (1 quart 2¾ cups) granulated sugar

1 ounce (1 tablespoon) salt

1⅛ ounces (2⅓ tablespoons) baking powder

1⅓ ounces (2⅔ tablespoons) baking soda

½ ounce (2 tablespoon) ground cinnamon

¾ ounce (¼ cup ⅓ tablespoon) ground ginger

1⅓ pounds (3 cups) shortening

2⅞ pounds (1 quart) molasses

1¼ pounds (2¼ cups) whole fresh eggs

2⅝ pounds (1 quart 1 cup) warm water

2⅝ pounds (1 quart 1 cup) ice water

2 ounces (¼ cup ⅓ tablespoon) nonstick cooking spray

■ Directions

1. Sift together flour, sugar, salt, baking powder, baking soda, cinnamon, and ginger into mixer bowl.

2. Add shortening, molasses, and eggs to dry ingredients. Beat at low speed for one minute until blended, and then continue beating at medium speed for two minutes. Scrape down the sides of the bowl.

3. Add water to mixture, and mix at low speed only until batter is smooth.

4. Lightly spray each pan with nonstick cooking spray. Pour about 3½ quarts batter into each sprayed and floured pan.

5. Using a convection oven, bake at 300 degrees for 25 to 35 minutes or until done on low fan, open vent. If using a standard oven, bake at 325 degrees.

6. Cut each cake into rows of six by nine for 54 pieces each. Serve warm if possible.

■ Notes

If desired, top each portion with ¼ cup whipped cream, or dust with powdered sugar.

Do not freeze frosting. The consistency of the frosting will change for the worse as it thaws.

■ Freezing Instructions

Can be frozen in individual servings or as an entire cake. Wrap in wax paper and place in a freezer bag after Step 5. Allow cake to cool before freezing. Allow to thaw overnight in refrigerator.

Brownies

Serving size: 1 piece
Pan size: 16 x 24 x 2 (two pans)

■ Ingredients

3 pounds (2 quarts 3 cups) general-purpose
  wheat flour

5 ¼ pounds (3 quarts) granulated sugar

1 ⅓ pounds (1 quart 3 cups) cocoa

1 ⅛ ounces (2 ⅓ tablespoons) baking powder

⅝ ounce (1 tablespoon) salt

2 ¾ pounds (1 quart 2 cups) shortening

2 ¾ pounds (1 quart 1 ¼ cups) whole fresh eggs

1 ⅞ pounds (2 ⅝ cups) chocolate syrup

1 ⅜ ounces (3 tablespoons) vanilla extract

1 ⅞ pounds (1 quart 2 cups) unsalted nuts, coarsely chopped

2 ounces (¼ cup ⅓ tablespoon) nonstick cooking spray

■ Directions

1. Place flour, sugar, cocoa, baking powder, and salt in mixer bowl. Blend well at low speed for one minute.

2. Add shortening, eggs, syrup, and vanilla to dry ingredients. Mix at low speed for one minute then scrape down bowl. Mix at medium speed for two minutes or until thoroughly blended.

3. Add nuts to batter, and mix at low speed for 30 seconds.

4. Lightly spray each pan with nonstick cooking spray. Spread 4 ¾ quarts batter in sprayed pans.

5. Using a convection oven, bake for 25 to 30 minutes or until done at 325 degrees on high fan, open vent. If using a standard oven, bake at 350 degrees. Do not bake for too long. Brownies are done when a toothpick inserted in the center of baked brownies comes out clean.

6. Cool and cut each pan into rows of six by nine for 54 brownies per pan.

■ Note

Do not freeze frosting. The consistency of the frosting will change for the worse as it thaws.

■ Freezing Instructions

Can be frozen in individual servings or as an entire cake. Wrap in wax paper, and place in a freezer bag after Step 5. Allow cake to cool before freezing. Allow to thaw overnight in refrigerator.

Butter Cream Frosting

Yield: 2 ½ quarts

■ Ingredients

1 ¼ pounds (2 ½ cups) softened butter

5 pounds (1 gallon ¾ quart) sifted powdered sugar

¼ ounce (⅛ teaspoon) salt

1 ounce (¼ cup 3 ⅓ tablespoons) dry nonfat milk

⅞ ounce (2 tablespoons) vanilla extract

6 ¼ ounces (¾ cups) water

■ Directions

1. Cream butter or margarine in mixer bowl at medium speed one to three minutes or until light and fluffy.

2. Sift together powdered sugar, salt, and milk. Add to creamed butter or margarine.

3. Add vanilla while mixing at low speed. Add just enough water to obtain a spreading consistency. Scrape down sides of the bowl. Beat at medium speed for three to five minutes or until mixture is light and well blended.

4. Spread immediately on cooled cakes.

■ **Note**

Do not freeze frosting. The consistency of the frosting will change for the worse as it thaws.

Chocolate Fudge Frosting

Yield: 2½ quarts

■ **Ingredients**

1 pound (2 cups) butter

8⅛ ounces (1⅛ cups) shortening

4¼ pounds (1 gallon) sifted powdered sugar

8⅛ ounces (2⅝ cups) cocoa

⅞ ounce (¼ cup 2⅓ tablespoons) dry nonfat milk

¼ ounce (⅛ teaspoon) salt

1 pound (1⅞ cups) warm water

⅞ ounce (2 tablespoons) vanilla extract

■ **Directions**

1. Melt butter or margarine and shortening; pour into mixer bowl.
2. Sift together powdered sugar, cocoa, milk, and salt. Add to melted fats, and mix at low speed until smooth.
3. Combine water and vanilla, and add to mixture in bowl. Beat at medium speed until mixture obtains desired spreading consistency.
4. Spread immediately on cooled cakes.

■ **Note**

Do not freeze frosting. The consistency of the frosting will change for the worse as it thaws.

Cream Cheese Frosting

Yield: 2 ½ quarts

■ Ingredients

4 pounds (1 quart 3 ⅞ cups) cream cheese, room temperature

3 ⅛ pounds (3 quarts) sifted powdered sugar

⅞ ounce (2 tablespoons) vanilla extract

■ Directions

1. Cream softened cream cheese, powdered sugar, and vanilla in mixer bowl at low speed for four minutes or until smooth and creamy.

2. Spread immediately on cooled cakes.

■ Note

Do not freeze frosting. The consistency of the frosting will change for the worse as it thaws.

Coconut Butter Cream Frosting

Yield: 2 ½ quarts

■ Ingredients

1 ¼ pounds (2 ½ cups) softened butter

5 pounds (1 gallon ¾ quarts) sifted powdered sugar

¼ ounce (⅛ teaspoon) salt

1 ounce (¼ cup 3 ⅓ tablespoons) dry nonfat milk

⅞ ounce (2 tablespoons) vanilla extract

6 ¼ ounces (¾ cups) water

9 ounces (2 ¾ cups) sweetened coconut flakes (mixed into frosting)

4 ⅞ ounces (1 ½ cups) sweetened coconut flakes (on top of cake)

▇ Directions

1. Cream butter or margarine in mixer bowl at medium speed one to three minutes or until light and fluffy.

2. Sift together powdered sugar, salt, and milk. Add to creamed butter or margarine.

3. Add vanilla while mixing at low speed, and add just enough water to obtain a spreading consistency. Scrape down bowl. Beat at medium speed three to five minutes or until mixture is light and well blended. Fold in coconut.

4. Spread immediately on cooled cakes. Sprinkle additional coconut evenly over each frosted cake.

▇ Note

Do not freeze frosting. The consistency of the frosting will change for the worse as it thaws.

Maple Butter Cream Frosting

Yield: 2 ½ quarts

▇ Ingredients

1 ¼ pounds (2 ½ cups) softened butter

5 pounds (1 gallon ¾ quarts) sifted powdered sugar

¼ ounce (⅛ teaspoon) salt

1 ounce (¼ cup 3 ⅓ tablespoons) dry nonfat milk

½ ounce (1 tablespoon) vanilla extract

1 ⅜ ounces (3 tablespoons) maple flavoring

6 ¼ ounces (¾ cup) water

▇ Directions

1. Cream butter or margarine in mixer bowl at medium speed for one to three minutes or until light and fluffy.

2. Sift together powdered sugar, salt, and milk. Add to creamed butter or margarine.

3. Add vanilla and maple flavoring while mixing at low speed. Add just enough water to obtain a spreading consistency. Scrape down sides of the bowl. Beat at medium speed for three to five minutes or until mixture is light and well blended.

4. Spread immediately on cooled cakes.

■ Note

Do not freeze frosting. The consistency of the frosting will change for the worse as it thaws.

Piecrust

Yield: 100 crusts

■ Ingredients

6 ⅞ pounds (1 gallon 2 ¼ quarts) general-purpose wheat flour

1 ⅞ ounces (3 tablespoons) salt

3 ⅝ pounds (2 quarts) shortening

2 ⅛ pounds (1 quart) cold water

■ Directions

1. Sift together flour and salt in mixer bowl.

2. Add shortening to dry ingredients. Using pastry knife attachment, mix at low speed for 30 seconds or until shortening is evenly distributed and mixture is granular in appearance.

3. Add water and mix at low speed for one minute until dough is just formed.

4. Chill dough for at least one hour for ease in handling.

5. Divide dough into 13 7 ½-ounce pieces for bottom crust and 13 7-ounce pieces for top crust. Place on lightly floured board.

6. Sprinkle each piece of dough lightly with flour and flatten gently. Using a floured rolling pin, roll lightly with quick strokes from center out to edge in all directions. Form a circle 1 inch larger than pie pan and about ⅛ inch thick. Bottom crust will be slightly thicker. Shift or turn dough occasionally to prevent sticking. If edges split, pinch cracks together.

7. To make the bottom crust, rolled dough in half and carefully place it into ungreased pie pan with fold at center. Unfold and fit carefully into pie pan, being careful not to leave any air spaces between pan and dough.

8. To make the top crust, roll it in the same manner as bottom crust and fold it in half. With a knife, make several small slits near center fold to allow steam to escape during baking. Brush outer rim of bottom crust with water. Lay top crust over filling with fold at center. Unfold, and press edges of two crusts together lightly.

9. Trim overhanging edges of dough by using a knife or spatula. (Incorporate excess dough into next crust, if needed.) There should be little excess if skill is used in weighing and rolling dough.

10. To seal the pie, press the edges of crust firmly together, or crimp with the thumb and forefinger to make a fluted edge.

11. For a washed top, brush pies with appropriate wash as follows:

    Egg and milk wash - This wash is used for fruit pies (apple, blueberry, cherry, peach, pineapple) that are baked 30 to 35 minutes. It should not be used for pies requiring longer baking time as the crust will brown excessively.

    Egg and water wash - This wash is used for berry and mincemeat pies that are baked 40 to 45 minutes. It should not be used for pies that are baked 30 to 35 minutes as the crusts will be too pale. Allow glaze to dry on crust before baking to eliminate dark spots.

12. Bake the pies specified on individual recipe card.

13. To bake just the crusts, bake at 425 degrees for about 15 to 18 minutes, or until light golden brown. (Bake at 400 degrees in a convection oven.) Cool before filling. Proceed with the recipe directions.

■ **Freezing Instructions**

Piecrust can be frozen before or after you roll it out. Freeze individual portions (single crust amounts) by wrapping in wax paper and placing in freezer bags. Allow to thaw overnight in refrigerator before rolling out for a pie.

You may also roll out an individual crust before freezing. Roll out dough on a piece of wax paper. Roll into a tube shape. Place tube in freezer bag. Freeze. Allow to thaw overnight in refrigerator.

Graham Cracker Crust (Chocolate Wafer Variation)

■ **Ingredients**

1 ⅞ pounds (3 ¾ cups) margarine

3 ⅝ pounds graham cracker crumbs

1 ⅓ pounds (3 cups) granulated sugar

■ **Directions**

1. Grind graham crackers or crush on board with rolling pin or in bowl of a food processor. Combine butter or margarine, crumbs, and sugar in mixer bowl. Mix at low speed until well blended, about two minutes.

2. Place about 8 ounces or 1 ¾ cups crumb mixture in each pie pan. Press firmly into an even layer against bottom and sides of each pan.

3. Chill at least one hour before filling is added.

■ **Notes**

For a firmer shell, omit Step 3. Instead, using a convection oven, bake at 325 degrees for seven minutes or until lightly browned on low fan, open vent. (Bake at 350 degrees in a conventional oven.)

Chocolate wafer cookies may be used in place if graham crackers may be used.

Freezing Instructions

Form crust in an aluminum pie tin. Place tin with crust in a freezer bag. Freeze. May be used frozen or after thawing in refrigerator.

Apple Pie Filling

Yield: fruit for 13 pies

Ingredients

45 cups apples, thinly sliced

⅓ cup 2 tablespoons lemon juice

11 ¼ cups white sugar

2 ½ cups cornstarch

1 tablespoon 2 teaspoons ground cinnamon

2 ½ teaspoons salt

½ teaspoon ground nutmeg

25 cups water

Directions

1. In a large bowl, toss apples with lemon juice, and set aside. Pour water into a Dutch oven over medium heat. Combine sugar, cornstarch, cinnamon, salt, and nutmeg. Add to water, stir well, and bring to a boil. Boil for two minutes, stirring constantly.

2. Add apples and return to a boil. Reduce heat, cover, and simmer until apples are tender, about six to eight minutes.

3. Cool for 30 minutes.

4. Ladle into 13 freezer containers, leaving ½ inch headspace.

5. Cool at room temperature no longer than one and a half hours.

6. Seal, and freeze. This filling can be stored for up to 12 months.

Freezing Instructions

Place 5 to 6 cups of cooled filling in a freezer bag. Freeze. Allow to thaw in refrigerator overnight before using for a pie.

Blueberry Pie

Yield: 13 double-crust pies
Serving size: 1 piece

Ingredients

26 pie crusts

13 ½ pounds (2 gallons 1 ⅞ quarts) frozen unsweetened blueberries

2 ⅓ pounds (1 quart ½ cup) water

5 ¼ pounds (3 quarts) granulated sugar

⅓ ounce (¼ teaspoon) salt

11 ¼ ounces (2 ½ cups) cornstarch

2 ⅓ pounds (1 quart ½ cup) cold water

6 ounces (¾ cups) butter

Directions

1. Prepare one recipe for piecrust (*see recipe earlier in this chapter*).

2. Divide dough into 13 7½-ounce pieces for bottom crust and 13 7-ounce pieces for top crust. Place on lightly floured board.

3. Sprinkle each piece of dough lightly with flour and flatten gently. Using a floured rolling pin, roll lightly with quick strokes from center out to edge in all directions. Form a circle 1 inch larger than pie pan and about ⅛ inch thick. Bottom crust will be slightly thicker. Shift or turn dough occasionally to prevent sticking. If edges split, pinch cracks together.

4. For the bottom crust, fold rolled dough in half, and carefully place it into ungreased pie pan with fold at center. Unfold, and fit carefully into pie pan, being careful not to leave any air spaces between pan and dough.

5. For the top crust, roll top crust in same manner as bottom crust and fold it in half. With a knife, make several small slits near center fold to allow steam to escape during baking. Brush outer rim of bottom crust with water. Lay top crust over filling with fold at center. Unfold, and press edges of two crusts together lightly.

6. To remove the excess dough, trim overhanging edges of dough by using a knife or spatula. (Incorporate excess dough into next crust, if needed.) There should be little excess if skill is used in weighing and rolling dough. To seal the pie, press edges of crust firmly together, or crimp with the thumb and forefinger to make a fluted edge.

7. Use frozen blueberries for your pie filling. Thawing is not necessary.

8. Combine water, sugar, and salt, and bring to a boil.

9. Combine cornstarch and water, and stir until smooth. Add gradually to boiling mixture. Cook at medium heat, stirring constantly, until thick and clear. Remove from heat.

10. Fold berries and butter or margarine carefully into thickened mixture.

11. Pour 3 cups filling into each unbaked 9-inch pie shell. Cover with top crust and seal edges.

12. Bake at 425 degrees for 45 minutes or until lightly browned. (Bake at 400 degrees in a convection oven.)

13. Cut eight wedges per pie.

▪ Freezing Instructions

Freeze after Step 11, prior to baking. Wrap pies in plastic wrap prior to freezing. To bake, remove from freezer and unwrap. Bake in preheated 425 degree oven for one hour or until lightly browned.

Peach Pie Filling

Yield: fruit for 13 pies

■ Ingredients

15 pounds (45 cups) peaches, thinly sliced

4 pounds (9 ⅓ cups) white sugar

6 ounces (¾ cup 1 teaspoon) cornstarch

4 ounces (¾ cup 2 teaspoons) minute
 tapioca (quick-cook tapioca)

⅒ ounce (2 teaspoons) ground nutmeg

■ Directions

1. Place sliced peaches in a bowl with sugar, cornstarch, tapioca, and nutmeg. Toss until evenly coated and sugar is dissolved.

2. Transfer peaches to a 9-inch foil-lined pie plate. Cover with another piece of foil, and freeze immediately to prevent peaches from discoloring. Once frozen solid, remove peaches from pie plate, with foil, and transfer to a zipper locked plastic bag for later use.

3. When ready to use, line a pie plate with prepared crust, and place frozen peaches on top.

4. Preheat oven to 450 degrees. (Bake at 400 degrees in a convection oven.)

5. Bake in the preheated oven on the bottom rack for 20 minutes.

6. Lower heat to 350 degrees, and continue baking for 30 to 35 minutes.

■ Freezing Instructions

Place 5 to 6 cups of cooled filling in a freezer bag. Freeze. Allow to thaw in refrigerator overnight before using for a pie.

Pumpkin Pie

Serving size: 1 piece

■ Ingredients

13 counts piecrust (*see recipe earlier in this chapter*)

3 ⅝ pounds (2 quarts ¼ cup) granulated sugar

1 ⅛ ounce (1 tablespoon) salt

6 ⅝ ounces (1 ½ cups) general-purpose wheat flour

8 ounces (3 ⅜ cups) dry nonfat milk

1 ½ ounces (¼ cup 2 ⅓ tablespoons) ground cinnamon

⅜ ounce (1 tablespoon) ground nutmeg

⅓ ounce (1 tablespoon) ground ginger

10 ½ pounds (1 gallon ⅞ quart) canned pumpkin, packed

9 ⅜ pounds (1 gallon ½ quart) water

2 ⅓ pounds (1 quart ⅜ cup) whole fresh eggs

■ Directions

1. Prepare dough for 13 single crust pies as described in pie dough recipe earlier this chapter (half the given recipe).

2. Combine sugar, salt, flour, milk, cinnamon, nutmeg, and ginger in mixing bowl.

3. Add pumpkin to dry ingredients; mix at low speed until well blended. Mixture must set for one hour under refrigeration 41 degrees or lower.

4. Add water and eggs, and mix at low speed until well blended.

5. Pour 3 ¾ cups filling into each unbaked pie shell.

6. Bake at 375 degrees for 50 to 55 minutes or until center is firm. (Bake at 350 degrees in a convection oven.) Cool thoroughly.

7. Cut eight wedges per pie.

■ Freezing Instructions

Cover cooked and cooled pie with aluminum foil. Place pie in plastic wrap, and freeze immediately. Allow to thaw overnight in refrigerator before serving.

Pecan Pie

Serving size: 1 piece
Recipe yields 13 9-inch pie pans

■ Ingredients

13 counts piecrust (*see recipe earlier in this chapter*)

6 pounds (2 quarts 3¼ cups) whole fresh eggs

4⅞ pounds (2 quarts 3 cups) granulated sugar

12 ounces (1½ cups) melted butter

11⅝ pounds (1 gallon) light corn syrup

1⅞ ounces (¼ cups ⅓ tablespoon) vanilla extract

1½ ounces (2⅓ tablespoons) salt

2½ pounds chopped pecans

■ Directions

1. Prepare dough for 13 single crust pies as described in pie dough recipe earlier this chapter (half the given recipe).

2. Place eggs in mixer bowl, and add sugar gradually while beating at low speed. Add butter or margarine, and mix thoroughly.

3. Add corn syrup, vanilla, and salt to mixture and beat at low speed until smooth.

4. Place ¾ cup pecans into each unbaked pie shell.

5. Pour 2¾ cups filling over pecans in each 9-inch pie pan.

6. Bake at 350 degrees for 35 minutes or until filling is set. (Bake at 325 degrees in a convection oven.)

7. Refrigerate until ready to serve.

8. Cut eight slices per pie.

9. Hold for service at 41 degrees or lower.

■ Freezing Instructions

Cover cooked and cooled pie with aluminum foil. Place pie in plastic wrap, and freeze immediately. Allow to thaw overnight in refrigerator before serving.

Conclusion

This book has taken you through the process of preparing to shop, cook, preserve, and serve large amounts of food. Whether you are cooking for a large gathering of friends and family or you plan on stocking your freezer for those times when you need a quick, wholesome, home-cooked meal but just do not have time to cook, everything you need to know has been provided to get you started. This book guided you through every aspect of cooking in bulk to make it as manageable as cooking regular-sized meals. The book detailed all the essential appliances and utensils you need in your kitchen, as well as how to take inventory of the supplies and foods you already have. You have been provided with tips so you know where and how to do your grocery shopping. In addition to these basic details, you have learned everything you need to know on cooking day, from planning, to cooking, cooling, properly storing, and serving your meals. Once you are ready to eat your frozen meal, you know how to thaw and reheat each recipe and how to detect foods gone bad — which probably will not happen if you follow the simple instructions in this book.

101 Recipes for Preparing Food in Bulk

The recipes included here offer a wide range of dishes and food types, giving you a good basis for menu experimentation and expansion. Even if you just prepare and can or freeze a large quantity of chicken, beef, or vegetable stock, a variety of good home-cooked meals can be just minutes away.

The following appendices offer still more useful information on the topic of preparing food in bulk. Take your time to become familiar with everything this book has to offer before you get started. The resources, charts, and safety information offered here are a great help.

Enjoy your cooking, and enjoy your meals. Bon appétit.

Conversion Charts

Throughout this section, you will find equivalency charts that can be useful to use as you begin your bulk cooking way of life. The charts featured throughout this section will show you conversions, how long things last, and easy multiplication charts so you do not have to take the time to figure out how much you need when you are doubling your chosen recipe.

Multiplication Chart

1	2	3	4	5	6
⅛ tsp	¼ tsp	¼ + ⅛ tsp	½ tsp	½ + ⅛ tsp	¾ tsp
¼ tsp	½ tsp	¾ tsp	1 tsp	1 ¼ tsp	1 ½ tsp
½ tsp	1 tsp	1 ½ tsp	2 tsp	2 ½ tsp	1 tbsp
1 tsp	2 tsp	1 tbsp	1 tbsp + 1 tsp	1 tbsp + 2 tsp	2 tbsp
1 ⅛ tsp	2 ¼ tsp	1 tbsp + ⅜ tsp	1 tbsp + 1 ½ tsp	1 tbsp + 2 ½ tsp + ⅛ tsp	2 tbsp + ¾ tsp

101 Recipes for Preparing Food in Bulk

1	2	3	4	5	6
1¼ tsp	2½ tsp	1 tbsp + ¾ tsp	1 tbsp + 2 tsp	2 tbsp + ¼ tsp	2 tbsp + 1½ tsp
1½ tsp	1 tbsp	1 tbsp + 1½ tsp	2 tbsp	2 tbsp + 1½ tsp	3 tbsp
2 tsp	1 tbsp + 1 tsp	2 tbsp	2 tbsp + 2 tsp	3 tbsp + 1 tsp	¼ cup
1 tbsp	2 tbsp	3 tbsp	¼ cup	¼ cup + 1 tbsp	¼ cup + 2 tbsp
1½ tbsp	3 tbsp	¼ cup + 1½ tsp	¼ cup + 2 tbsp	¼ cup + 3½ tbsp	½ cup + 1 tbsp
2 tbsp	¼ cup	¼ cup + 2 tbsp	½ cup	½ cup + 2 tbsp	¾ cup
2½ tbsp	⅓ cup	¼ cup + 3½ tbsp	½ cup + 2 tbsp	¾ cup + 1½ tsp	¾ cup + 3 tbsp
3 tbsp	¼ cup + 2 tbsp	½ cup + 1 tbsp	¾ cup	¾ cup + 3 tbsp	1 cup + 2 tbsp
3½ tbsp	¼ cup + 3 tbsp	⅔ cup	¾ cup + 2 tbsp	1 cup + 1½ tbsp	1⅓ cup
¼ cup	½ cup	¾ cup	1 cup	1¼ cup	1½ cups
⅓ cup	⅔ cup	1 cup	1⅓ cup	1⅔ cups	2 cups
½ cup	1 cup	1½ cups	2 cups	2½ cups	3 cups
⅔ cup	1⅓ cups	2 cups	2⅔ cups	3⅓ cups	4 cups
¾ cup	1½ cups	2¼ cups	3 cups	3¾ cups	4½ cups
1 cup	2 cups	3 cups	4 cups	5 cups	6 cups
1¼ cups	2½ cups	3¾ cups	5 cups	6¼ cups	7½ cups
1⅓ cups	2⅔ cups	4 cups	5⅓ cups	6⅔ cups	8 cups
1½ cups	3 cups	4½ cups	6 cups	7½ cups	9 cups

Appendix A: Conversion Charts

1	2	3	4	5	6
1 ⅔ cups	3 ⅓ cups	5 cups	6 ⅔ cups	8 cups	9 ⅔ cups
1 ¾ cups	3 ½ cups	5 ¼ cups	7 cups	8 ¾ cups	10 ½ cups
2 cups	4 cups	6 cups	8 cups	10 cups	12 cups
2 ¼ cups	4 ½ cups	6 ¾ cups	9 cups	11 ¼ cups	13 ½ cups
2 ½ cups	5 cups	7 ½ cups	10 cups	12 ½ cups	15 cups
2 ⅔ cups	5 ⅓ cups	8 cups	10 ⅔ cups	13 ⅓ cups	16 cups
2 ¾ cups	5 ½ cups	8 ¼ cups	11 cups	13 ¾ cups	16 ½ cups
3 cups	6 cups	9 cups	12 cups	15 cups	18 cups
3 ¼ cups	6 ½ cups	9 ¾ cups	13 cups	16 ¼ cups	19 ½ cups
3 ⅓ cups	6 ⅔ cups	10 cups	13 ⅓ cups	16 ⅔ cups	20 cups
3 ½ cups	7 cups	10 ½ cups	14 cups	17 ½ cups	21 cups
3 ⅔ cups	7 ⅓ cups	11 cups	14 ⅔ cups	18 ⅓ cups	22 cups
3 ¾ cups	7 ½ cups	11 ¼ cups	15 cups	18 ¾ cups	22 ½ cups
4 cups	8 cups	12 cups	16 cups	20 cups	24 cups
4 ¼ cups	8 ½ cups	12 ¾ cups	17 cups	21 ¼ cups	25 ½ cups
4 ⅓ cups	8 ⅔ cups	13 cups	17 ⅓ cups	21 ⅔ cups	26 cups
4 ½ cups	9 cups	13 ½ cups	18 cups	22 ½ cups	27 cups
4 ⅔ cups	9 ⅓ cups	14 cups	18 ⅔ cups	23 ⅓ cups	28 cups
4 ¾ cups	9 ½ cups	14 ¼ cups	19 cups	23 ¾ cups	28 ½ cups
5 cups	10 cups	15 cups	20 cups	25 cups	30 cups

Equivalency Charts

Assorted Baking Ingredients & Measures

Dry Measure	Pinch = a little less than ⅛ teaspoon
	3 tsp = 1 tbsp
	2 tbsp = 1 oz = ⅛ cup
	4 tbsp = 2 oz = ¼ cup
	5⅓ tbsp = 2.7 oz = ⅓ cup
	8 tbsp = 4 oz = ½ cup
	10⅔ tbsp = 5.4 oz = ⅔ cup
	12 tbsp = 6 oz = ¾ cup
	16 tbsp = 8 oz = 1 cup
	2 cups = 1 pint
	4 cups = 1 quart
	4 quarts = 1 gallon
	16 oz = 1 lb
Bread Cubes and Crumbs	4 slices of bread = 2 cups fresh soft crumbs
	4 slices of bread = ¾ cup dry bread crumbs
	6 oz dried bread crumbs = 1 scant cup
	16 oz loaf = 14 cup one inch cubes
Cereal	21 oz box corn flakes = 7 cups
	2 cups of flakes = ¾ cup crumbs
	15 oz box crisp rice cereal = 11 cups
	13 oz box of crisp rice = 6 cup crumbs
	42 oz box rolled oats = 10 cups

Assorted Baking Ingredients & Measures

Flours/Meal	1 lb white flour = 3 ½ cups or 4 cups sifted
	1 lb whole wheat flour = 3 ¼ cups or 3 ½ cups sifted
	1 cup flour = 4 oz
	14 oz cracker meal = 3 ¾ cups
Leavening Agents	16 oz baking soda = 2 ⅓ cups = 37 tbsp
	16 oz baking powder = 2 ⅓ cups = 37 tbsp
	14 oz can baking powder = 1 ¾ cups = 28 tbsp
	5 ½ oz baking powder = 1 cup
	.25 oz active dry yeast = 1 tbsp
	1 oz active dry yeast = 3 ⅓ tbsp
	16 oz active dry yeast = 3 ⅓ cup
	.60 oz compressed yeast = 4 tsp
Cracker and Cookie Crumbs	28 soda or saltine crackers = 1 cup crumbs
	16 oz crackers = 6 cup fine crumbs
	15 square graham crackers = 1 cup crumbs
	16 oz graham crackers = 70 crackers
	1 roll snack crackers = approx. 1 ⅓ cups crumbs
	16 oz snack crackers = approx. 5 ⅓ cup crumbs
	24 round butter crackers = 1 cup fine crumbs
	14 oz box cracker meal = 3 ¾ cups crumbs
	22 vanilla wafers = 1 cup crumbs
	14 Oreo cookies = 1 cup crumbs

Assorted Baking Ingredients & Measures

Liquid Measure	A dash = a few drops
	3 tsp = 1 tbsp
	2 tbsp = 1 oz
	4 tbsp = 2 oz = ¼ cup
	5⅓ tbsp = 2.7 oz = ⅓ cup
	8 tbsp = 4 oz = ½ cup
	10⅔ tbsp = 6 oz = ¾ cup
	16 tbsp = 8 oz = 1 cup
	2 cup = 1 pint = ½ quart
	4 cup = 2 pints = 1 quart
	4 quarts = 16 cups = 1 gallon = 128 oz
Butter/Margarine/ Shortening	1 tbsp = ½ oz = ⅛ stick
	4 tbsp = 2 oz = ¼ cup = ½ stick
	8 tbsp = 4 oz = ½ cup = 1 stick
	16 tbsp = 8 oz = 1 cup = 2 sticks
	32 tbsp = 16 oz = 2 cup = 4 sticks = 1 lb
	3 lb can of shortening = 6 cups
Sweeteners	12 oz honey = 1 cup
	16 oz honey = 1½ cups
	16 oz corn syrup = 1½ cups
	11 oz molasses = 1 cup
	16 oz white sugar = 2⅓ cups
	11 oz maple syrup = 1 cup
	4 lb white sugar = 10 cups
	16 oz brown sugar = 2¼ cups packed
	16 oz powdered sugar = 3½ cups

Appendix A: Conversion Charts

Fruits	
Apples	1lb = 3 medium
	1 medium = 1 cup chopped
Applesauce	16 oz = 2 cups
Bananas	1 lb = 3 medium = 2 ½ cups diced, or 3 cups sliced
	1 medium = ⅓ cup mashed
Strawberries/Raspberries	1 lb = 2 cups sliced
Blueberries	1 lb = 3 cups
Cranberries	1 lb = 4 cups
Limes	1 medium = 1 ½ to 2 tbsp fresh juice
Raisins	1 lb = 3 ½ cups
	6 oz = approx. 1 cup
Pineapple	1 lb = 2 ½ cups diced
Grapes	1 lb = 2 ½ cups
Melon	1 lb = 1 cup diced
Lemons	1 medium = 3 tbsp juice, or 1 tbsp grated rind
Oranges	1 = ⅓ cup fresh juice

Vegetables	
Carrots	1 lb = 3 cups sliced = 2 cups diced = 6 to 8 medium
	1 medium carrot = ½ cup grated
Onions	1 lb = 3 medium = 3 cups sliced, or chopped
	1 medium = 1 cup chopped = ⅔ cup sautéed
	10 oz frozen peppers, and onion = 2 ¼ cups
Green Onions	7 medium green onions = ½ cup sliced
Green Beans	1 lb fresh = 3 cups = 2 ½ cups cooked
Broccoli	1 lb fresh, or frozen = 2 cups florets

Vegetables

Cabbage	1 lb = 4 cups shredded
Cauliflower	1 lb = 1 ½ cups cooked = 3 cups florets
Celery	1 medium bunch = 2 ½ to 3 cups sautéed
	1 medium bunch = 3 cups diced = 3 ½ cups sliced
	3 large ribs = approx. 1 ½ cups diced
	1 cup diced = ⅔ cup sautéed
	1 rib = ½ cup sliced, or diced
Corn	2 to 3 fresh ears = 1 cup kernels
	1 lb frozen = 3 cups kernels
Peas	4 oz = 1 cup
	10 oz frozen = 1 ½ cups
Potatoes	1 lb = 3 medium = 2 ¾ cups diced = 3 cups sliced
	1 lb = 2 cups mashed
	5 lbs = 10 cups diced, or mashed
	1 lb frozen wedges = 3 cups cooked
	1 lb hash brown potatoes = 2 ½ cups cooked
Sweet Potatoes	1 lb = 3 medium = 2 ½ to 3 cups diced
Spinach, and other greens	1 lb raw = 10 to 12 cups torn = 1 cup cooked
	10 oz frozen = 1 ½ lb fresh = 1 ½ cups cooked
Sweet Bell Peppers	1 medium = ½ cup finely chopped
	1 lb = 5 medium = 3 ½ cups diced
Mushrooms	4 oz fresh = 1 cup whole = ½ cup cooked
	1 lb = approx. 20 large, or 40 medium, whole
Tomatoes	1 lb = 4 small = 1 ½ cups cooked
Garlic	1 medium clove = ½ tsp minced
Fennel	1 lb bulb = 3 cups, sliced

Vegetables

Lettuce	1 medium head = 4 to 6 cups torn
Water Chestnuts	8 oz sliced, or whole = 1 cup, drained
Frozen Vegetables	10 oz package = 1 ½ cups
	¼ cup buttermilk powder = 1 cup buttermilk

Dairy Products

Shredded and Cubed Cheese	16 oz = 4 cup cubed, or shredded
Heavy Whipping Cream	1 cup, or 8 oz carton = 2 cups whipped
Parmesan or Romano Cheese	4 oz = 1 cup cubed, or shredded
	6 oz = 1 cup
	16 oz = 2 ⅔ cups
	24 oz = 3 cups
Cottage Cheese	6 oz = 1 cup, 16 oz = 2 ⅔ cups
Sour Cream	16 oz = 1 ¾ cups
	9 oz = 1 cup
Cream Cheese	3 oz = 6 tbsp, or approx. ⅓ cup
	8 oz = 1 cup
	1 lb, or 16 oz = 2 cups
Sweetened Condensed Milk	14 oz can = 1 ¼ cups
Evaporated Milk	14 ½ oz can = 1 ⅔ cups
	6 oz = ⅔ cup
Dry Milk Powder	16 oz = 4 cups dry, or 4 to 5 quarts of liquid
Buttermilk Powder	12 oz = 3 ¾ quarts of liquid buttermilk

Meats

Bacon	8 slices = ½ cup cooked, and crumbled
	16 oz = approx. 18 slices
Beef	1 lb ground = 2 ½ cups browned
	10 lbs ground = 25 cups browned
	1 lb beef cuts = 3 ½ cups sliced
	1 ½ lb roast = 3 cups cooked, cubed
Bulk Sausage	1 lb raw = 2 ½ cup cooked and crumbled
Chicken, boneless, skinless	7 ½ lbs raw = approx. 25 pieces
	1 lb raw = 2 cups raw, ground = 2 ⅔ cups raw, diced
	5 lbs raw = 12 cups cooked, diced
	1 large breasts = ¾ cup cooked, diced
	2 ½ lbs = 7 to 8 large pieces
Chicken Thighs	5 lbs = approx. 25 pieces
Whole Chicken	2 ½ lb chicken 2 ½ cups cooked, diced
	3 ½ to 4 lb = 4 cups, cooked, diced
	4 ½ to 5 lb = 6 cups, cooked, diced
Crab Meat (real, or imitation)	1 lb cooked, and boned = 2 cups
Ham	1 lb whole ham = 2 ½ cups ground ham
	1 lb whole ham = 3 cups, cubed
Turkey Breast	5 lb raw = 10 cups cooked, diced
	1 lb drumstick, or thigh = 1 ⅛ cups diced
Whole Turkey	Each pound = approx. 1 cup cooked
Tuna Fish	6 oz = ¾ cup, lightly packed
Lamb	1 lb chops = 2 chops

Dry Beans/Grains/Pasta/Nuts

Lentils	6 oz dry = 1 cup
Kidney Beans	11 oz dry = 1 cup dry = 3 cups cooked
	15 oz can = 1 ¾ cups
	16 oz dry = 5 cups cooked
Barley	¾ cups pearl barley = 3 cups cooked
	1 cup quick cooking barley = 2 ½ cups cooked
Long Grain White Rice	16 oz dry = 2 ½ cups dry = 10 cups cooked
	1 cup dry = 7 oz dry = 3 cups cooked
Quick Cooking Brown Rice	1 cup dry = 2 cups cooked
	12 oz box = 5 ⅓ cups fully cooked = 4 ½ cups half cooked
White Converted Rice	1 cup dry = 4 cups cooked
Couscous	1 cup dry = 2 ½ to 3 cups cooked
Oatmeal	42 oz dry = 10 cups dry
Spaghetti	2 oz = 1 serving = ½ inch diameter dry portion
	16 oz = 4 to 5 cups dry = 10 cups cooked
Elbow Macaroni	4 oz dry = 1 cup dry = 3 cups cooked
	16 oz dry= 4 cups dry =12 cups
Tiny Pasta (acini pepe, orzo, ditalini, alphabets)	8 oz dry = 1 ⅓ cups dry
Pecans	6 oz pieces = 1 ½ cups

1 oz of Weight to Measurement of Herbs and Spices

Allspice, ground = 4 tbsp	Mustard, dry, ground = 6 tbsp + 1 tsp
Basil = ½ cup	Nutmeg, ground = 5 tbsp

1 oz of Weight to Measurement of Herbs and Spices

Bay Leaf, whole = 7 tbsp	Onion Powder = 4 ½ tsp
Black Pepper, ground = ½ cup	Oregano = 6 tbsp
Celery Seed = ¼ cup	Paprika = 5 tbsp
Chili Pepper = ½ cup + 1 ½ tsp	Parsley Flakes = ½ cup + 1 ½ tsp
Cinnamon = 5 ½ tbsp	Poppy Seeds = 3 ¾ tbsp
Cloves, ground = 5 ½ tbsp	Red Pepper Flakes = ½ cup + 1 ½ tsp
Cumin Seed = 6 tbsp	Rosemary = ½ cup
Curry Powder = 5 ½ tbsp	Sage = ½ cup + 1 ½ tbsp
Dill Weed = 6 tbsp	Savory = 6 ¾ tbsp
Dill Seed = 4 ½ tbsp	Sesame Seed = 5 tbsp
Garlic Powder = 6 ⅓ tbsp	Tarragon = 6 ¾ tbsp
Ginger = 6 tbsp	Thyme = 6 ⅓ tbsp
Marjoram = ½ cup	Turmeric = 5 tbsp

Miscellaneous

Jams/Jellies/Preserves	6 oz = ⅔ cup
	10 oz = about 1 cup
	16 oz = 94 tsp = 32 tbsp = 2 cups
Nuts	16 oz = 4 cups
	2 oz = ½ cup
Cocoa Powder	8 oz = 2 cups
	16 oz = 4 cups
Chocolate Chips	6 oz = 1 cup
Shredded Coconut	16 oz = 5 cups
Peanut Butter	16 oz = 1 ¾ cups
	18 oz = 2 cups

Miscellaneous	
Ice Cubes	11 cubes = 1 cup liquid
Mayonnaise	1 quart = 32 oz = 4 cups
Marshmallows	16 oz = 9 cups
Broth	10 oz can = 2 ½ cups

Freezer Time Chart

Food	Freezer Life
Baked Goods:	
Bread dough, yeast unbaked	2 weeks
Baked bread	12 months
Rolls	
Unbaked	2 weeks
Half baked	12 months
Fully baked	12-15 months
Muffins	
Unbaked	2 weeks
Baked	3 months
Waffle/pancake batter	2-4 weeks
Waffle/pancake batter cooked	6 months
Dairy Products	
Butter - Salted	3 months
Butter - Unsalted	6 months
Margarine	5 months
Hard cheese	3 months
Cream cheese	3 months

Food	Freezer Life
Milk	1 month
Eggs, raw and out of shell	6 month
Produce	
All vegetables	12 months
Exceptions	
Asparagus	8-12 months
Onions	6 months
Jerusalem artichokes	3 months
Potatoes	3-6 months
Beets	6 months
Green beans	8-12 months
Leeks	6 months
Winter squash	10 months
Mushrooms	8 months
Corn on the cob	8-10 months
Herbs	6 months
Vegetable Purees	6-12 months
Prepared Vegetable Dishes	3 months
Miscellaneous	
Pasta, cooked	3-4 months
Pasta, mixed into dishes	3-4 months
Rice, cooked	3-4 months
Rice, mixed into dishes	3-4 months
Beef	
Raw ground beef/stew beef	3-4 months
Fresh beef steak	6-12 months

Appendix A: Conversion Charts

Food	Freezer Life
Fresh beef roast	6-12 months
Fresh beef sausage	3-4 months
Smoked beef links or patties	1-2 months
Cooked beef dishes	2-3 months
Fresh beef in marinade	2-3 months
Pork	
Ground pork	3-4 months
Fresh pork sausage	1-2 months
Fresh pork chops	4-6 months
Fresh pork roast	4-6 months
Bacon	1 month
Pepperoni	1-2 months
Smoked pork links or patties	1-2 months
Canned ham	Don't freeze
Whole	1-2 months
Half or slices	1-2 months
Pre-stuffed pork chops	Don't freeze
Cooked pork chops	2-4 months
Uncooked pork chops	2-4 months
Uncooked casseroles w/ham	1 month
Cooked casseroles w/ham	1 month
Fresh pork in marinade	2-3 months
Poultry	
Fresh ground turkey	2-3 months
Fresh turkey sausage	1-2 months
Fresh whole turkey	12 months

Food	Freezer Life
Chicken or turkey	
Fresh pieces	9 months
Cooked pieces	4 months
Cooked nuggets	3-4 months
Pre-stuffed chicken breast	Don't freeze
Cooked poultry dishes	4-6 months
Fresh chicken in marinade	2-3 months
Fish	
Fresh pieces	6-12 months
Cooked pieces	2-3 months
Cooked fish dishes	2-3 months
Fish in marinade	2-3 months
Miscellaneous	
Vegetable or meat soups/stews	2-3 months
Ground veal and lamb	3-4 months
Gravy and meat broths	2-3 months
Cooked meat pies	3-4 months
Cooked meatloaf	1-3 months

APPENDIX B

Information & Resources

From *The Complete Guide to Food Preservation: Step-by-Step Instructions on How to Freeze, Dry, Can, and Preserve Food* by Angela Williams Duea

Altman, Elissa. *Big Food: Amazing Ways to Cook, Store, Freeze, and Serve Everything You Buy in Bulk*. United States of America: Holtzbrinck Publishers, 2005.

Garcia, Bonnie, Howell, Vanda, and Martinez, Susie. *Don't Panic- Dinner's in the Freezer: Great Tasting Meals You Can Make Ahead*. Grand Rapids: Revell, 2007.

Lagerborg, Mary Beth, Wilson, Mimi. *Once-a-Month Cooking*. New York: St. Martin's Press, 2007.

Larsen, Linda. *The Everything Meals For A Month Cookbook: 300 Smart Recipes to Help You Plan Ahead, Save Time, and Stay on a Budget*. Avon: Adams Media, 2005.

Neville, Katie, and Tkacsik, Lindsay. *Fix, Freeze, Feast: Prepare in Bulk and Enjoy by the Serving*. North Adams: Storey Publishing, 2007.

Molt, Mary. *Food for Fifty*. Upper Saddle River: Simon & Schuster, 1997.

Slagle, Nanci. *The Freezer Cooking Manual From 30 Day Gourmet: A Month of Meals Made Easy*. Brownsburg: 30 Day Gourmet Press, 2008.

Canning

The following resources and canning experts can help you with canning supplies, questions, advice, and other guidelines.

National Presto Industries
(Presto canners, parts)
(800) 877-0441

National Center for Home Food Preservation (**www.uga.edu/nchfp**) Guidelines posted to this site have been scientifically tested to make sure that foods that are preserved at home are safe to eat.

Wisconsin Aluminum Foundry Company
(Makers of All-American canners)
(920) 682-8627

Putting Food by Ruth Hertzberg

Pressure Cooker Outlet
(Presto, Mirro, All American & Maitres Pressure Cookers & Parts; canning books and supplies)
(800) 251-8824

Canning supplies

Alltrista Corp.
(Manufactures Ball and Kerr canning lids, produces the Ball Blue Book of canning and other publications); Hotline: (800) 240-3340; Order: (800) 392-2575

Kitchen Krafts
(Free catalog)
(800) 776-0575 or (563) 535-8000

Home Canning Supply
(Free catalog)
(800) 354-4070

Lip Smackin' Jams and Jellies by Amy and Dave Butler
(**www.amybutlerdesign.com**)

Freezing

The National Center for Home Food Preservation
(**www.uga.edu/nchfp/how/freeze**)

USDA Food Storage and Inspection Service
(**www.fsis.usda.gov/home/index.asp**)

APPENDIX C

More Information on Canning

Canning is one of the most popular preservation methods for food. However, it can be much more labor-intensive than freezing or drying foods, and you will need special equipment to process the food correctly. The benefits to canning, in spite of the extra trouble, are that many foods taste better when they are canned rather than frozen. Some produce, such as plums, apples, and carrots, develop a richer, complex taste in the canning process. In addition, your freezer usually has a small amount of room for storage, whereas canned foods can be piled up in a pantry, basement, or closet for years. Finally, there are some foods, such as pickles, that cannot complete the fermenting process in a freezer.

A Glossary of Canning Terms

Acid foods: Foods that contain enough acid to result in a pH of 4.6 or lower. Includes all fruits except figs; most tomatoes; fermented and pickled vegetables; relishes; and jams, jellies, and marmalades. Acidic foods may be processed in boiling water.

Altitude: The vertical elevation of a location above sea level.

Ascorbic acid: The chemical name for vitamin C. Lemon juice contains large quantities of ascorbic acid and is commonly used to prevent browning of peeled, light-colored fruits and vegetables.

Bacteria: A large group of one-celled microorganisms widely distributed in nature. See microorganism.

Blancher: A 6- to 8-quart lidded pot designed with a fitted perforated basket to hold food in boiling water, or with a fitted rack to steam foods. Useful for loosening skins on fruits to be peeled, or for heating foods to be hot packed.

Boiling-water canner: A large standard-sized lidded kettle with jar rack, designed for heat-processing 7 quarts or 8 to 9 pints in boiling water.

Botulism: An illness caused by eating toxin produced by growth of *Clostridium botulinum* bacteria in moist, low-acid food, containing less than 2 percent oxygen, and stored between 40 and 120 degrees. Proper heat processing destroys this bacterium in canned food. Freezer temperatures inhibit its growth in frozen food. Low moisture controls its growth in dried food. High oxygen controls its growth in fresh foods.

Canning: A method of preserving food in airtight, vacuum-sealed containers and heat processing sufficiently to enable storing the food at normal home temperatures.

Canning salt: Also called pickling salt, this is regular table salt without the anticaking or iodine additives.

Citric acid: A form of acid that can be added to canned foods. It increases the acidity of low-acid foods and may improve the flavor and color.

Cold pack: Canning procedure in which jars are filled with raw food. "Raw pack" is the preferred term for describing this practice. "Cold pack" is often used incorrectly to refer to foods that are open-kettle canned or jars that are heat-processed in boiling water.

Enzymes: Proteins in food that accelerate many flavor, color, texture, and nutritional changes, especially when food is cut, sliced, crushed, bruised, and exposed to air. Proper blanching or hot-packing practices destroy enzymes and improve food quality.

Exhausting: Removing air from within and around food and from jars and canners. Blanching exhausts air from live food tissues. Exhausting or venting pressure canners is necessary to prevent a risk of botulism in low-acid canned foods.

Fermentation: Changes in food caused by intentional growth of bacteria, yeast, or mold. Native bacteria ferment natural sugars to lactic acid, a major flavoring and preservative in sauerkraut and in naturally fermented dills. Alcohol, vinegar, and some dairy products are also fermented foods.

Headspace: The unfilled space above food or liquid in jars. Allows for food expansion as jars are heated, and for forming vacuums as jars cool.

Heat processing: Treating jars with sufficient heat to enable storing food at normal home temperatures.

Hermetic seal: An absolutely airtight container seal that prevents air or microorganisms from re-entering into packaged foods.

Hot pack: Heating raw food in boiling water or steam and filling it hot into jars.

Low-acid foods: Foods that contain very little acid and have a pH above 4.6. The acidity in these foods is insufficient to prevent the growth of the bacterium Clostridium botulinum. Vegetables, some tomatoes, figs, all meats, fish, seafoods, and some dairy foods are low acid. To control all risks of botulism, jars of these foods must be (1) heat processed in a pressure canner, or (2) acidified to a pH of 4.6 or lower before processing in boiling water.

Microorganisms: Independent organisms of microscopic size, including bacteria, yeast, and mold. When alive in a suitable environment, they grow rapidly and may divide or reproduce every ten to 30 minutes, reaching high populations very quickly. Undesirable microorganisms cause disease and food spoilage. Microorganisms are sometimes intentionally added to ferment foods, make antibiotics, and for other reasons.

Mold: A fungus-type microorganism whose growth on food is usually visible and colorful. Molds may grow on many foods, including acidic foods like jams and jellies and canned fruits. It is recommended to use heat processing and sealing practices to prevent mold growth on these foods.

Mycotoxins: Toxins produced by the growth of some molds on foods.

Open-kettle canning: A non-recommended canning method. Food is supposedly adequately heat processed in a covered kettle, and then filled hot and sealed in sterile jars. Foods canned this way have low vacuums or too much air, which permits rapid loss of quality in foods. Moreover, these foods often spoil because they become recontaminated while the jars are being filled.

Pasteurization: Heating a specific food enough to destroy the most heat-resistant pathogenic or disease-causing microorganism known to be associated with that food.

pH: A measure of acidity or alkalinity. Values range from 0 to 14. A food is neutral when its pH is 7.0, lower values are increasingly more acidic; higher values are increasingly more alkaline.

Pickling: The practice of adding enough vinegar or lemon juice to a low-acid food to lower its pH to 4.6 or lower. Properly pickled foods may be safely heat processed in boiling water.

Pressure canner: A specifically designed metal kettle with a lockable lid used for heat processing low-acid food. These canners have jar racks, one or more safety devices, systems for exhausting air, and a way to measure or control pressure. Canners with 16- to 23-quart capacity are common. The minimum volume of canner that can be used is one that will contain 4-quart jars. Using pressure saucepans with smaller capacities is not recommended.

Raw pack: The practice of filling jars with raw, unheated food. Acceptable for canning low-acid foods, but allows more rapid quality losses in acidic foods heat processed in boiling water.

Spice bag: A closeable fabric bag used to extract spice flavors in pickling solution.

Style of pack: Form of canned food, such as whole, sliced, piece, juice, or sauce. The term may also be used to reveal whether food is filled raw or hot into jars.

Vacuum: The state of negative pressure. Reflects how thoroughly air is removed from within a jar of processed food — the higher the vacuum, the less air left in the jar.

Yeasts: A group of microorganisms that reproduce by budding. They are used in fermenting some foods and in leavening breads.

The Proper Techniques of Canning

The goal of proper canning is to remove oxygen, destroy enzymes, and kill harmful microorganisms such as mold, bacteria, and yeast. Proper canning will also produce jars with a strong vacuum seal that will prevent liquid from leaking out or microorganisms from getting into the food. Properly canned foods can last for several years. Proper canning practices include:

- ▸ Selecting fresh, undamaged foods
- ▸ Carefully inspecting and washing fruits and vegetables
- ▸ Peeling fresh foods, if necessary
- ▸ Using the hot packing method where appropriate
- ▸ Adding acids (lemon juice or vinegar) to foods that need acid-packing
- ▸ Following recipes and directions precisely
- ▸ Using clean jars and lids that seal properly
- ▸ Using the right processing time when canning jars in a boiling-water or pressure canner.

Collectively, these practices remove oxygen; destroy enzymes; prevent the growth of undesirable bacteria, yeasts, and molds; and help form a high vacuum in jars. Good vacuums form tight seals that keep liquid in and air and microorganisms out. Most health-related problems arise when people do not follow the canning directions properly. Today's canning experts agree that old methods of canning and outdated cookbooks give unhealthy or inaccurate directions for food safety. However, The Center for Home Food Preservation, working with the University of Georgia, interviewed home canners and found that they often used unsafe directions or instructions solely from friends or relatives.

Different methods are now considered best for different types of foods. The USDA recommends water bath or pressure-canning methods when preserving high-acid products such as pickles, fruits, and tomatoes. In the past, people canned these products with open-kettle canning, but experts no longer considered this a safe canning method. Oven and microwave procedures are also considered unsafe.

Courtesy of the USDA — *Equipment and methods not recommended*

Open-kettle canning and processing freshly filled jars in conventional ovens, microwave ovens, and dishwashers are not recommended because these practices do not prevent all risks of spoilage. Steam canners are not recommended because processing times for use with current models have not been adequately researched. Because steam canners do not heat foods in the same manner as boiling-water canners, using them with boiling-water process times may result in spoilage. It is not recommended that pressure processes in excess of 15 PSI be applied when using new pressure canning equipment. So-called canning powders are useless as preservatives and do not replace the need for proper heat processing. Jars with wire bails and glass caps make attractive antiques or storage containers for dry food ingredients but are not recommended for use in canning. One-piece zinc porcelain-lined caps also are no longer recommended. Both glass and zinc caps use flat rubber rings for sealing jars, but too often fail to seal properly.

The canning process sterilizes food and then seals the foods so that no contamination can enter the jar. Sterilization happens during the hot water processing, which also creates a vacuum seal in the jar. In the past, many homemakers poured a layer of wax over foods such as jams and preserves before processing the seal. Most experts now consider this unsafe and unnecessary. In fact, modern lids produce a good vacuum seal without this additional step.

The vacuum seal is crucial and is affected by the quality of the lids as well as the proper level of food and liquid in the jar — which is known as headspace. Each type of food has a different headspace depending on the food's shrinkage or swelling during the boiling process. Be sure to follow the directions closely, and use a ruler if you have any doubts. *More information on headspace can be found later in this section.*

Each food has a different processing time to allow enough heat to kill microorganisms. In addition, these times increase with your altitude above sea level because water boils at lower temperatures at higher altitudes. Foods with a lot of acid, such as citrus fruits, tomatoes, and recipes with added vinegar or lemon juice, have an additional antiseptic agent. The acid itself helps to sterilize the foods. Low-acid foods like meat and beans will need a much longer sterilization period.

Canning tools

You will need a few items to can your foods properly. The good news is that most of these items are probably already in your kitchen. Before you get started on a canning recipe, make sure you have the following accessories handy:

Canning supplies that are part of a kit

1. A jar lifter, which is a set of tongs specially made for canning jars with rubber-coated handles to lift hot jars out of the boiling water in the canner.

2. A small-bladed spatula — either plastic or rubber — to push out bubbles from jars before processing. Some instructions say to use a metal knife, but this may cause some fruits to change color.

3. An accurate kitchen timer, measuring cups, and spoons. Canning recipes are very exact, and proper timing and measuring are crucial to your success.

4. Saucepans to cook sauces and warm lids.

5. Colanders to drain.

6. Knives and cutting boards to cut and process fruits and vegetables.

7. Pot holders or mitts to protect hands from hot surfaces.

8. A large spoon for stirring.

9. Towels to use while cooling your canning jars.

Canning jars

Before you start canning any of the sauces or other items you may have created in bulk, you will need to purchase or borrow canning jars. There are still many old-fashioned jars in circulation — perhaps you inherited some from a relative. These could be old, cracked jars or

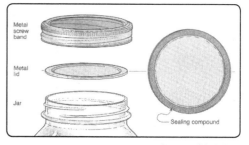

Courtesy of the USDA

ones with a rubber gasket and clasp; these are likely to break during processing, and the clasp-type lids are not as safe for canning as modern jars and lids. Some recycled food containers are safe for use in a water-bath process but cannot stand a pressure canner. Commercial mayonnaise jars are a particular concern due to their lack of heat-tempering and thin walls. They also have narrow rims that prevent a proper seal. Of course, many types of recycled food jars can be used for foods that you will refrigerate and use within a week or two. If you borrow or re-use canning jars, be sure to inspect them for nicks, cracks, or lid wear that could cause

Appendix C: More Information on Canning

breakage — or even explosion in a pressure canner. Jars are safe to reuse if they can accommodate modern, flat canning lids and screw-on rings.

Your best choice is to purchase new jars made especially for canning from grocery stores, hardware stores, and the like. Quart jars are best for larger produce or meat pieces; pint and half-pint sizes are ideal for sauces, condiments, chutneys, jams, and jellies. Jars come in standard and wide-mouth varieties. Many prefer wide-mouth jars that are easier to fill and wash. Regular and wide-mouth Mason-type, threaded, home-canning jars with self-sealing lids are the best choice. They are available in ½ pint, pint, 1 ½ pint, quart, and ½ gallon sizes. The standard jar mouth opening is about 2⅜ inches. Wide-mouth jars have openings of about 3 inches, which makes them easier to fill and empty. You can use half-gallon jars to can very acidic juices. Regular-mouth decorator jelly jars are available in 8- and 12-ounce sizes. With careful use and handling, Mason jars may be reused many times, requiring only new lids each time. When jars and lids are used properly, jar seals and vacuums are excellent, and jar breakage is rare.

Today, safe canning requires the self-sealing, two-piece vacuum lid that can be found anywhere canning jars are purchased. These flat metal lids have a rubber gasket strip molded to a crimped underside. A metal band screws onto the jar to hold the lid in place. When you process the jars in a hot water bath, the compound softens and begins to seal while still allowing air to escape from the jar. When you allow the jars to cool after processing, the lid seals itself and creates a vacuum within the jar. This is why you should never reuse lids, but the metal bands can be removed after canning and used repeatedly. Be sure to check the metal bands for any signs of rust before using, as the rust can prevent a proper seal. Buy only the quantity of lids you will use in a year. To ensure a good seal, carefully follow the manufacturer's directions in preparing lids for use. Examine all metal lids carefully. Do not use old, dented, or deformed lids, or lids with gaps or other defects in the sealing gasket.

Jar cleaning and preparation

Before every use, wash empty jars in hot water with detergent, and rinse well by hand, or wash in a dishwasher. Unrinsed detergent residues may cause unnatural flavors and colors. Jars should be kept hot until you are ready to fill them with food. Submerge the clean empty jars in enough water to cover them in a large stockpot or boiling water canner. Bring the water to a simmer (180 degrees), and keep the jars in the simmering water until it is time to fill them with food. A dishwasher may be used to preheat jars if they are washed and dried on a complete regular cycle. Keep the jars in the closed dishwasher until you are ready to fill them.

Sterile jars and utensils ready for canning

These washing and preheating methods do not sterilize jars. Some used jars may have a white film on the exterior surface caused by mineral deposits. This scale or hard-water film on jars is easy to remove by soaking jars several hours in a solution containing 1 cup of vinegar (5 percent acidity) per gallon of water prior to washing and preheating the jars.

Another method is to put all of the jars, lids, bands, tongs, and any other items that will come into contact with the food into a large pot and boil the items for ten minutes. Keep the sterile items in the pot until you are ready to use them. Do not touch sterilized supplies with your hands or any unsterilized tools — this will contaminate your sterile supplies. If you boil the equipment while you are preparing your foods for packing, the hot-pack foods will go straight into hot jars and minimize stress on the glass.

Canning Guidelines

Hot pack vs. raw pack

When packing food (and any juices or spices) into canning jars, there are two ways you can do it: hot pack or raw pack. To hot pack food, you will boil some kind of liquid, juice, or broth and cook the food slightly before putting it into hot jars. The raw pack method requires you to tightly pack raw food into jars and then cover with boiling water, syrup, juice, or broth to the proper headspace. Each canning recipe will indicate which method is best, though some items can be packed either raw or hot.

The hot pack method works best for firm produce or meats that either need a cooked sauce or will taste best with a processed syrup or broth. In addition, hot-packed foods will

These peppers were hot packed to preserve their bright colors

contain less air, will inactivate enzymes, and will preserve the bright color of the produce. To hot pack foods, fold them into a boiling syrup, juice, or water. Then pack the produce into hot, sterile jars to prevent the glass from cracking, and to eliminate food-borne illnesses. Ladle the juice or broth into the jars until it reaches the required headspace. You may need to tap the jar on a counter or slide a spatula down between the jar and produce to remove any bubbles. Seal the jars, and then process them in a water-bath canner. Because these foods are partially cooked, hot packed produce requires less processing time. Recipes should indicate the proper processing time and the hot pack process.

Raw pack (or cold pack) works best for delicate foods like berries or some types of pickles. Cold packing is quicker and easier, but the processing time is longer. Make sure to pack the produce as tightly as possible into hot, sterile jars. Then pour in the hot syrup, juice, or water to fill spaces and submerge the contents. Again, you may need to tap the jar on a counter or slide a spatula down the insides of the jars to remove any bubbles. Seal the jars, and follow the recipe's directions to process them in a hot water canner.

Illustration courtesy of the USDA

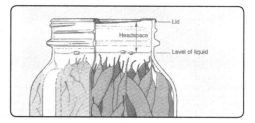

Illustration courtesy of the USDA

Headspace

The space between the food and liquid and the top rim of the jar is called the headspace. Proper headspace is crucial to a good seal. This space will allow the food and air to expand and move while it is heated. The air will expand much

Illustration courtesy of the USDA

more than the food does, and the higher the temperature, the more the air will expand. If you fill the jar too full, the food will swell and spurt out of the jar, ruining the seal. This causes a mess in your canner, too. Even if you wipe off the jar, food may be trapped under the seal and will cause the food to rot. The best remedy is to sterilize the jar and lid and reprocess that jar with the correct headspace.

As the jars cool, the food, liquid, and air begins to contract; this pulls down the lid to create a vacuum seal that protects your food. You have probably noticed the characteristic hiss as you open a jar of food and the vacuum releases. However, if there is too much headspace for the specific food, the product has too much room to set a strong vacuum as the jars cool. Always make sure the lid is concave when fully cooled, as this indicates a good seal.

Canning recipes should always indicate the right amount of headspace. Make sure you follow the instructions carefully. As a general guideline, vegetables and fruits usually need ½ inch of headspace if processed in a boiling water canner. Produce, meat, and other recipes processed in a pressure canner should generally have 1 inch of headspace. Jams and jellies need ¼ inch of headspace.

Altitude adjustments

The canning recipes in this book call for a specific processing time and, with pressure canners, a specific amount of pressure. These instructions are intended for people who are processing food at altitudes ranging from sea level to 1,000 feet above sea level. However, the processing times used at higher altitudes may not be sufficient and can cause the food to spoil. This is because water boils at a lower temperature at higher altitudes; the lower temperature may not be sufficient to destroy all the bacteria and mold.

If you live at a high altitude, you are probably familiar with adjusting many types of recipes to work with your area. When using a pressure canner at altitudes above 1,000 feet, add ½ pound more pressure for each 1,000 in altitude. If your pressure canner does not have a dial gauge that allows you to make small adjustments, increase the weighted gauge to the next mark. For example, if your recipe calls for 10 pounds of pressure at 1,000 feet, process it at 15 pounds of pressure at high altitudes. When processing high-acid foods in a water-bath canner at altitudes above 1,000 feet, add five minutes of processing time. For low-acid foods, add ten minutes for each 1,000 in altitude. These are only general guidelines; your particular area may vary. If you have questions about your altitude, proper pressures, or canning times, check with your county extension office.

Determining Your Altitude Above Sea Level, courtesy of the USDA

It is important to know your approximate elevation or altitude above sea level in order to determine a safe processing time for canned foods. Because the boiling temperature of liquid is lower at higher elevations, it is critical that additional time be given for to safely process foods at altitudes above sea level.

It is not practical to include a list of altitudes in this guide because there is wide variation within a state and even a county. For example, Kansas has areas with altitudes varying between 75 feet and 4,039 feet above sea level. Kansas is not generally thought to have high altitudes, but there are many areas of the state where adjustments for altitude must be considered. Colorado, on the other hand, has people living in areas between 3,000 and 10,000 feet above sea level. They tend to be more conscious of the need to make altitude adjustments in the various processing schedules. Listing altitudes for specific counties may actually be misleading due to the differences in geographic terrain within a county.

If you are unsure about the altitude where you will be canning foods, consult your county extension agent. An alternative source of information would be your local district conservationist with the Soil Conservation Service.

Boiling water bath canners

These types of canners are large metal or porcelain-lined pots that have a removable canning rack and a lid. These are inexpensive and easy to find in department or hardware stores. Buy a size that will be no more than 4 inches wider than your stove burners so the water will process food evenly.

During water bath processing, jars are placed on top of the canning rack, and then the pot is filled with water. Make sure you fill the canner so at least 1 inch of water covers the tops of the jars. The water is heated to boiling, and once a full rolling boil is attained, start timing the processing according to the recipe's directions. Some boiling-water canners do not have flat bottoms. A flat bottom must be used on an electric range. Either a flat or ridged bottom can be used on a gas burner. To ensure uniform processing of all jars with an electric range, the canner should be no more than 4 inches wider in diameter than the element on which it is heated.

Boiling water bath canning is suitable only for foods containing high acid, like many fruits and pickles; the acid content helps to destroy toxins and harmful microorganisms. Lower-acid foods need a longer processing time and the heat concentration of a pressure canner to raise the temperature high enough to kill the same microorganisms.

How to use a water bath canner — instructions courtesy of the USDA

1. Before you start preparing your food, fill the canner halfway with clean water. This is approximately the level needed for a canner load of pint jars. For other sizes and numbers of jars, the amount of water in the canner will need to be adjusted so it will be 1 to 2 inches over the top of the filled jars.

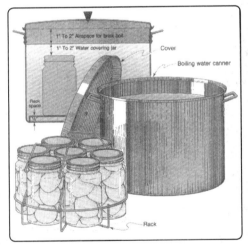

Illustration courtesy of the USDA. Example of a boiling water bath canner.

2. Preheat water to 140 degrees for raw packed foods and to 180 degrees for hot packed foods. You can start preparing the food while this water is preheating.

3. Load filled jars, fitted with lids, into the canner rack, and use the handles to lower the rack into the water; or fill the canner with the rack in the bottom, one jar at a time, using a jar lifter. When using a jar lifter, make sure it is securely positioned below the neck of the jar (below the screw band of the

lid). Keep the jar upright at all times. Tilting the jar could cause food to spill into the sealing area of the lid.

4. Add more boiling water, if needed, so the water level is at least 1 inch above jar tops. For process times over 30 minutes, the water level should be at least 2 inches above the tops of the jars.

5. Turn heat to its highest position, cover the canner with its lid, and heat until the water in the canner boils vigorously.

6. Set a timer for the total minutes required for processing the food.

7. Keep the canner covered, and maintain a boil throughout the process schedule. The heat setting may be lowered a little as long as a complete boil is maintained for the entire process time. If the water stops boiling at any time during the process, bring the water back to a vigorous boil, and begin the timing of the process over from the beginning.

8. Add more boiling water, if needed, to keep the water level above the jars.

9. When jars have been boiled for the recommended time, turn off the heat and remove the canner lid. Wait five minutes before removing jars.

10. Using a jar lifter, remove the jars and place them on a towel, leaving at least 1-inch spaces between the jars during cooling. Let jars sit undisturbed to cool at room temperature for 12 to 24 hours.

Pressure canners

Pressure canners have been extensively redesigned in recent years. Models made before the 1970s were heavy walled kettles with clamp-on or turn-on lids. They were fitted with a dial gauge, a vent port in the form of a petcock or counterweight, and a safety fuse. All low-acid foods must be processed in a pressure canner. This is a different kitchen appliance

A 16-quart pressure canner

than a pressure cooker — it is designed to accommodate large canning jars and produces the proper temperature for canned food processing. An average canner can hold about seven quart jars or up to nine pint jars. Smaller canners can hold four quart jars.

Pressure does not destroy microorganisms, but high temperatures applied for an adequate period of time do kill microorganisms. Whether you are able to destroy all microorganisms capable of growing in canned food is based on the temperature obtained in pure steam, free of air, at sea level. At sea level, a canner operated at a gauge pressure of 10.5 pounds provides an internal temperature of 240 degrees.

A pressure canner has a locking lid that holds in the steam and allows the pressure and heat to build up. Either a pressure canner has a pressure gauge that shows the settings — 5, 10, or 15 pounds — or a dial gauge that monitors rises in pressure from 5 to 15 pounds. If you live at a higher altitude, the dial gauge will be easier for you to use because you must increase the pressure by ½ pound for each 1,000 feet above sea level. If you use a dial gauge, be sure to have it checked every year at your county extension office.

Two serious errors in temperatures obtained in pressure canners occur because:

1. **Internal canner temperatures are lower at higher altitudes.** To correct this error, canners must be operated at the increased pressures.

2. **Air trapped in a canner lowers the temperature obtained at 5, 10, or 15 pounds of pressure and results in under processing.** The highest volume of air trapped in a canner occurs in processing raw packed foods in dial-gauge canners. These canners do not vent air during processing. To be safe, all types of pressure canners must be vented ten minutes before they are pressurized.

To vent a canner, leave the vent port uncovered on newer models or manually open petcocks or vent ports on some older models. Heating the filled canner with its lid locked into place boils water and generates steam that escapes through the petcock or vent port. When steam first escapes, set a timer for ten minutes. After venting ten minutes, close the petcock or place the counterweight or weighted gauge over the vent port to pressurize the canner.

Weighted gauge models exhaust tiny amounts of air and steam each time their gauge rocks or jiggles during processing. They control pressure precisely and need neither watching during processing nor checking for accuracy. The sound of the weight rocking or jiggling indicates that the canner is maintaining the recommended pressure. The single disadvantage of weighted-gauge canners is that they may be imprecise at higher altitudes. At altitudes above 1,000 feet, they must be operated at canner pressures of 10 instead of 5, or 15 instead of 10, PSI.

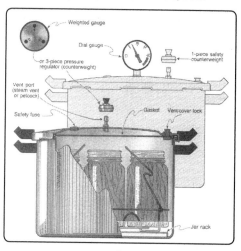

Illustration courtesy of the USDA

Check dial gauges for accuracy before use each year. Gauges that read high cause under-processing and may result in unsafe food. Low readings cause over-processing. Pressure adjustments can be made if the gauge reads up to 2 pounds high or low. Replace gauges that differ by more than 2 pounds. Every pound of pressure is very important to the temperature needed inside the canner for producing safe food, so accurate gauges and adjustments are essential when a gauge reads higher than it should. If a gauge is reading lower than it should, adjustments may be made to avoid over processing but are not essential to safety. Gauges may be checked at many county Cooperative Extension offices, or contact the pressure canner manufacturer for other options.

Handle canner lid gaskets carefully, and clean them according to the manufacturer's directions. Nicked or dried gaskets will allow steam leaks during pressurization of canners. Keep gaskets clean between uses. Gaskets on older model canners may require a light coat of vegetable oil once per year. Gaskets on newer model canners are prelubricated and do not benefit from oiling. Check your canner's instructions if there is doubt that the particular gasket you use has been prelubricated.

Lid safety fuses are thin metal inserts or rubber plugs designed to relieve excessive pressure from the canner. Do not pick at or scratch fuses while cleaning lids. Use only canners that have the Underwriter's Laboratory (UL) approval to ensure their safety.

Replacement gauges and other parts for canners are often available at stores that offer canning equipment or from canner manufacturers. When ordering parts, give your canner model number, and describe the parts needed.

Using pressure canners — instructions courtesy of the USDA

Follow these steps for successful pressure canning:

1. Put 2 to 3 inches of hot water in the canner. Some specific products may require that you start with even more water in the canner. Always follow the directions for specific foods if they require more water added to the canner. Place filled jars on the rack using a jar lifter. When using a jar lifter, make sure it is securely positioned below the neck of the jar (below the screw band of the lid). Keep the jar upright at all times. Tilting the jar could cause food to spill into the sealing area of the lid. Fasten canner lid securely.

Illustration courtesy of the USDA

2. Leave weight off vent port or open petcock. Heat at the highest setting until steam flows freely from the open petcock or vent port.

3. While maintaining the high heat setting, let the steam flow (exhaust) continuously for ten minutes, and then place the weight on the vent port or close the petcock. The canner will pressurize during the next three to five minutes.

4. Start timing the process when the pressure reading on the dial gauge indicates that the recommended pressure has been reached, or when the weighted gauge begins to jiggle or rock as the canner manufacturer describes.

5. Regulate heat under the canner to maintain a steady pressure at or slightly above the correct gauge pressure. Quick and large pressure variations during processing may cause unnecessary liquid losses from jars. Follow the canner manufacturer's directions for how a weighted gauge should indicate it is maintaining the desired pressure.

    IMPORTANT: If at any time pressure goes below the recommended amount, bring the canner back to pressure, and begin the timing of the process over from the beginning (using the total original process time). This is important for the safety of the food.

6. When the timed process is completed, turn off the heat, remove the canner from heat if possible, and let the canner depressurize. **Do not force cool the canner.** Forced cooling may result in unsafe food or food spoilage. Cooling the canner with cold running water or opening the vent port before the canner is fully depressurized will cause loss of liquid from jars and seal failures. Force cooling may also warp the canner lid of older model canners, causing steam leaks. Depressurization of older models without dial gauges should be timed. Standard-size heavy-walled canners require about 30 minutes when loaded with pints and 45 minutes with quarts. Newer thin-walled canners cool more rapidly and are equipped with vent locks. These canners are depressurized when their vent lock piston drops to a normal position.

7. After the canner is depressurized, remove the weight from the vent port or open the petcock. Wait ten minutes, unfasten the lid, and remove it carefully. Lift the lid away from you so the steam does not burn your face.

8. Remove jars with a jar lifter, and place them on a towel, leaving at least 1-inch spaces between the jars during cooling. Let jars sit undisturbed to cool at room temperature for 12 to 24 hours.

Cooling jars

When you remove hot jars from a canner, do not retighten their jar lids. Retightening hot lids may cut through the gasket and cause seal failures. Cool the jars at room temperature for 12 to 24 hours. Jars may be cooled on racks or towels to minimize heat damage to counters. The food level and liquid volume of raw-packed jars will be noticeably

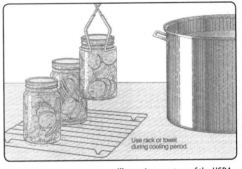

Illustration courtesy of the USDA

lower after cooling. Air is exhausted during processing and food shrinks. If a jar loses excessive liquid during processing, do not open it to add more liquid.

Testing jar seals

After cooling jars for 12 to 24 hours, remove the screw bands and test seals with one of the following options:

▶ Press the middle of the lid with a finger or thumb. If the lid springs up when you release your finger, the lid is unsealed.

Illustration courtesy of the USDA

▶ Tap the lid with the bottom of a teaspoon. If it makes a dull sound, the lid is not sealed. If food is in contact with the underside of the lid, it will also cause a dull sound. If the jar is sealed correctly, it will make a ringing, high-pitched sound.

▶ Hold the jar at eye level, and look across the lid. The lid should be concave (curved down slightly in the center). If center of the lid is either flat or bulging, it may not be sealed.

Reprocessing unsealed jars

If a lid fails to seal on a jar, remove the lid and check the jar-sealing surface for tiny nicks. If necessary, change the jar; add a new, properly prepared lid; and reprocess within 24 hours using the same processing time. Headspace in unsealed jars may be adjusted to 1 ½ inches, and jars could be frozen instead of reprocessed. Foods in single unsealed jars could be stored in the refrigerator and consumed within several days.

Storing jars

Store your jars in a dark, dry cool place away from heat sources, and protect from freezing. You can remove the screw bands from the lids if you wish, but some prefer to use those bands to secure the lids after the first time you open the jar. Label and date the jars, and store them in a clean, cool, dark, dry place. Do not store jars above 95 degrees. Do not store in locations near hot pipes, a range, a furnace, under a sink, in an uninsulated attic, or in direct sunlight. Under these conditions, food will lose quality in a few weeks or months and may spoil. Dampness may corrode metal lids, break seals, and allow recontamination and spoilage.

Common Canning Problems

Because the canning process requires several steps and careful attention to details, many things can go wrong. In addition, before you eat food from any jar, check it again for problems. Once you complete a batch of canning and allow it to cool for 24 hours, check each jar for problems. Do not diagnose problems by tasting the food.

This guide will describe some common problems, how they occurred, and how to avoid these problems next time you can. Some of the problems are merely appearance issues, while other problems will affect the taste or texture of the food and hamper how you can enjoy your products.

However, some of the problems are health issues. These are the most important problems for you to monitor. Once you complete a batch of canning, always check your food against these health signs to be sure you do not harm anyone with the food. If you see signs that food has become contaminated, take care with your disposal method. Some bacteria are deadly even in small amounts; you could spill a tiny splash on your hand and then wipe your mouth, and then the bacterium has entered your system. It is best to dump bad products down the drain where the water treatment plants will neutralize contaminants and then scrub your sink and sterilize the jars. Make sure you always discard the self-seal lids after using them. The screw ring can be re-used once it is sterilized. Alternatively, you can boil the jars in a water bath canner for 30 minutes to neutralize the contents, and then place the unopened jars in the trash.

Spoiled food

Spoiled food usually has several indicators; just one sign may not be a problem. For example, some foods, such as juices, may be cloudy after processing because of the pulp present in the juice. However, if you open the jar and the food smells off, rather than the food's ordinary smell, or if you see feathery mold growing on the rim or in the jar, it is clearly a spoiled product. For this reason, if you notice something odd with the food, check for anything else that may indicate a problem:

the color, smell, increase in bubbles, seepage from the jar, obvious growth of bacteria or contaminants, etc. Remember, do not test food by tasting it.

If you notice the following problems with your jars, carefully discard the food and lid, and sterilize the jar immediately. It is better to lose a little food than make yourself sick. To prevent these problems in the future, take these precautions to process the food properly:

Illustration courtesy of the USDA

- ▶ Make sure the jars are not overstuffed and that they are filled to the proper headspace. Remove air bubbles before putting the lids on the jars.

- ▶ Follow the processing method and time exactly.

- ▶ Check to be sure you have a good seal: concave, good vacuum, and no bulging at the lid.

- ▶ Make sure the pressure gauge on your pressure canner is checked and calibrated for accuracy at the beginning of each canning season.

- ▶ Check jars and lids for cracks, chips, rust, or damage. Always use new lids and sterilized equipment.

- ▶ Choose the freshest foods that have no rotten or moldy parts. Prepare the product properly.

- ▶ Carefully wipe the rim of each jar after it is filled. Make sure no food remains on the rim to hamper the seal or cause spoilage later.

Problem	Possible Causes
Product at the top of the jar is dark and/or thicker than normal.	This may not be a sign of spoiled food; check the table on appearance changes to rule out other problems. If other signs of spoilage exist, this is probably the result of improper processing.
The liquid in the jar is cloudy.	This may not be a sign of spoiled food; check the table on appearance changes to rule out other problems. If other signs of spoilage exist, this is probably the result of improper processing.
The liquid in the jar contains sediment.	This may not be a sign of spoiled food; check the table on appearance changes to rule out other problems. If other signs of spoilage exist, this is probably the result of improper processing.
Nonpickled or fermented food has a sour, strange, or foul smell.	The food or jar has been contaminated — especially if bubbles also appear within the jar.
Nonpickled or fermented food is bubbly.	The food or jar has been contaminated and fermentation has occurred, especially if the food has a strange or foul smell.
Food has an unusual color.	This may not be a sign of spoiled food; check the table on appearance changes to rule out other problems. If other signs of spoilage exist, this is probably the result of improper processing.
Jar lid, rim, or the surface of the food contains mold.	While some molds are harmless and can be removed so the rest of the food can be eaten, it is best to be safe and discard the entire contents. This is the result of improper processing.

Color or appearance changes

Problem	Possible Causes	How To Avoid
Product at the top of the jar is dark and/or thicker than normal.	Too much air in the jar has caused the top layer of food to become oxidized.	Do not overstuff jars, but be careful that the food and liquid reach the recipe's proper headspace. Remove bubbles from the jar before processing.
	The food in the jar is not completely covered with liquid.	Do not overstuff jars, but be careful that the liquid completely covers the food and reaches the recipe's proper headspace.

Problem	Possible Causes	How To Avoid
	Food is spoiled because it was not processed correctly.	Follow preparation and processing instructions exactly.
Food has an unusual color.	Some substances in foods react to the canning process by changing color. For example, peaches, pears, cauliflower, or apples may turn slightly pink or blue.	If no other signs of spoilage exist, this is a natural reaction, and no action is needed.
	Food that is white, blue, black, or green (unless it is naturally that color) is spoiled. If other signs of spoilage exist, the food has been contaminated.	Follow preparation and processing instructions exactly.
Food has pale color.	The jars have been stored improperly.	Store the jars in a cool, dark place, free from drafts or excess humidity.
The liquid in the jar is cloudy.	Minerals or additives in the water or salt may have clouded the liquid.	Choose pure salt with no additives, and use soft or distilled water for canning.
	The starchy foods have released some starch, which has clouded the liquid. Meat products often produce cloudy liquid during processing; this is normal.	Choose fresh, ripe products that are not overripe. If cutting up starchy foods like potatoes, rinse them in cold water before processing; then when you add liquid to the jars, use fresh water instead of the cooking water.
	If the product is juice, it is possible that extra pulp has drained into the juice.	This is not a problem — the pulp will add extra flavor and nutrients to the finished product. However, if you prefer a clear juice, strain the juice several times before processing, and do not squeeze or press the pulp while straining.
	If other signs of spoilage exist, the food has been contaminated.	Follow preparation and processing instructions exactly.
The liquid in the jar contains sediment.	Minerals or additives in the water or salt may have clouded the liquid.	Choose pure salt with no additives, and use soft or distilled water for canning.
	If other signs of spoilage exist, the food has been contaminated.	Follow preparation and processing instructions exactly.

Problem	Possible Causes	How To Avoid
Food is floating in the jar.	The syrup used in canning is heavier than the product.	Prepare ripe, firm fruit properly, and use the hot pack method. Use thinner syrup that contains less sugar.
	The produce or jar contains too much air.	Use the hot pack method to remove more air from the product. Make sure all bubbles are removed from the jar before processing. Pack the produce firmly in the jar.
Tomato juice has separated into yellow liquid on top and thick red juice at the bottom.	This is a natural enzymatic action that occurs when tomatoes are cut up for processing.	If you prefer not to shake up the jar before pouring some juice, then make sure during the hot pack process that you bring the tomatoes to a boil immediately after chopping them.

Jar is not sealed properly

If you discover any of the following problems, you can refrigerate the food and eat it within a few days. Alternatively, if you discover a bad seal within the first 12 to 24 hours and the band and lid are undamaged, you can re-process the jar using the original method and timing.

Problem	Possible Causes	How To Avoid
Not enough liquid in jars.	Uneven pressure in the pressure canner	Make sure pressure remains constant during processing. Allow pressure canner to release the pressure and heat naturally. Wait at least ten minutes before opening the canner.
	Bubbles were left in the jar while packing food.	Slide a knife or spatula inside the jar to remove air bubbles; adjust headspace if necessary.
	Liquid escaped through a bad seal.	Use new, undamaged lids and ring bands that screw on properly. Make sure the jars do not have any chips or cracks. Make sure no food is on the rim of the jar by wiping the rims before putting on the lids. Wipe sealing surface of jar clean after filling, before applying lid.

Problem	Possible Causes	How To Avoid
	The water bath canner did not have sufficient water.	Make sure the water is at least 2 inches over the tops of the jars throughout the entire processing time.
	The food absorbed too much liquid.	Starchy foods will need a larger ratio of liquid to product. Make sure you hot pack these items.
	The food was packed too tightly.	Allow enough headspace so the food does not boil out of the jars.
The jar did not seal; the lid is not concave and does not have a vacuum seal.	There was food between the rim and seal, or the rim was damaged.	Check jars before using. Wipe the rims of jars after filling them.
	Ring bands were damaged or not screwed on properly.	Check ring bands before using. Always screw bands on finger-tight.

Special problems with jams and jellies

Problem	Possible Causes	How to Avoid
The product contains crystals.	Too much sugar may have been added, or the sugar was not completely dissolved during processing.	Reduce the amount of sugar; follow tested recipes exactly, and remove from heat once the product reaches the jellying point.
	If appearing in products made from grape juice, naturally occurring tartrate crystals may have formed.	Settle the crystals in the juice by refrigerating overnight and then straining the juice before making the product.
Bubbles	Jelly set while air bubbles were still in the jar.	Skim foam from the liquid before filling jars, and quickly slide a spatula through the product to remove air bubbles.
	If other signs of spoilage exist, the food has been contaminated.	Follow preparation and processing instructions exactly.

Problem	Possible Causes	How to Avoid
Jam or jelly is too soft.	There may be several causes: The juice was overcooked. Too much water was used to make the juice. The sugar and juice proportions were not correct. The product was undercooked, so that the sugar was not concentrated enough.	Follow tested recipes exactly.
	The product did not contain enough acid.	Add a small amount of lemon juice to the juice before making the jam or jelly.
	Making too much jelly/jam at once.	Process jams and jellies in small batches, such as 4-6 pint jars at a time. You will need approximately 8-12 cups of fruit juice to produce 4-6 pint jars; follow recipes for specific amounts.
	Not allowing enough time before moving jars.	Wait at least 12 hours after processing before you move the jars.
	Using the product before it has had time to properly gel.	Most jams or jellies will take about two weeks to completely gel; jellies take a little longer than jams. Some fruits, such as plums, will take longer than two weeks; fruit butters will not completely gel. Shaking the jar might help you determine if the product is ready.
The product is darker than normal.	The juice may have cooked too long, or the sugar may have scorched.	Follow the instructions precisely; smaller batches of product will be easier to manage.
	The jam or jelly may be too old or may have been stored in a very warm environment.	Once the product has set, store it in a cool, dark place and use within the next year. Refrigerate the jar after it has been opened.

Problem	Possible Causes	How to Avoid
The product is cloudy.	The juice used to make the jam/jelly has too much pulp drained into the juice.	This is not a problem – the pulp will add extra flavor and nutrients to the finished product. However, if you prefer a clear juice, strain the juice several times before processing, and do not squeeze or press the pulp while straining.
	The completed jelly/jam sat before it was poured into the jars or was poured too slowly.	The product will begin to gel immediately upon removal from the heat. Pour into the jars quickly and carefully.
The jam or jelly is stiff or too thick.	The product has been overcooked so that too much of the liquid has boiled away.	Follow cooking instructions precisely, and stop cooking once the product forms a sheet on the cooking spoon.
	Inaccurate proportion of pectin to fruit.	Use less pectin; tested recipes should not present this problem.

Index

Index